PRENTICE HALL

HISTORY OF OUR WORLD

Reading and Vocabulary Study Guide

Needham, Massachusetts
Upper Saddle River, New Jersey

ISBN 0-13-130789-4

5 6 7 8 9 10 08 07 06 05

Contents for History of Our World, The Early Ages

Contents for History of Our World, Survey Edition

How to Use This Book

The Reading and Vocabulary Study Guide was designed to help you understand World History content. It will also help you build your reading and vocabulary skills. Please take the time to look at the next few pages to see how it works!

The Prepare to Read page gets you ready to read each section.

Objectives from your textbook help you focus your reading.

With each chapter, you will study a Target Reading Skill. This skill is introduced in your textbook, but explained more here. Later, questions or activities in the margin will help you practice the skill.

You are given a new Vocabulary Strategy with each chapter. Questions or activities in the margin later will help you practice the strategy.

CHAPTER 1 **Prepare to Read**

Section 1
Geography and History

Objectives

1. Learn what tools are used to understand history.
2. Find out how geography and history are connected.

Target Reading Skill

Preview and Set a Purpose Reading a textbook is different from reading a novel or the newspaper. To read to learn effectively, you must preview and set a purpose for your reading.

Before you read this section, take a moment to preview it. Look at the title "Geography and History" and the objectives. Now flip through the next two pages. Read each heading. They tell you about the section's contents. They tell you what to expect to learn from each section. As you preview, use this information to give yourself a reason to read the section. Are you curious about anything in the section, like how people learn about history? Read to satisfy that curiosity—that's your purpose for reading.

Vocabulary Strategy

Using Context Clues Words work together to explain meaning. The meaning of a word may depend on its **context**. A word's context is the other words and sentences that surround it. The context gives you clues to a word's meaning.

Try this example. Say that you do not know the meaning of the word *history* in the following sentence:

"History began when people started to keep written records of their experiences."

You could ask yourself: "What information does the sentence give me about the word?" Answer: "I know that history began when people started writing down their experiences. This tells me that history must be the written record of human experience."

6 Reading and Vocabulary Study Guide

Section Summary pages provide an easy-to-read summary of each section.

Provides a summary of the section's most important ideas.

Large blue headings correspond to large red headings in your textbook.

This checkmark tells you when to answer the Reading Check question.

Key Terms, in blue within the summary, are defined at the bottom of the page.

Section 1 Summary

In 1991 two hikers found the frozen body of a man in the Alps. They called the frozen man the Iceman. Scientists studied his clothing, tools, and body. They hoped to learn about the Iceman's life and death. The scientists learned that he lived about 5,000 years ago. The most important clue was the Iceman's copper ax. Europeans first used copper in about 4000 B.C. The ax told scientists that the Iceman lived after people had learned to use copper.

Understanding History

Humans want to know what life was like long ago. About 5,000 years ago, people began writing down what happened to them. That was the beginning of history. The time before people learned to write is called prehistory.

To learn about life in prehistoric times, scientists can't study written records. They must use other kinds of clues. Archaeologists are scientists who study objects to learn about the past. Objects such as bones and tools tell them how people lived. For example, the size of a spear point can tell whether it was used to kill a large or small animal.

Historians don't just use objects to learn about the past. They also study written records. Many written records began as oral traditions. They were passed down by word of mouth. They tell stories about heroes or things that happened. Not all oral stories are accurate. People often mix facts with tall tales about heroes. Still, oral stories tell historians how people lived and what they thought was important. ✓

Target Reading Skill

If you want to learn about studying history, how does reading about archaeologists help you meet your goal?

✓ Reading Check

Why are historians interested in oral traditions?

Key Terms

history (HIS tuh ree) *n.* the written events of people
prehistory (pree HIS tuh ree) *n.* time before writing was invented
archaeologist (ahr kee AHL u jist) *n.* a scientist who studies objects to learn about the past
oral traditions (AWR ul truh DISH unz) *n.* stories passed down by word of mouth

Questions and activities in the margin help you take notes on main ideas, and practice the Target Reading Skill and Vocabulary Strategy.

Vocabulary Strategy

What does the word *civilization* mean in the underlined sentence? What clues can you find in the surrounding words, phrases, or sentences? Circle the words in this paragraph that could help you learn what *civilization* means.

Mark the Text

✓ Reading Check

Give one example of geography's effect on history.

____

____

____

Linking Geography and History

It is important to know when something happened. But historians want to know more. They want to understand *why* things happened. To do this, they often look at geography. Geography is the study of the earth's surface and how it was shaped. It also refers to a place's climate, landscape, and location.

Often geography and history are linked. Many things affect people's lives. Whether a place is hot or cold affects the lives of the people who live there. So does its water supply. For example, the geography of Egypt helps explain why the ancient Egyptians had a successful civilization.

Egyptian civilization was built on the banks of the Nile River in Africa. Each year, the Nile flooded. Rich soil was left on the river banks. Because of this, Egyptian farmers were able to grow large crops. They were able to feed large numbers of people in cities. That meant that not everyone had to farm. Some people could do other kinds of jobs. That helped develop the civilization. Without the Nile and its floods, Egyptian civilization would not have done so well. This is one way geography affects history. ✓

Review Questions

1. What do scientists study to learn about prehistory?

____

____

____

2. How can geography help us understand history?

____

____

____

Key Term

geography (jee AHG ruh fee) *n.* the study of Earth's surface and how it is shaped

Use write-on lines to answer the questions. You can also use the lines to take notes.

When you see this symbol, mark the text as indicated.

Chapter 1 Assessment

…me before writing was invented is known as
…l tradition.
…tory.
…ehistory.
…ography.

…ians often look at geography to tell them
…en people lived.
…out religion.
…out wars and rulers.
…w a location affected the lives of the people who lived there.

… did early humans cross from Asia to North America?
A. more than a million years ago
B. about 30,000 years ago
C. more than 100,000 years ago
D. 500,000 years ago

4. Which of the following describes the Old Stone Age?
A. People learned to domesticate animals.
B. People began to grow their own food.
C. Some people became pastoral nomads.
D. People survived by hunting animals and gathering wild plants.

5. What did people need to grow farming settlements into cities?
A. a large supply of slaves
B. tame animals and grazing land
C. rich soil, drinking water, and building materials
D. large public buildings

Short Answer Question

How did the start of farming change people's lives?

____

____

____

____

____

Questions at the end of each section and chapter help you review content and assess your own understanding.

Prepare to Read

Section 1
Geography and History

Objectives

1. Learn what tools are used to understand history.
2. Find out how geography and history are connected.

Target Reading Skill

Preview and Set a Purpose Reading a textbook is different from reading a novel or the newspaper. To read to learn effectively, you must preview and set a purpose for your reading.

Before you read this section, take a moment to preview it. Look at the title "Geography and History" and the objectives. Now flip through the next two pages. Read each heading. They tell you about the section's contents. They tell you what to expect to learn from each section. As you preview, use this information to give yourself a reason to read the section. Are you curious about anything in the section, like how people learn about history? Read to satisfy that curiosity—that's your purpose for reading.

Vocabulary Strategy

Using Context Clues Words work together to explain meaning. The meaning of a word may depend on its **context**. A word's context is the other words and sentences that surround it. The context gives you clues to a word's meaning.

Try this example. Say that you do not know the meaning of the word *history* in the following sentence:

> "<u>History</u> began when people started to keep written records of their experiences."

You could ask yourself: "What information does the sentence give me about the word?" Answer: "I know that history began when people started writing down their experiences. This tells me that history must be the written record of human experience."

Section 1 Summary

In 1991 two hikers found the frozen body of a man in the Alps. They called the frozen man the Iceman. Scientists studied his clothing, tools, and body. They hoped to learn about the Iceman's life and death. The scientists learned that he lived about 5,000 years ago. The most important clue was the Iceman's copper ax. Europeans first used copper in about 4000 B.C. The ax told scientists that the Iceman lived after people had learned to use copper.

Understanding History

Humans want to know what life was like long ago. About 5,000 years ago, people began writing down what happened to them. That was the beginning of **history**. The time before people learned to write is called **prehistory**.

To learn about life in prehistoric times, scientists can't study written records. They must use other kinds of clues. **Archaeologists** are scientists who study objects to learn about the past. Objects such as bones and tools tell them how people lived. For example, the size of a spear point can tell whether it was used to kill a large or small animal.

Historians don't just use objects to learn about the past. They also study written records. Many written records began as **oral traditions**. They were passed down by word of mouth. They tell stories about heroes or things that happened. Not all oral stories are accurate. People often mix facts with tall tales about heroes. Still, oral stories tell historians how people lived and what they thought was important. ✓

Target Reading Skill

If you want to learn about studying history, how does reading about archaeologists help you meet your goal?

___

___

___

✓ Reading Check

Why are historians interested in oral traditions?

___

___

___

Key Terms

history (HIS tuh ree) *n.* the written events of people
prehistory (pree HIS tuh ree) *n.* time before writing was invented
archaeologist (ahr kee AHL u jist) *n.* a scientist who studies objects to learn about the past
oral traditions (AWR ul truh DISH unz) *n.* stories passed down by word of mouth

Linking Geography and History

It is important to know when something happened. But historians want to know more. They want to understand *why* things happened. To do this, they often look at **geography**. Geography is the study of the earth's surface and how it was shaped. It also refers to a place's climate, landscape, and location.

Often geography and history are linked. Many things affect people's lives. Whether a place is hot or cold affects the lives of the people who live there. So does its water supply. For example, the geography of Egypt helps explain why the ancient Egyptians had a successful civilization.

Egyptian civilization was built on the banks of the Nile River in Africa. Each year, the Nile flooded. Rich soil was left on the river banks. Because of this, Egyptian farmers were able to grow large crops. They were able to feed large numbers of people in cities. That meant that not everyone had to farm. Some people could do other kinds of jobs. That helped develop the civilization. Without the Nile and its floods, Egyptian civilization would not have done so well. This is one way geography affects history. ✓

Vocabulary Strategy

What does the word *civilization* mean in the underlined sentence? What clues can you find in the surrounding words, phrases, or sentences? Circle the words in this paragraph that could help you learn what *civilization* means.

✓ Reading Check

Give one example of geography's effect on history.

____

____

____

Review Questions

1. What do scientists study to learn about prehistory?

____

____

____

2. How can geography help us understand history?

____

____

____

Key Term

geography (jee AHG ruh fee) *n.* the study of Earth's surface and how it is shaped

Prepare to Read

Section 2 Prehistory

Objectives

1. Discover how hunter-gatherers lived during the Stone Age.
2. Learn about the beginning of farming.

Target Reading Skill

Preview and Predict Making predictions about what you will learn from your text helps you set a purpose for reading. It also helps you remember what you have read. Before you begin reading, preview the section. Look at the section title and objectives above, then the headings. Then predict what the section will tell you. Based on your preview, you will probably predict that this section will tell you about how early humans lived.

List two facts that you expect to learn about how early humans lived.

Prediction 1: ____

Prediction 2: ____

As you read, check your predictions. Were they right? If they were not very accurate, you may need to pay closer attention while you preview the section.

Vocabulary Strategy

Using Context Clues Sometimes you can pick up clues about an unfamiliar word's meaning from the words, phrases, and sentences around it. The underlined words in the paragraph below give clues to the meaning of the word *nomad*.

> Many of our Old Stone Age ancestors were **nomads**. They moved around to places where they thought they would find food. They stayed there for several days. When they had gathered all the food around them, they moved on.

A nomad is a person who travels from place to place instead of settling in one place. The underlined phrases told you that information.

Section 2 Summary

Stone Age Hunting and Gathering

The **Stone Age** was the earliest known period of human culture. People began using stone to create tools. They also made tools from wood and animal bones. The Stone Age continued until people learned to use metal for tools.

Archaeologists divide the Stone Age into three periods: the Old Stone Age, the Middle Stone Age, and the New Stone Age. During the Old Stone Age, early humans did not yet know how to farm. They lived by hunting animals and gathering wild plants. Over time they learned to hunt in groups. Most of human prehistory took place during the Old Stone Age.

Early humans first learned to use fire between 1,400,000 and 500,000 years ago. Humans later learned to create fire. With fire to keep them warm, people could move to areas with cold climates.

As our ancestors learned to use tools, they left their original homes in Africa. This may have occurred as early as one million years ago. Many of our Old Stone Age ancestors were **nomads**. They moved around to places where they thought they would find food. When they had finished gathering all the food around them, they moved on. ✓

Humans eventually spread over much of Earth.

When	Event
At least 500,000 years ago	Human ancestors are living in Asia and Europe
More than 100,000 years ago	Modern humans originated in Africa
About 30,000 years ago	Humans cross Asia to North America

Key Terms

Stone Age (stohn ayj) *n.* a period of time during which people made tools and weapons from stone

nomad (NOH mad) *n.* a person who has no settled home

Target Reading Skill

Based on what you have read so far, are your predictions on target? If not, change your predictions now.

New Predictions: ______________

____

____

____

✓ Reading Check

What was life like during the Stone Age?

____

____

____

The Beginning of Farming

People lived by hunting and gathering food for tens of thousands of years. During the Middle Stone Age, people learned to make better tools. About 11,000 years ago, people learned to grow their own food. This was the beginning of the New Stone Age. They no longer had to be nomads.

At the same time, some people became pastoral nomads. Pastoral nomads raised livestock. They traveled in search of grass for their animals. There are still pastoral nomads in some countries today.

In most societies, women were in charge of farming. Men were usually hunters.

Some places were better for farming than others. Soil in some areas was very **fertile**. In several places around the world, the soil, water, and length of growing seasons were good for plants. People there became farmers. Over time, people learned how to grow better, more useful plants.

During the New Stone Age, humans learned to **domesticate** animals. Dogs were used for hunting. Sheep, goats, and pigs gave meat, milk, wool, and skins. By about 2400 B.C., cattle, camels, horses, and donkeys were used to carry heavy loads. Domesticated animals helped people make sure they would have a steady supply of food. ✓

Review Questions

1. What important skills did people of the Old Stone Age use to find food?

2. What marked the start of the New Stone Age?

Key Terms

fertile (FUR tul) *adj.* able to grow plants well
domesticate (duh MES tih kayt) *v.* tame wild plants and animals for human use

Vocabulary Strategy

Mark the Text

Look at the phrase *pastoral nomads* in the underlined sentence. The term is not defined for you. But there are clues to what it means. Write the definition below, then circle the words or phrases that helped you learn its meaning.

✓ Reading Check

What skills did people develop during the New Stone Age?

Prepare to Read

Section 3 The Beginnings of Civilization

Objectives

1. Find out the advantages people gained from settling in one place.
2. Learn about the growth of early cities.
3. Understand how the first civilizations formed and spread.

Target Reading Skill

Preview and Ask Questions Before you read this section, preview the section title, objectives, and headings to see what the section is about. What do you think are the most important concepts in the section? How can you tell?

After you preview the section, write two questions that will help you understand or remember important concepts or facts in the section. For example, you might ask yourself

- How did the first cities grow?
- How did early civilizations form?

Find the answers to your questions as you read.

Keep asking questions about what you think will come next. Does the text answer your questions? Were you able to predict what would be covered under each heading?

Vocabulary Strategy

Using Context Clues Many English words have more than one meaning. You can use context clues to figure out the meaning of these words. For example, in the sentences below, the word *back* is used in two different ways.

He wrote his answers on the **back** of the worksheet.

From the rest of the sentence, you can figure out that *back* means "reverse side."

She asked her friends to **back** her plan.

By using context clues, you can figure out that in this sentence, *back* means "support."

Section 3 Summary

Advantages of a Settled Life

Farming was hard work. But it had advantages. People who grew their own food could stay in one place. They could store **surplus** food for later use. People could have larger families. The world's population grew quickly. About 10,000 years ago, the population of the world was about 5 million people. By 7,000 years ago, the world's population had grown to as much as 20 million.

People lived in New Stone Age farming settlements for many centuries. Settlements grew into towns. With food surpluses, people did not have to spend all their days getting food. Some people switched to other kinds of work. Some became **artisans**. They made things such as baskets, tools, pottery, and cloth. ✓

The Growth of Cities

Not all farming settlements grew into cities. Cities started in areas with rich soil. Rich soil led to large surpluses of food. People also needed plenty of drinking water and materials to build homes. Some of the earliest cities grew along rivers, such as the Nile in Egypt. Cities grew there because the soil is rich near rivers. ✓

Early cities were different from farming villages. They were larger. They had large public buildings. Some buildings were used to store crops. Other buildings were for worshiping the gods. Still others were places where people could buy and sell goods. In villages, most people were farmers. In cities, most people worked at a craft.

As the population grew, governments formed. Governments kept order. They settled disputes and managed **irrigation** projects.

Key Terms

surplus (SUR plus) *n.* more than is needed
artisan (AHR tuh zun) *n.* a worker who is especially skilled at crafting items by hand
irrigation (ihr uh GAY shun) *n.* supplying land with water through a network of canals

✓ Reading Check

What effect did food surpluses have on people living in towns?

____
____
____

✓ Reading Check

Why did cities often grow up along rivers?

____
____
____

Target Reading Skill

Ask and answer a question about how settlements grew into cities.

Question: ______________________________
____

Answer: ______________________________
____

The First Civilizations

Over time, some New Stone Age societies became **civilizations**. A civilization has cities, a central government, and specialized workers. It also has writing, art, and architecture.

By 6600 B.C., artisans in Europe and Asia had learned to get copper from certain rocks. By 3000 B.C., they mixed copper and tin to make bronze. This was the start of the Bronze Age. Bronze was much harder than copper and was used to make longer-lasting weapons, tools, and shields.

Traders took precious items to faraway cities. They traded for goods that people at home wanted. Then they brought these goods back home. Around 3500 B.C., the wheel and axle were invented. Now goods could be carried farther and more easily. Merchant ships carried goods across seas and rivers. New ideas spread from one society to another. ✓

Cities developed **social classes**. In the large cities, the king was the most powerful person. Next were two other classes. One was the priests of the city's religion. The other was made up of nobles. They were government officials and military officers. Below them were artisans and merchants. At the bottom were workers and farmers. Slaves, or human beings who are owned by other people, ranked below free people.

Vocabulary Strategy

The word *noble* has several meanings. You may already know one of its meanings. Read the underlined sentences below. What is its meaning in this context?

✓ Reading Check

What skills and practices were important in the growth of early civilizations?

Review Questions

1. What helped villages grow into cities?

2. What happened as societies grew into civilizations?

Key Terms

civilization (sih vuh luh ZAY shun) *n.* a society with cities, a central government, job specialization, and social classes

social class (SOH shul klas) *n.* a group of people with similar backgrounds, income, and ways of living

Chapter 1 Assessment

1. The time before writing was invented is known as
   A. oral tradition.
   B. history.
   C. prehistory.
   D. geography.

2. Historians often look at geography to tell them
   A. when people lived.
   B. about religion.
   C. about wars and rulers.
   D. how a location affected the lives of the people who lived there.

3. When did early humans cross from Asia to North America?
   A. more than a million years ago
   B. about 30,000 years ago
   C. more than 100,000 years ago
   D. 500,000 years ago

4. Which of the following describes the Old Stone Age?
   A. People learned to domesticate animals.
   B. People began to grow their own food.
   C. Some people became pastoral nomads.
   D. People survived by hunting animals and gathering wild plants.

5. What did people need to grow farming settlements into cities?
   A. a large supply of slaves
   B. tame animals and grazing land
   C. rich soil, drinking water, and building materials
   D. large public buildings

Short Answer Question

How did the start of farming change people's lives?

____

____

____

____

____

Prepare to Read

Section 1
Land Between Two Rivers

Objectives

1. Find out how geography made the rise of civilization in the Fertile Crescent possible.
2. Learn about Sumer's first cities.
3. Examine the characteristics of Sumerian religion.

Target Reading Skill

Reread Rereading is a skill that can help you understand words and ideas. Rereading means to read something again. Sometimes you may not understand a word or idea the first time you read it. There may be words you do not recognize.

When this happens, rereading can help. Sometimes you may need to reread two or three times. As you reread, look for specific information that will clarify the word or idea you didn't understand. Look for connections among the words and sentences. Put together the facts that you do understand. See if you can find the main idea. Think about how the idea you don't understand relates to the main idea.

Vocabulary Strategy

Using Context to Clarify Meaning When you come across new words in your text, they are often defined for you. Sometimes the definition appears in a separate sentence or in the same sentence. Sometimes the word *or* is used to introduce the definition. Look at the following examples.

scribes, or *professional writers*

myths, or *stories about gods that explain a people's beliefs*

polytheism comes from Greek words that mean *"a belief in many gods"*

The underlined words are defined in context. In these examples, brief definitions appear in italics. Look for definitions in the context as you come across unfamiliar words in your reading.

Section 1 Summary

The first known schools were set up in the land of Sumer (SOO mur) over 4,000 years ago. They taught the new invention of writing. People who went to these schools became **scribes**. Scribes kept records that help tell the story of this early civilization.

The Geographic Setting

Sumer was located in an area called Mesopotamia (mes uh puh TAY mee uh). It had rich soil. The rivers provided water. The people who settled there became farmers, city builders, and traders.

The word *Mesopotamia* comes from Greek words that mean "between the rivers." The region lies between the Tigris and Euphrates rivers. It is part of a larger area called the **Fertile Crescent**. This area was a very good place for growing crops.

Each spring, the Tigris and Euphrates rivers flooded. The floods left rich topsoil on the land. Farmers grew crops in this soil. The floods did not always happen at the same time each year. Sometimes they took people by surprise. When this happened, the flood waters washed away people, animals, crops, and houses. ✓

The First Cities

Success in farming led to surpluses of food. This helped cities grow. By 3500 B.C., cities arose in Sumer, along the Tigris and Euphrates rivers.

These cities shared the same culture and language. But they did not all have the same ruler. Instead, they were independent **city-states**. Each Sumerian city acted as a state with its own government, and its own king.

Key Terms

scribe (skryb) *n.* someone who writes for a living
Fertile Crescent (FUR tul KRES unt) *n.* a region in Southwest Asia; site of the first civilizations
city-state (SIH tee stayt) *n.* a city with its own government and king; both a city and an independent state

Vocabulary Strategy

Mark the Text

The term *Mesopotamia* is defined in context in the bracketed paragraph. Circle its definition. *Hint:* Look in the first *and* second sentences of the paragraph.

✓ Reading Check

List how flooding rivers affected people who settled in Mesopotamia.

____

____

____

Target Reading Skill

Reread this paragraph. In what ways did Sumerian cities act as states?

____

____

____

Life was bustling in these cities. Merchants displayed goods in outdoor market places. Streets were crowded with musicians, acrobats, beggars, and water sellers. Sumerian houses faced onto inner courtyards. On hot nights, people slept on their flat roofs. ✓

✓ Reading Check

Describe the cities of Sumer.

____

____

____

Sumerian Religion

At the heart of a Sumerian city was the ziggurat (ZIG oo rat). It was the temple to the city's main god. Much of the town's activity took place there. A ziggurat was a tall pyramid. It had a shrine on top. Sumerians believed that gods used the ziggurat as a stairway to come down to Earth.

The people of Sumer practiced **polytheism**. Their **myths** promised that the gods would punish people who angered them. The gods would reward those who pleased them. The Sumerians honored their gods with ceremonies. The Sumerians' religion gives us an idea of what mattered to them.

Sumer's wealth led to its downfall. Sumerian city-states fought each other over land. They also fought over who could use the river water. Rulers of several city-states won and lost power. Around 2300 B.C. King Sargon of Akkadia (uh KAY dee uh) united the city-states of Sumer. He improved Sumer's government and army. Sumer stayed united for about 100 years. Then it split up again. After 2000 B.C., Sumer was no longer a main power. In the 1700s B.C., Babylonia took control of Sumer. ✓

✓ Reading Check

What forces weakened the cities of Sumer?

____

____

____

Review Questions

1. How did Mesopotamia's geography help civilizations grow in the area?

____

____

2. Describe the religious beliefs of the people of Sumer.

____

____

Key Terms

polytheism (PAHL ih thee iz um) *n.* the belief in many gods

myth (mith) *n.* a traditional story or a legend that explains people's beliefs

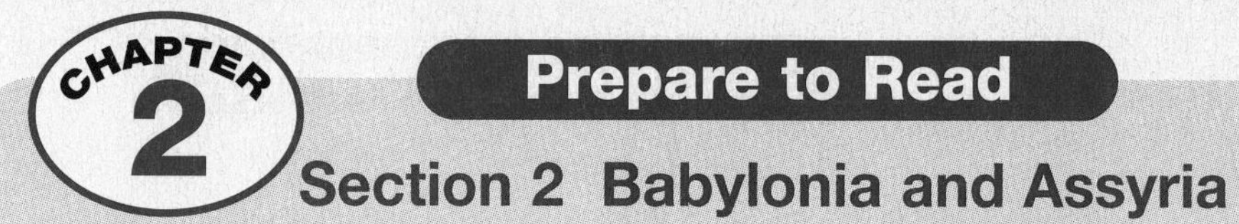
CHAPTER
2

Prepare to Read

Section 2 Babylonia and Assyria

Objectives

1. Learn about the two most important empires of Mesopotamia.
2. Find out what characterized the Babylonian and Assyrian empires.
3. Understand how Babylonia was able to rise again after defeat.

Target Reading Skill

Paraphrase When you paraphrase, you put something into your own words. Paraphrasing is another skill that can help you understand what you read. Putting ideas into your own words will also help you remember what you have read.

For example, look at this sentence: "King Sargon II of Assyria heard the news: Assyria had attacked the nearby kingdoms of Urartu and Zikirtu as planned." You could paraphrase it this way: "King Sargon II of Assyria learned that his country had attacked two kingdoms."

As you read, paraphrase the information following each heading.

Vocabulary Strategy

Using Context to Clarify Meaning Social studies textbooks often contain words that you may not know. Look at a word's context, or the words and sentences just before and after the word, to figure out its meaning. Clues in a word's context can include examples, explanations, or definitions. Use the graphic organizer as a guide to help you figure out the meaning of hard words.

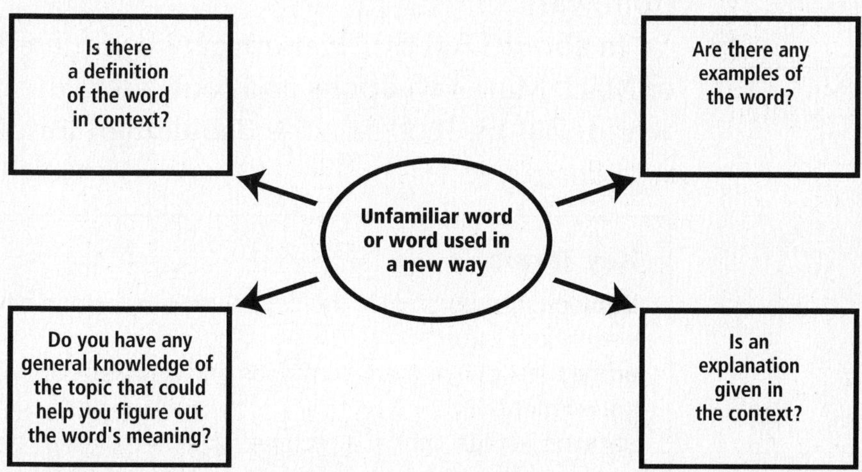
Is there a definition of the word in context?
Are there any examples of the word?
Unfamiliar word or word used in a new way
Do you have any general knowledge of the topic that could help you figure out the word's meaning?
Is an explanation given in the context?

Section 2 Summary

Vocabulary Strategy

As you read this section, look for at least one word that is new to you or that is used in a new way. Use the graphic organizer on the previous page to help you figure out what it means. Use the word's context for help. Write the word below, followed by a brief definition. (**Do not** use any of the Key Terms in blue.)

____

____

____

✓ Reading Check

Why did many rulers wish to conquer Mesopotamia?

____

____

____

✓ Reading Check

Who was Hammurabi and what did he accomplish?

____

____

____

The Two Empires of Mesopotamia

The army that could conquer Mesopotamia gained great wealth. The most important Mesopotamian civilizations were Babylonia (bab uh LOH nee uh) and Assyria (uh SEER ee uh). ✓

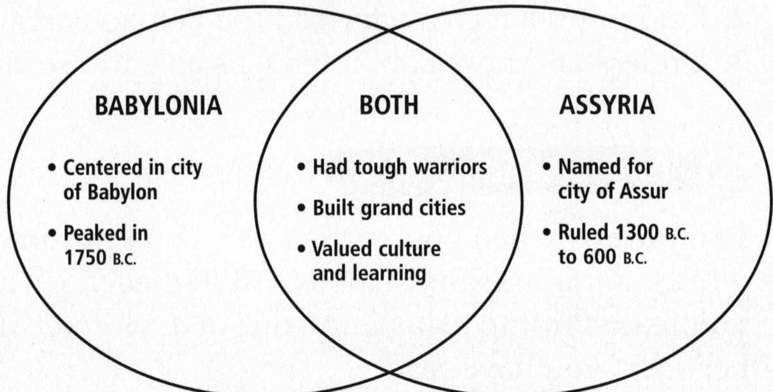

Keep reading to learn more about these empires.

The Babylonian Empire

There was a Babylonian king named Hammurabi (hahm uh RAH bee). He united the cities of Sumer. He created the Babylonian **Empire**. He then conquered lands all the way to Asia Minor. This is where the country of Turkey is today. The Babylonians built many roads. ✓

Babylon's location made it a crossroads of trade. **Caravans** from the north and the south stopped in Babylon. Many exotic goods were sold in the city's **bazaars**. Babylon got rich from trade. It also got rich from wars.

In about 1760 B.C., Hammurabi conquered the city of Mari. Mari's weapons and tools were the best in the world. But by 1600 B.C., the Babylonian Empire itself was destroyed.

Key Terms

Babylon (BAB uh lahn) *n.* the capital of Babylonia; a city of great wealth and luxury

empire (EM pyr) *n.* many territories and peoples controlled by one government

caravan (KA ruh van) *n.* a group of traders traveling together

bazaar (buh ZAHR) *n.* a market selling different kinds of goods

The Empire of the Assyrians

Assyria was a small kingdom north of Babylon. Assyria lay on open land so it was easily invaded. As a result, the Assyrians became skilled warriors. They decided that the best way to defend themselves was to attack others. By 650 B.C., Assyria had conquered a large empire. It stretched from the Nile River to the Persian Gulf.

The Assyrians were very good at waging war. They invented the **battering ram** to pound down city walls. Their armed chariots were able to slash their way through enemy troops.

Assyria's capital was Nineveh (NIN uh vuh). It was a city of great learning with a great library. It had writings from Sumer and Babylon. From these records, we know a great deal about early Mesopotamia. ✓

The people the Assyrians conquered fought against their rule. Two groups, the Medes (meedz) and Chaldeans (kal DEE unz), beat the Assyrians in 612 B.C.

Babylonia Rises Again

The Chaldeans made Babylon the center of a new empire. It was called the New Babylonian Empire. King Nebuchadnezzar (neb you kud NEZ ur) II rebuilt the city. He put up huge walls to protect the city. The New Babylonian Empire was a center of learning and science. ✓

In 539 B.C., the New Babylonian Empire was conquered by the Persians. But the city of Babylon was spared.

Review Questions

1. What are Babylonia and Assyria?

____

____

2. How was the New Babylonian Empire created?

____

____

Key Term

battering ram (BAT ur ing ram) *n.* a powerful weapon with a wooden beam mounted on wheels

Target Reading Skill

Paraphrase the bracketed paragraphs. In your paraphrase, give all the examples that show how good the Assyrians were at waging war.

____

____

____

____

✓ Reading Check

How has the library at Nineveh helped us learn about early Mesopotamia?

____

____

____

✓ Reading Check

Who was Nebuchadnezzar II?

____

____

____

Prepare to Read

Section 3
The Legacy of Mesopotamia

Objectives

1. Learn about the importance of Hammurabi's Code.
2. Find out how the art of writing developed in Mesopotamia.

Target Reading Skill

Summarize You will learn more from your text if you summarize it. When you summarize text, you use your own words to restate the key points. A good summary includes important events and details. It notes the order in which the events occurred. It also makes connections between the events.

Use the table below to summarize what you will read on the next two pages.

The Legacy of Mesopotamia	
Hammurabi's Code	**The Art of Writing**

Vocabulary Strategy

Using Context to Clarify Meaning When you come across a word that you do not know, you may not need to look it up in a dictionary. In this workbook, key terms appear in **blue**. The definitions are in a box at the bottom of the page. Looking at the definition breaks up your reading. Before you do that, continue to read to the end of the paragraph. See if you can figure out what the word means from its context. Clues can include examples and explanations. Then look at the definition on the bottom of the page to see how accurate you were. Finally, reread the paragraph to make sure you understood what you read.

Section 3 Summary

Hammurabi's Code

The Babylonians thought there should be a **code** of law. This code needed to be written down. It should be applied fairly. **Hammurabi** ruled Babylonia from about 1792 to 1750 B.C. He set rules for all to follow. These rules were known as Hammurabi's Code. The code told the people how to settle disputes. The code covered all parts of life.

Hammurabi's Code was based partly on the older Sumerian laws. It had 282 laws. The laws were grouped in categories. They included trade, labor, property, and family laws. There were laws for adopting children, practicing medicine, and hiring wagons. There were even laws dealing with wild animals.

Hammurabi's Code was based on the idea of "an eye for an eye." In other words, the punishment should be similar to the crime. However, the code did not apply equally to all people. The punishment depended on how important the victim was. The higher the class of the victim, the worse the punishment. A person who accidentally broke a rule was just as guilty as someone who meant to break it. ✓

Hammurabi's Code is important because it was written down. With written laws, everyone knew the rules and the punishments. It was not the first time a society had set up a code of laws. But it is the first organized set that we have found.

The Art of Writing

Humans were not always able to read and write. Writing began in Mesopotamia around 3100 B.C. The Sumerians used it to keep records. The first records were about farm animals. Only a few people knew how to write. Writing was an important skill. Scribes were well respected.

Key Terms

code (kohd) *n.* an organized list of laws and rules
Hammurabi (hah muh RAH bee) *n.* the king of Babylon from about 1792 to 1750 B.C.; creator of the Babylonian empire

Target Reading Skill

Summarize the bracketed paragraph. Give the main point and two details.

Main point: ____________________

____

Detail: ____________________

____

Detail: ____________________

____

✓ Reading Check

What was Hammurabi's Code?

____

____

____

The scribes of Sumer recorded many different types of information. For example, they kept track of the payments, sales, how much food was needed to feed the army and more.

Scribes wrote on clay from the rivers. First they shaped the clay into smooth, flat surfaces called tablets. They used sharp tools to mark letters in the clay. When the clay dried, it left a permanent record.

The size and shape of a tablet depended on its use. Larger tablets were used for reference purposes. They stayed in one place. Smaller tablets were the size of letters or postcards. They were used for personal messages. They even had clay envelopes.

Writing developed over time. At first, shaped pieces of clay were used as tokens, or symbols. Tokens could be used to keep track of how many animals had been bought or sold, or how much food had been grown. By about 3100 B.C., this form of record keeping had developed into writing.

At first, people drew pictures to show what they wanted to say. Each main object had a symbol. The symbols changed when people learned to record ideas as well as facts. Eventually, scribes developed **cuneiform**. Cuneiform script could be used to stand for different languages. This was helpful in a land of many peoples. ✓

Vocabulary Strategy

From context clues, write a definition of the word *token*. Circle words or phrases in the text that helped you write your definition.

Mark the Text

____

____

____

✓ Reading Check

When, where, and how did writing first develop?

When: ______________________

Where: ______________________

How: ______________________

Review Questions

1. How does the expression "an eye for an eye" fit Hammurabi's Code?

____

____

____

2. What were some of the tasks of early Mesopotamian scribes?

____

____

____

Key Term

cuneiform (kyoo NEE uh fawrm) *n.* groups of wedges and lines used to write several languages of the Fertile Crescent

Prepare to Read

Section 4
Mediterranean Civilizations

Objectives

1. Learn how the sea power of the Phoenicians spread civilization.
2. Learn about the major events in the history of the Israelites.

Target Reading Skill

Read Ahead Reading ahead can help you understand something you are not sure of in the text. If you do not understand a word or passage, keep reading. The word or idea may be explained later. Sometimes a word is defined after it has been used. The main idea of one paragraph may be discussed in later paragraphs.

When you read the sentence about Phoenicia's resources in this section, you may not understand what a resource is. By reading ahead, you will find out that resources are things that grow or live in Phoenicia.

Vocabulary Strategy

Using Context to Clarify Meaning When you come across a new word while reading, you should look for context clues to help you figure out what the word means. The chart below shows how the subject of the section and word clues can help you determine meaning.

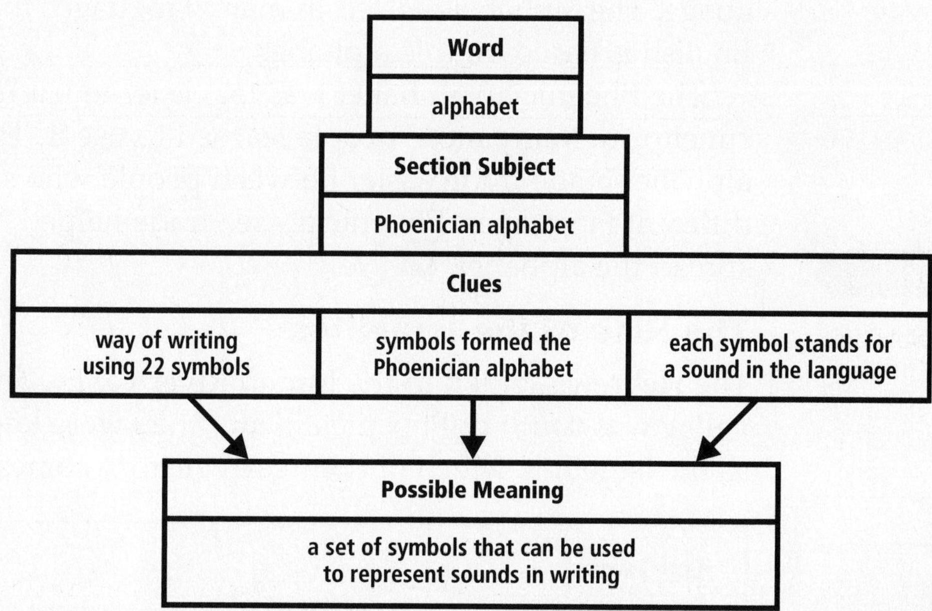

Section 4 Summary

Phoenician Sea Power

Tyre (tyr) was the major city of a region called Phoenicia (fuh NISH uh). Phoenicia was a Fertile Crescent civilization that looked west. It faced the Mediterranean Sea. There were many growing cities around this sea.

Phoenicia had few resources, but they were important. There were snails that produced a rich purple dye. The purple color was highly valued by wealthy people. There were also cedar forests. Phoenicians sold the dyed cloth and wood to neighboring peoples. ✓

✓ Reading Check

Circle the names of the two resources the Phoenicians first used to build their wealth.

Mark the Text

The Phoenicians traded by sea to gain wealth. In time, they controlled trade in much of the Mediterranean. From about 1100 B.C. to 800 B.C., Phoenicia was a great sea power. Phoenician ships sailed as far as the Atlantic Ocean.

Trade brought goods from lands around the Mediterranean to the Phoenician cities of Tyre and Sidon (SY dun). Bazaars were full of foods and animals from faraway places.

The Phoenician Alphabet

The Phoenicians used writing to help them with trade. They created a way of writing that used just 22 symbols. These symbols formed the Phoenician **alphabet**. Each of the symbols stands for a sound of the language. The alphabet is used in many languages today. English is based on this alphabet.

The Phoenician alphabet was far easier to learn than cuneiform. Many more people learned to use it. The alphabet made trade easier between people who spoke different languages. Phoenicia's sea trade helped spread the alphabet. ✓

How did the Phoenician alphabet differ from cuneiform script?

______

______

______

The Rise of the Israelites

The Hebrews settled in the Jordan River valley. This valley was south of Phoenicia. Later they were known as the Israelites. Much of their early history comes

Key Term

alphabet (AL fuh bet) *n.* a set of symbols that represent the sounds of the language

from stories in religious books. One of these books is the Torah (TOH rah). The Torah is the Hebrew Bible. The Israelites greatly influenced our civilization.

The Israelites came from Mesopotamia. According to the Torah, their leader was named Abraham. The Torah says that God told Abraham to leave Mesopotamia. He taught his people to practice **monotheism**. Abraham led the Israelites to the land of Canaan (KAY nun). Then a **famine** caused them to flee to Egypt.

An Israelite named Moses led his people out of Egypt. The flight from Egypt is called the Exodus (EKS uh dus). For 40 years, the Israelites lived in the desert on the Sinai (SY ny) Peninsula. There, God gave them the Ten Commandments, a code of laws. Later, the Israelites went back to Canaan.

The Israelites united under King Saul. The next king was named David. He made Jerusalem his capital. Later the country split into two kingdoms—Israel and Judah. Judah was conquered by its neighbor, Assyria.

In 722 B.C., the Assyrians **exiled** thousands of Israelites to far-off parts of their empire. In 612 B.C., Judah was taken over by Chaldean Babylonians. In 587 B.C., the King of Judah rebelled. King Nebuchadnezzar destroyed Jerusalem and exiled the people of Judah to Babylonia. ✓

Review Questions

1. How did the Phoenicians gain their wealth and power?

____

____

2. What was the Exodus?

____

____

Key Terms

monotheism (MAHN oh thee iz um) *n.* the belief in one god
famine (FAM in) *n.* when there is so little food that people starve
exile (EK syl) *v.* to force someone to live in another country

Vocabulary Strategy

The word *Torah* is not a Key Term. But, it is defined in context. Use the chart on the first page of this section to help you find clues to clarify its meaning. Circle the words or phrases that tell you what the word *Torah* means.

Mark the Text

Target Reading Skill

The Torah says that Abraham was told to leave Mesopotamia and live elsewhere. Keep reading to see what that means.

Where did Abraham lead the Israelites?

____

____

____

✓ Reading Check

Who were the Israelites?

____

____

____

Prepare to Read

Section 5 Judaism

Objectives

1. Learn about the basic beliefs of Judaism.
2. Find out about the impact that Judaism has had on other religions.

Target Reading Skill

Summarize When you summarize, you focus on the main points. You leave out the less important details. A summary is shorter than the original text. When you summarize, keep the main ideas or facts in the correct order.

Look at the following sentence: "At the same time, religious teachers called on government leaders to temper the laws with justice and mercy." It could be summarized like this: "Religious leaders also called for justice and mercy."

As you read, pause to summarize the main ideas about Judaism.

Vocabulary Strategy

Using Context to Clarify Meaning Sometimes you may read a word you recognize, but the word does not seem to make sense in the sentence. Most words have more than one meaning. What a word means depends on its context. Look for clues in the surrounding words or sentences. For example, the word *temper* has many meanings. You cannot know what meaning the author had in mind unless you look at the context.

Some of the most common meanings of *temper* are listed in the chart below. The chart also has examples in context.

	Definitions	**Examples**
temper	mood or state of mind	She is in a good temper today.
	self-control	He lost his temper.
	a tendency to get angry	What a temper you have!
	anger or rage	She went into a temper.
	to lessen or soften	He tries to temper justice with mercy.

Section 5 Summary

The Beliefs of Judaism

To the Israelites, history and religion were closely linked. Each event showed God's plan for the Israelite people. These beliefs became the religion we know as Judaism. It was always monotheistic. It differed in other ways from the beliefs of nearby peoples.

Most ancient people thought that their gods were connected to certain places or people. The Israelites believed that God is present in all places. They believed that God knows everything. They believed that God has complete power.

The Torah says that God promised Abraham that his people would become kings. God said they would build nations. God made a **covenant** with Abraham. The Israelites considered themselves to be God's "chosen people." **Moses** later renewed this covenant. He told the Israelites that God would lead them to Canaan. Canaan was the "promised land." In return, the Israelites had to obey God faithfully.

The Israelites believed God gave Moses the Ten Commandments. They set religious duties toward God. The Torah set many other laws. Some had to do with everyday matters. Others had to do with crimes. Like Hammurabi's Code, many laws demanded an eye for an eye. At the same time, religious teachers called on government leaders to temper the laws with justice and mercy.

Some laws protected women. For example, mothers were to be treated with respect. But women were of lower status than men. A man who was head of a family owned his wife and children. Early on, there were some women leaders, such as the judge Deborah, who won honor and respect. But later, women were not allowed to be religious leaders.

Target Reading Skill

Summarize the first bracketed paragraph. Be sure to include the key points. Also include the important details about God's promise to the Israelites.

Key point: ____________________

Detail: ____________________

Detail: ____________________

Detail: ____________________

Vocabulary Strategy

Mark the Text

The word *temper* is used in the second bracketed paragraph. Find it and circle it. How is it used here? Copy the correct definition from the chart at the beginning of this section.

____

____

____

Key Terms

covenant (KUV uh nunt) *n.* a promise made by God

Moses (MOH zuz) *n.* an Israelite leader whom the Torah says led the Israelites from Egypt to Canaan

The history of the Israelites tells of **prophets**. They told the Israelites what God wanted them to do. Prophets urged the Israelites to live by the idea of right and wrong. They called on the rich and powerful to protect the poor and weak. All people were equal before God. Kings were not gods. They had to obey God's law just like anyone else. ✓

✓ Reading Check

What did the prophets tell the Israelites?

____

____

____

The Effects of Judaism

People who follow Judaism are known as Jews. The Romans drove the Jews out of their homeland in A.D. 135. The Jews then scattered to many parts of the world. The Assyrians and Chaldeans had begun this **diaspora**.

Wherever they lived, Jews preserved their heritage. They lived in close communities. They obeyed their religious laws. They worshiped at their temples. They followed traditions such as Passover. These traditions helped unite Jews. ✓

✓ Reading Check

Name four ways the Jews preserved their heritage.

1. _______________
2. _______________
3. _______________
4. _______________

Judaism had an important effect on two later religions, Christianity and Islam. Both of these faiths came from the same area. Both were monotheistic. Jews, Christians, and people who follow Islam all honor Abraham, Moses, and the prophets. They share the Israelite moral point of view.

Review Questions

1. Why did the Israelites believe that they were God's chosen people?

____

____

____

2. What religious laws did the Israelites follow?

____

____

____

Key Terms

prophet (PRAHF it) *n.* a religious teacher who people believe speaks for God or a god

diaspora (dy AS pur uh) *n.* the scattering of people who have a common background or beliefs

Chapter 2 Assessment

1. *Mesopotamia* means "between the rivers." Which two rivers is it between?
   - **A.** Sumer and Tigris rivers
   - **B.** Phoenicia and Assur rivers
   - **C.** Tigris and Euphrates rivers
   - **D.** Akkadia and Sumer rivers

2. Which of these is true of the Babylonian Empire?
   - **A.** It was created by Hammurabi.
   - **B.** It was on open land, which was easily invaded.
   - **C.** It had its capital at the city of Nineveh.
   - **D.** It was conquered by Mari.

3. Hammurabi's Code was
   - **A.** a secret code known only to the Babylonian rulers.
   - **B.** used as a model for the laws of the United States.
   - **C.** based on justice and mercy.
   - **D.** the first organized set of laws that we have found.

4. The Phoenician alphabet was
   - **A.** the model of the alphabet used today in the United States.
   - **B.** so hard to learn that people had to study it for years.
   - **C.** a system that used wedges and lines scratched into clay tablets.
   - **D.** made up of symbols that stood for objects and ideas.

5. Why did the Israelites make such a deep impact on our civilization?
   - **A.** They ruled one of the largest empires in history.
   - **B.** They developed the moral point of view shared by Judaism, Christianity, and Islam.
   - **C.** They developed the alphabet that is used today.
   - **D.** They were the only people in southwest Asia that were never conquered by another nation.

Short Answer Question

How did the Jews preserve their heritage in exile?

Prepare to Read

Section 1
The Geography of the Nile

Objectives

1. Find out how the geography of the Nile changes along its course.
2. Learn about the first communities that settled along the Nile, and how people used the Nile for trade.

Use Context Clues When you are reading, you will sometimes see an unfamiliar word. Or you may find a word you recognize, but the word is used in a new way. This is the time to look for clues to the word's meaning in the context. Context is the surrounding words, phrases, and sentences.

As you read this section, find details in the context that give clues to the meaning of *course* in the blue heading "The Course of the Nile River." What do you think *course* means?

Vocabulary Strategy

Finding Roots Many words have a few letters attached to the beginning or the end to make another word. For example, the letters *un-* may be attached at the beginning of a word. Or the letters *-ing* may be attached at the end of a word. When you remove these added letters, you end up with what is called the root. A root is a word that is used to make another word.

Attached Letters	Word	Root
un-	unwell	well
-ing	doing	do

When you come across a new word, look at it closely. See if it contains any other words that you already know. Often, you can use the root to help you figure out what the word means.

Section 1 Summary

The Course of the Nile River

The Nile River is the world's longest river. It is more than 4,000 miles (6,400 kilometers) long. It flows north to the Mediterranean Sea. It has two main sources. The Blue Nile starts in the highlands of what is now Ethiopia. The White Nile begins in East Africa and flows northward through swamps. The two rivers meet in what is now Sudan.

North of the point where the Blue Nile and White Nile meet, the Nile makes an S shape. The northern tip of the S is at the city of Aswan in Egypt. This area was **Nubia**.

Nubia has six **cataracts**. Between the first and second cataracts was Lower Nubia. It is a land of desert and granite mountains, so people lived close to the Nile for water. Between the second and sixth cataracts is Upper Nubia.

From the first cataract, the Nile passed through Upper Egypt. In the north, the Nile formed a fertile, marshy area called Lower Egypt.

Also, in the north, the Nile split into several streams that flowed into the Mediterranean Sea. These streams formed the **delta**. The water deposited sediment that was rich in minerals. Because of this, the delta contained very fertile farmland.

Every spring, waters came rushing down from the highlands. They brought a rich, fertile sediment called **silt**. Each spring, the Nile flooded the dry land and deposited a layer of thick silt. The silt was ideal for farming. Because of this dark soil, the ancient Egyptians called their land Kemet (KEH meht), "the black land." Unlike the Mesopotamians, the Egyptians usually did not have to worry about flash floods. ✓

Key Terms

Nubia (NOO bee uh) *n.* an ancient region in the Nile River Valley, now in southern Egypt and northern Sudan
cataract (KAT uh rakt) *n.* a large waterfall; any strong flood or rush of water
delta (DEL tuh) *n.* a plain at the mouth of a river, formed where flowing water deposits soil
silt (silt) *n.* fine soil found on the bottom of rivers

Target Reading Skill

If you do not know what the word *sediment* is, consider the context clues. Sediment is described as being carried by water and rich in minerals. If you read ahead, you will learn that silt is a kind of sediment. What is the meaning of *sediment*?

✓ Reading Check

How did the people of Nubia and Egypt benefit from the geography of the Nile?

Vocabulary Strategy

The words below appear in the bracketed paragraph. Each of these words contains another word that is its root. Underline the roots.

Mark the Text

useless

farming

protected

completely

traveled

Circle the words in the text. Did knowing the root help you figure out the meaning?

Beyond the fertile riverbanks was the vast desert, or "red land." These lands were useless for farming. But the rocks and hot sands protected the Egyptians and Nubians from foreign attacks. The people of Egypt and Nubia faced few invasions for about 2,000 years. But they were not completely cut off. The Nile valley was used as a highway to central Africa. People traveled to Southwest Asia by boat on the Mediterranean Sea and the Red Sea.

The Growth of Communities and Trade Along the Nile

Hunting and fishing communities may have started in Nubia around 6000 B.C. Farming communities began to appear in both Egypt and Nubia around 5000 B.C. In Egypt, villages formed near the Nile delta and in the valley. Nubia had less farmland, so people also fished in the river and hunted.

Egyptians used the Nile like a highway to carry goods for trade. Ships could float downriver because the Nile flowed north. They could sail upriver because the winds blew toward the south. Egyptians also traveled across the desert to the Red Sea or to Mesopotamia. ✓

Because of the cataracts, Nubians could travel only on land. The Nubians became famous traders of the ancient world. They brought goods from central Africa and Nubia to sell in Egypt and southwest Asia. They also brought goods home.

✓ Reading Check

How did the Nile work as a highway?

____

____

____

Review Questions

1. How did Egyptians and Nubians use the Nile River?

____

____

____

2. How did the Nile's cataracts affect Nubian trade?

____

____

____

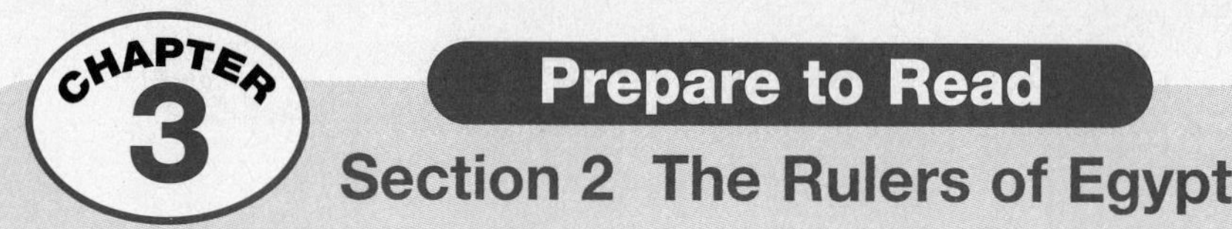

CHAPTER 3

Prepare to Read

Section 2 The Rulers of Egypt

Objectives

1. Learn the history of ancient Egyptian kingship.
2. Find out about Egypt's three kingdom periods.
3. Understand how the pharaohs ruled Egypt during the New Kingdom period.

Target Reading Skill

Use Context Clues When you need help figuring out the meaning of an unfamiliar word, use context. Context includes the surrounding words, phrases, and sentences. Sometimes the context will actually include a definition of the word.

> This was a giant sphinx, *a legendary creature with a lion's body and a human head.*

Your textbook often gives you definitions of new words in the same sentence. Other times, it may be in the sentence before or after the new word. Whenever you see a new word, watch for a definition.

Vocabulary Strategy

Finding Roots Words often have a few letters added to the beginning or the end to make another word. The original word is called a root. The letters attached to the beginning or end form one or more syllables. A syllable is a group of letters that is spoken as a single sound. Below are some common syllables added to the beginning or end of words.

Beginning Syllables	Ending Syllables
de-	*-ed*
non-	*-ment*
anti-	*-ern*

What words do you know that begin or end with these syllables? What are their roots?

When you come across a new word, look to see if contains any other words that you already know.

Section 2 Summary

Egyptian Kingship

Ancient Egypt had 31 **dynasties** from about 3100 B.C. until 332 B.C. Historians group the dynasties into three kingdoms. The earliest is called the Old Kingdom. Next comes the Middle Kingdom. The last time period is the New Kingdom.

According to legend, a pharaoh, or king, named Menes (MEE neez) united Upper Egypt and Lower Egypt. That is when the first dynasty began. Menes built a city named Memphis near where Cairo (KY roh) now is. From there, he ruled over the Two Lands of Upper Egypt and Lower Egypt. This began one of the most stable civilizations in history. ✓

Egypt's **pharaohs** had **absolute power**. People thought that their pharaohs were gods.

The Three Kingdoms

Each kingdom is known for an important event or an achievement. The Old Kingdom is known for its well-run government. The pharaohs kept peace and traded with Nubia. They sent buyers to the eastern Mediterranean to find <u>timber</u>. Timber is trees used for building. This timber was used to build houses, boats, and furniture. Toward the end of the Old Kingdom, governors in the provinces challenged the pharaohs' rule. Egypt's unity crumbled, and the dynasties grew weak.

The Middle Kingdom returned order and reunited the country. Pharaohs spent the nation's wealth on public works, not war. Egypt grew richer. But weaker rulers followed. Then foreign invaders took over the country.

Key Terms

dynasty (DY nus tee) *n.* a series of rulers from the same family or ethnic group
pharaoh (FEHR oh) *n.* the title of the kings of ancient Egypt
absolute power (AB suh loot POW ur) *n.* complete control over someone or something

✓ Reading Check

Who was Menes and what did he do?

____

____

____

Target Reading Skill

The word *timber* is underlined below. If you do not know what *timber* means, look for context clues. Find a restatement of *timber*. Reread what the Egyptians used timber for. What is timber?

____

____

____

Vocabulary Strategy

The words below appear in the summary after the heading "The Three Kingdoms." Each of these words contains another word that is its root. Underline the roots.

government

eastern

building

reunited

Mark the Text

Circle the words in the text. Did knowing the roots help you figure out the meaning of any new words?

In time, strong Egyptian princes drove out the invaders. This was the start of the New Kingdom in 1567 B.C. The first pharaohs of the New Kingdom wanted to build an empire. They created huge armies with good weapons. One pharaoh, King Tutankhamen, became more well known after the discovery of his tomb. He had died at the young age of 18 and was buried with many precious objects. ✓

Rule During the New Kingdom

In 1504 B.C., a child named Thutmose III (thoot MOH suh) began to rule. His stepmother was made **regent**. Her name was Hatshepsut (haht SHEP soot). She had herself made pharaoh and ruled for 15 years. She created a time of great peace and economic success. When Thutmose grew up, she refused to step down. Thutmose became pharaoh after her death.

Thutmose III was one of the greatest pharaohs of the New Kingdom. His armies went east to the Euphrates River. They also went south into Nubia. But Thutmose was also an educated man. Unlike past rulers, he treated the people he defeated with mercy.

Toward the end of the New Kingdom, Egypt declined again. Civil war left Egypt weak. Then Egypt fell to Alexander the Great of Macedonia. The Macedonians ruled Egypt for about 300 years. In 51 B.C., Queen Cleopatra VII became the last Macedonian ruler. Egypt became part of the Roman Empire in 31 B.C. Egypt would not govern itself again for almost 2,000 years. ✓

Review Questions

1. What powers did Egyptians believe their kings had?

___

___

2. Describe the New Kingdom under Thutmose III.

___

___

___

Key Term

regent (REE junt) *n.* someone who rules for a child until the child is old enough to rule

✓ Reading Check

Name an important event or achievement in each of the three kingdoms.

Old Kingdom: ___

Middle Kingdom: ___

New Kingdom: ___

✓ Reading Check

Why did Egypt decline during the New Kingdom period?

___

Prepare to Read

Section 3 Egyptian Religion

Objectives

1. Learn about Egyptian gods and goddesses.
2. Find out about the Egyptians' belief in the afterlife.
3. Discover how and why the pharaohs had tombs built.

Target Reading Skill

Use Context Clues Lots of words in English have more than one meaning. This can cause confusion when you read. Sometimes you come across a word you know, but it doesn't seem to make sense in the sentence. When this happens, you could look up the word in a dictionary. Or you can use context clues and your own general knowledge to figure out what the word means.

The body was then wrapped in layers of long linen bandages.

The word *linen* may not seem to make sense here. Perhaps you know that *linen* is used to refer to tablecloths and napkins, or to sheets and pillowcases. These are all items made of a type of cloth. Linen bandages must be bandages made of cloth.

Vocabulary Strategy

Finding Roots Syllables or groups of syllables are often added at the beginning or the end of a word. This creates a new word. The meaning of the new word is related to the original word. But it is changed in some way. For example, we can add the syllable *un-* at the beginning of *well.* The new word, *unwell,* means the opposite of the original word, *well.* It is still related to the original word because it uses the original word as its root.

When you come across a new word, look to see if it has a root. If you know the word's root, it will help you to figure out the meaning of the whole word.

Section 3 Summary

Egyptian Gods and Goddesses

Religion was very important to ancient Egyptians. They believed that their gods and goddesses controlled the natural world. So, Egyptians built temples to honor their gods. They offered them food, gifts, and prayers.

Each town had its own gods and goddesses. But all Egyptians worshiped certain gods. Over time, they all began to believe in groups of gods. The chief god of the ancient Egyptians was Amon-Re (ah mun RAY). He protected rich and poor alike. Another powerful god was Osiris (oh SY ris), the god of the living and the dead. The goddess Isis (EYE sis) was his wife. Horus, the sky god, was their son. ✓

Belief in an Afterlife

Ancient Egyptians believed in an **afterlife**. If they had pleased the gods, their spirits joined Osiris. They lived a life of ease and pleasure. However, the souls of the dead could not survive without food, clothing, and other items from this life. So, their personal items were buried with them. ✓

At first, most Egyptians were buried in the desert in shallow pits. The climate dried out the body, creating a **mummy**. The Egyptians believed the soul left the mummy, but returned to it for food offerings. The body had to be preserved so that the soul could find it. Later, the Egyptians began to preserve bodies artificially. This process was expensive. It took two or three months. Workers removed the organs. The body was filled with a natural salt and stored until it dried out. Then it was cleaned and bathed with spices. Finally, it was wrapped in layers of long linen bandages.

While the mummy was being prepared, workers carved the coffin. Pharaohs had three or four coffins that fit inside one another. The first coffin inside was usually shaped like a human body. The dead person's face was painted on the top.

Key Terms

afterlife (AF tur lyf) *n.* a life after death
mummy (MUM ee) *n.* a dead body preserved in lifelike condition

Vocabulary Strategy

The word below appears in the first sentence after the heading "Egyptian Gods and Goddesses." Underline the word's root.

Egyptians

What clue to the whole word's meaning comes from the root?

___

___

___

✓ Reading Check

Who was Osiris?

___

___

___

✓ Reading Check

Why did ancient Egyptians bury their dead with food and personal items?

___

___

___

The Pharaohs' Tombs

The earliest royal tombs were made of mud brick. The pharaohs of the Fourth Dynasty built the largest and most famous tombs. These were the **pyramids**. The largest is the Great Pyramid in **Giza**. It was built for Khufu (KOO foo), the second king of this dynasty.

Pyramid building took great organization. For example, the Great Pyramid is made up of more than 2 million stones. The average weight is 5,000 pounds (2,270 kilograms). Each stone had to be hauled up the side and put into its place.

Target Reading Skill

What does *hauled* mean in the bracketed paragraph? Look for context clues in the text.

It could take more than 20 years to build a pyramid. First a site was selected on the west bank of the Nile. Engineers set the pyramid square with the main points of the compass. Workers then cut the building blocks. Stone for the inside came from nearby. But fine stone for the outside came from farther away. Some stone came by boat.

Sleds, wooden rollers, and levers were used to get the blocks into place. They dragged and pushed the blocks up ramps of packed rubble. It was dangerous work. Men were killed in accidents. But the workers believed that their work was important. It meant the pharaoh had a place in the afterlife. ✓

✓ Reading Check

Why did the Egyptians build pyramids?

Review Questions

1. What was the purpose of a mummy for ancient Egyptians?

2. How do we know that the afterlife was important to the ancient Egyptians?

Key Terms

pyramid (PIH ruh mid) *n.* a huge building with four sloping triangular-shaped sides; built as royal tombs in Egypt

Giza (GEE zuh) *n.* an ancient Egyptian city; the site of the Great Pyramid

Prepare to Read

Section 4 Ancient Egyptian Culture

Objectives

1. Find out how ancient Egyptians lived everyday.
2. Learn about writing in ancient Egypt.
3. Discover Egyptian achievements in science and medicine.

Target Reading Skill

Use Context Clues You have learned that using context can help you figure out the meaning of an unfamiliar word. The words, phrases, and sentences around a word can provide clues.

In some cases, cause-and-effect clues can help you understand the meaning of the word. In the following sentence, a cause-and-effect clue points to the meaning of *scattered*:

The farmer <u>scattered</u> the seeds, which flew and landed all around.

Ask: What caused the seeds to land all around? What do you think *scattered* means?

Vocabulary Strategy

Finding Roots Often, syllables or groups of syllables are added at the beginning or the end of a word to make a new word. The meaning of the new word is related to the original word. But it is changed in some way. It is still related to the original word because it uses the original word as its root.

In some cases, the spelling changes slightly when a word becomes a root. Often, a final *e* is dropped when a new ending is added to a word. For example, if we add the ending *y* to the word *ease*, it is spelled *easy* (and **not** *easey*!).

If you keep this in mind, you can see that the word *writing* contains the root *write*.

Section 4 Summary

The Lives of the Egyptians

Egyptian society was built like a pyramid.

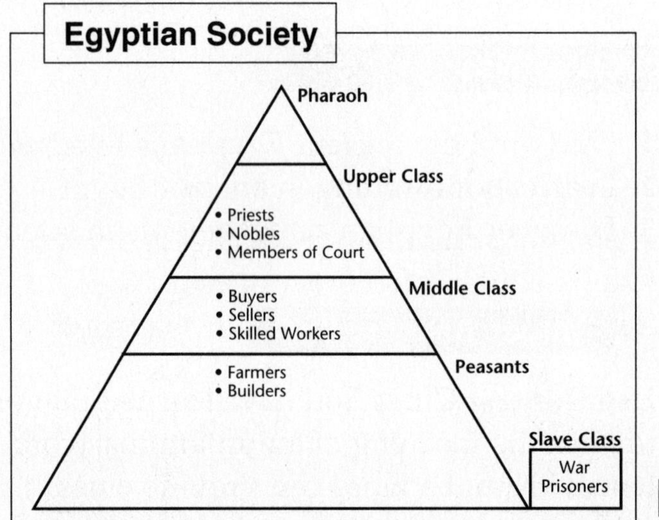

✓

During the flood season, peasants worked on roads, temples, and other buildings. After the floods, they farmed the land of the rich or their own land.

Women had most of the rights of men. They could own property, run businesses, and travel. Even slaves had rights. The could own personal items and inherit land. They could also be set free.

Writing in Ancient Egypt

The ancient Egyptians had a special way of writing. They used **hieroglyphs** to keep records of the kingdom's growing wealth.

At first, the Egyptians wrote on clay and stone. But then they made something better—**papyrus**. Inner stalks of the papyrus plant were cut into narrow strips. Next, strips were placed side by side in one layer. Another layer of strips was placed crosswise. Then, strips were soaked, pounded flat, and dried. Finally, sap from the plant glued the strips together.

Key Terms

hieroglyphs (HY ur oh glifs) n. pictures and other written symbols that stand for ideas, things, or sounds

papyrus (puh PY ruhs) *n.* an early form of paper made from a reed plant found in the marshy areas of the Nile delta

Vocabulary Strategy

The words below appear after the heading "The Lives of the Egyptians." Each of these words contains a root. Underline the root.

worked

buildings

businesses

Mark the Text

Circle the word in the text. Did knowing any of these roots help you figure out its meaning in context?

✓ Reading Check

How was Egyptian society organized?

____

____

____

Target Reading Skill

What does *sap* mean in the underlined sentence below? Look for cause-and-effect clues in the text. Sap from the plant glues the strips of papyrus together. What is sap?

____

____

____

After the A.D. 400s, people had forgotten what the symbols of hieroglyphs meant. But, in 1799, a soldier dug up a large black stone near the Nile. Two parts of the stone had different forms of hieroglyphs. A third part had Greek letters. In the 1820s, a French scholar used the Greek letters to figure out the meanings of the hieroglyphs. This opened up a new window onto the world of ancient Egypt. The stone is called the Rosetta Stone because it was found near the city of Rosetta. ✓

Science and Medicine

As farmers, the ancient Egyptians needed to know when the Nile would flood every year. Their **astronomers** helped by figuring out the length of a year—365 days. ✓

The Egyptians had good math skills. Mathematics helped them measure rock to build pyramids. They were also able to measure the area of a plot of land.

The ancient Egyptians studied the human body. They learned to perform surgery and set broken bones. They also created medicines from plants.

Review Questions

1. How were the lives of Egypt's peasants ruled by the seasons?

____

____

____

2. What areas of science and medicine did the ancient Egyptians study?

____

____

____

Key Term

astronomer (uh STRAHN uh mur) *n.* a scientist who studies the stars and other objects in the sky

✓ Reading Check

Why was the Rosetta Stone an important discovery?

____

____

____

✓ Reading Check

Why was it important for the Egyptians to know the length of their year?

____

____

____

CHAPTER 3

Prepare to Read

Section 5 The Cultures of Nubia

Objectives

1. Look at the relationship between Nubia and Egypt.
2. Learn about the Nubian kingdoms centered in Kerma, Napata, and Meroë.

Target Reading Skill

Use Context Clues Context refers to the words, phrases, or sentences before or after the word. Context can offer clues to the meaning of words that are new to you.

One strategy for understanding unfamiliar words is to use synonyms. A synonym is a word that has a similar meaning.

Taharka received the <u>ultimate</u> prize, the greatest honor possible.

The word *greatest* is a synonym for *ultimate*. As you read, look for synonyms and other context clues.

Vocabulary Strategy

Finding Roots You now know that syllables or groups of syllables can be added at the beginning or the end of a word to make a new word. The meaning of the new word is related to the original word. But it is changed in some way.

In some cases, the spelling changes slightly when a word becomes a root. Often, a *y* at the end of a word is changed to *i* when the word becomes a root. For example, if we add the ending *-ly* to the word *easy*, it is spelled *easily* (and **not** *easyly*!).

If you keep this in mind, you can see that the word *geographic* comes from *geography*.

Section 5 Summary

Nubia and Egypt

For years, Nubia and Egypt were mostly peaceful neighbors. Egypt needed Nubia for its gold, copper, and iron **ores**. Also, **Lower Nubia** was a connection for goods between central Africa and Egypt. In time, powerful kingdoms arose in **Upper Nubia**. The most powerful were in the cities of Kerma, Napata, and Meroë. These kingdoms wanted land controlled by Egypt. The Nubians were ruled by the Kushites, people of southern Nubia. ✓

The Kerma Culture

When Egypt grew weak, the Kushites took control. By about 1600 B.C., the Kushite kingdom had expanded from the Nubian city of Kerma (KUR muh) into parts of Egypt. These Nubians are called the Kerma culture. Their kingdom lasted nearly 500 years.

Kerma was rich from its trading with central Africa. It was noted for its **artisans**. These craftsmen made beautiful pottery. Like Egyptians, the people of Kerma spent their resources on royal burials. They built mounds of earth as large as football fields. Inside, the kings' bodies were surrounded by gold, ivory, and jewels. ✓

Egypt grew stronger around the 1500s B.C. After 50 years of war, Egypt took control of part of Nubia. Egypt ruled this part of Nubia for about 700 years. During that period, the Nubians adopted many Egyptian ways. They even began to worship Egyptian gods along with their own. The two cultures began to mix.

Key Terms

ore (awr) *n.* a mineral or a combination of minerals mined for the production of metals

Lower Nubia (LOH ur NOO bee uh) *n.* the region of ancient Nubia between the First and Second Nile cataracts

Upper Nubia (UP ur NOO bee uh) *n.* the region of ancient Nubia between the Second and Sixth Nile cataracts

artisan (AHR tuh zun) *n.* a worker who is skilled in crafting goods by hand

✓ Reading Check

Why did Nubia and Egypt become rivals?

____

____

____

Target Reading Skill

Do you know what *artisan* means? Look for context clues. What does the word mean?

____

____

____

✓ Reading Check

What were some features of Kerma?

____

____

____

Vocabulary Strategy

The words below appear under the heading "Napata and Meroë." Each of these words contains a root. Underline the roots. If the spelling of the root has been changed, write the correct root after the word.

controlled

Nubians

moving

allowed

hieroglyphics

✓ Reading Check

How did the people of Meroë use iron ore?

____

____

____

Napata and Meroë

In the late 700s B.C., Egypt grew weak again. At the same time, the Kushites had grown strong. From their city Napata (nuh PAY tuh), the Kushites moved back into Egypt. They made their capital first in Thebes, then in Memphis. Soon, they controlled all of Egypt. The pharaohs of Egypt's Twenty-fifth Dynasty were Nubians. But their rule did not last very long. About 660 B.C., they were forced back to Napata. Then they moved their capital south to Meroë (MEHR oh ee). They never again controlled Egyptian land.

After moving as far from Egypt as possible, the Nubians started over. Meroë became the center of an empire that included much of Nubia and central Africa. Meroë's desert had large deposits of iron ore. The Nubians used the ore to make iron weapons and tools. Iron plows allowed them to grow large supplies of food. Iron weapons allowed them to control trade routes. Meroë became rich from trade. ✓

The Meroë culture created its own type of hieroglyphics. So far, scholars have not been able to understand the symbols. Because of this, Meroë is largely a mystery. It began to weaken in the A.D. 200s. Later, it fell to another African kingdom. But parts of Nubian culture such as braided hairstyles, clothing, pottery, furniture, and jewelry, are still found in present-day Sudan.

Review Questions

1. What was the relationship between Egypt and Nubia?

____

____

____

2. How is the history of Napata tied to Egypt?

____

____

____

Chapter 3 Assessment

1. The Nile River flows
   A. north for about 4,000 miles.
   B. south to the Mediterranean Sea.
   C. north to the Red Sea.
   D. south.

2. The three kingdoms of ancient Egypt refer to
   A. Upper Egypt, Lower Egypt, and Nubia.
   B. the three main time periods into which Egypt's history is grouped.
   C. Kerma, Napata, and Meroë.
   D. periods of trouble between Egypt's dynasties.

3. The chief Egyptian god was
   A. Amon-Re.
   B. Horus.
   C. Isis.
   D. Osiris.

4. Which of the following describes the Egyptian class system?
   A. It was shaped like a pyramid.
   B. A person could easily rise to a higher class.
   C. Only pharaohs could own property and inherit land.
   D. It was very rigid and people could not rise to a higher class.

5. Which of the following Nubian cultures created a system of hieroglyphic writing?
   A. Egypt
   B. Kerma
   C. Napata
   D. Meroë

Short Answer Question

Describe the locations of Upper and Lower Egypt, and Upper and Lower Nubia on the course of the Nile River.

____

____

____

____

____

Prepare to Read

Section 1 The Indus and Ganges River Valleys

Objectives

1. Learn about India's geographic setting.
2. Find out about life in an ancient city of the Indus River valley.
3. Learn about the rise of a new culture in the Indus and Ganges river valleys.

Target Reading Skill

Identify Causes and Effects A cause makes something happen. It is the reason that something happens. An effect is what happens. It is the result of the cause. As you read, pause to ask yourself what happened. The answer to that question is the effect. Then ask yourself why it happened. The answer to that question is the cause.

For example, millions of years ago India's landmass crashed into Asia. Think of this as the cause. The effect was the formation of the Himalaya Mountains.

Seeing causes and effects helps you understand how events are connected. It helps you understand why things happen as they do.

Vocabulary Strategy

Recognizing Compound Words When you come across a new word, you may be able to figure out what it means if you break it down into parts. For example, if you did not know what the word *snowball* means, you could break it down into its parts: *snow* and *ball*. A snowball is a ball of snow. Many words in English are made by combining two or more words. Such words are referred to as *compound words*. As you read, use what you know about compound words to help you understand new words.

Here are some common words that are made up of two words:

anybody	*homeland*	*seashore*
baseball	*landform*	*skyscraper*
countryside	*mainland*	*southwest*
downtown	*mountaintop*	*waterway*
farmland	*northeast*	*worldwide*

Section 1 Summary

India's Geographic Setting

The land of India sticks out from the rest of Asia into the Indian Ocean. India is a **subcontinent**. The Himalayas and the Hindu Kush mountain range cut India off from the rest of Asia. The Bay of Bengal, the Indian Ocean, and the Arabian Sea are on India's east and west. Because of this, India had little contact with the rest of the world for many years.

India's climate is ruled by **monsoons** or strong seasonal winds. From October to May, the winter monsoon blows from the northeast. It spreads dry air across the country. The summer monsoon comes in the middle of June. It picks up moisture from the Indian Ocean. The people rely on summer monsoons for rain. If the monsoon is late or weak, crops die and there is famine. If there is too much rain, rivers may flood. ✓

The first people of northern India probably came through openings in the Hindu Kush mountains. Great rivers rise in the mountains. The Indus (IN dus) River flows into the Arabian Sea. The Ganges (GAN jeez) River flows into the Bay of Bengal. The rivers let farmers grow crops in the plains of northern India.

Life in the Indus River Valley

The Indus Valley had rich soil. With surplus food, the number of people grew. From around 2500 B.C. to 1500 B.C., cities grew up in the valley. One large city was Mohenjo-Daro (moh HEN joh DAH roh). It was on the banks of the Indus River.

Mohenjo-Daro was well planned. It was built above ground level to protect it from floods. Homes and shops were on one side of the city. Public buildings were on the other side. A wall protected the city's most important buildings. These buildings included the **citadel**.

Key Terms

subcontinent (SUB kahn tih nunt) *n.* a large piece of land that sticks out from a continent
monsoon (mahn SOON) *n.* a strong wind that blows across East Asia at certain times of the year
citadel (SIT uh del) *n.* a fortress in a city

Target Reading Skill

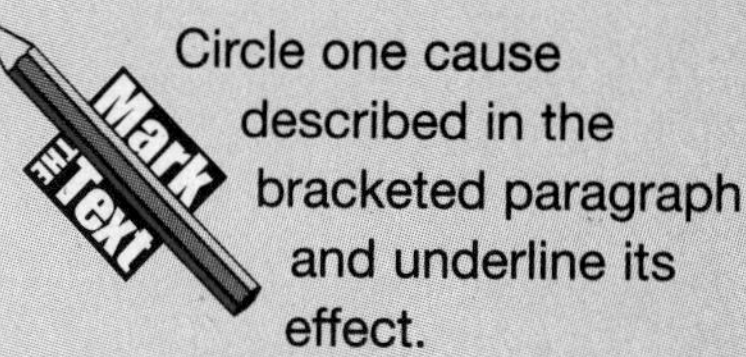

Circle one cause described in the bracketed paragraph and underline its effect.

✓ Reading Check

How do winter monsoons differ from summer monsoons?

____

____

____

✓ Reading Check

Describe the city plan for Mohenjo-Daro.

Vocabulary Strategy

Remember to look for compound words as you read. There are two on this page. As you find each one, draw a line between the two words that form the compound.

Mark the Text

Then write the words you found on the lines below.

1. ______________________

2. ______________________

✓ Reading Check

How was Aryan society organized?

Mohenjo-Daro had a means of draining water from the land. Clay pipes under the streets sent waste away from the city. Canals ran next to the Indus River. They helped to keep flood water from the city. ✓

Around 2000 B.C., the people of the Indus Valley began to leave their land. From 2000 B.C. to 1500 B.C., newcomers from the north came to the area.

A New Culture Arises

The new people were called Aryans (AYR ee uhnz). They **migrated** from their homelands in central Asia. They were nomadic herders. Local people adopted the Aryans' language. They also adopted some of their beliefs. A new, mixed Aryan culture began.

This new culture first started in the northern Indus Valley. It spread into the Ganges Valley to the east. By about 800 B.C., the people of northern India had learned to make tools and weapons of iron. With iron axes, they cleared the thick rain forests.

Aryan society was grouped into three classes. Priests, called Brahmans, performed religious services. Below them were warriors and nobles. Next came the artisans and merchants. Finally, a fourth class of people made up of farm workers, laborers, and servants was formed.

This division of classes is the **caste** system. People had to stay in the caste of their parents. Each caste had many groups. People did the same work as their parents and other members of their group. ✓

Review Questions

1. How do the monsoons affect India's climate?

2. Who were the Aryans?

Key Terms

migrate (MY grayt) *v.* to relocate; to move from one place and settle in another

caste (kast) *n.* a social class of people

Prepare to Read

Section 2 Hinduism in Ancient India

Objectives

1. Find out about the beginnings of Hinduism.
2. Learn about the basic beliefs of Hinduism.
3. Examine the practice of Hinduism.

Target Reading Skill

Recognize Cause-and-Effect Signal Words As you read, watch for clues that show cause and effect. Often, a word will give you a signal that what is being described is either a cause or an effect. Words such as *affect*, *as a result*, and *from* signal a cause or an effect.

In the following example, *from* signals a cause: "*From* this blend of ideas and beliefs came one of the world's oldest living religions, Hinduism." The cause is a blend of ideas and beliefs. The effect is Hinduism.

As you read, look for signals that explain other causes and effects.

Vocabulary Strategy

Using Prefixes and Roots A prefix is one or more syllables attached to the beginning of a word to make a new word. The word it is attached to is known as the root. When a prefix is added to a root, the new word has a new meaning. The meaning of the prefix is added to the meaning of the root.

Some common prefixes are listed below, along with their meanings and examples. Notice that some of them have more than one meaning. Learning to identify prefixes, and knowing what they mean, will help you understand what you read.

Prefix	Meaning	Example
in-, im-	in, into, within, on, toward	inject, immigrate
non-	not	nontoxic
pre-	before	prehistory
re-	again	reread

Section 2 Summary

Vocabulary Strategy

The words below appear in this section. Each word contains a prefix. Underline the prefix in each word.

reborn

nonviolence

Mark the Text

Now look at the chart on the previous page. Use the chart to find the prefix's meaning. Then, add the meaning of the prefix to the meaning of the root.

1. Reborn means ____________
____

2. Nonviolence means ________
____
____

✓ Reading Check

List the most important Hindu gods.

1. ____________________
2. ____________________
3. ____________________

The Beginnings of Hinduism

Aryan culture mixed with India's existing cultures. From this blend of ideas and beliefs came one of the world's oldest living religions, Hinduism. It has picked up beliefs from other religions in its 3,500 years. It became very complex. Hindus believe that there are many ways of coming to god.

Hinduism is one of the world's major religions. More than 850 million people in India follow it today. Its beliefs have influenced people of many religions. But it is different from other major world religions. There is no one founder. Hindus worship many gods and goddesses. But they believe in one single spiritual power. This power is called **brahman**.

The gods and goddesses of Hinduism stand for different parts of brahman. The three most important gods are Brahma the Creator, Vishnu the Preserver, and Shiva is the Destroyer. Each one takes many forms. These forms are called **avatars**. ✓

Hindus believe that Brahma created Earth and all that is on it. But he is not as widely worshiped as Vishnu and Shiva. Vishnu is kind. He tries to protect humans. Shiva is responsible for both the creative and destructive forces in the universe. Hindu gods have families. Many Hindus worship Shiva's wife, Shakti.

The Teachings of Hinduism

All Hindus share certain beliefs. They are in religious writings. One of these is the Upanishads (oo PAN uh shadz). *Upanishad* means "sitting near a teacher."

One of the shared ideas is **reincarnation**. Hindus believe that when a person dies, the soul is reborn in another living thing. They believe that every living thing has a soul.

Key Terms

brahman (BRAH mun) *n.* a single spiritual power that Hindus believe lives in everything
avatar (av uh TAHR) *n.* a Hindu god or goddess in human or animal form
reincarnation (ree in kahr NAY shun) *n.* rebirth of the soul in the body of another living thing

Hindus believe that a person's actions in this life affect his or her fate in the next. Good behavior is rewarded. Bad behavior is punished. Faithful followers of Hinduism will be born into a higher position. Those who have been bad may be born into a lower caste. They may even return as an animal. A perfect life may free a soul from the cycle of death and rebirth. As a result, this person's soul is united with brahman. ✓

To do this, a person must obey his or her **dharma**. The duties of dharma depend on a person's class, job, and age. **Ahimsa**, or nonviolence, is also important. To Hindus, all people and things are part of brahman. They must be treated with respect. That is why many Hindus do not eat meat. They try not to hurt living things.

The Practice of Hinduism

Hindus believe that there are many paths to the truth. They may worship in different ways. One way is by practicing yoga (YOH guh). Yoga means union. Hindus believe yoga exercises help free the soul from the cares of the world. It helps the soul unite with brahman. There are many yogas that lead to brahman. Physical activity is one yoga. Another is selfless deeds, such as giving to the poor. ✓

Review Questions

1. How did the early Aryan culture influence Hinduism?

2. What does Hinduism teach about the path to truth?

Key Terms

dharma (DAHR muh) *n.* the religious and moral duties of Hindus
ahimsa (uh HIM sah) *n.* the Hindu idea of nonviolence

Target Reading Skill

What does *As a result* signal?

✓ Reading Check

According to Hindu belief, what happens to a person's soul after death?

✓ Reading Check

How is yoga practiced by Hindus?

Prepare to Read

Section 3 The Beginnings of Buddhism

Objectives

1. Learn about the Buddha and his teachings.
2. Find out how Buddhism was received inside and outside India.

Target Reading Skill

Recognizing Multiple Causes A cause makes something happen. An effect is what happens. Often, an effect can have more than one cause. For example, in the story that begins this section, Gautama sees three events that cause him to change his life. Can you identify the three causes?

Looking for more than one cause will help you fully understand why something happened. As you read this section, look for other things that have multiple causes.

Vocabulary Strategy

Using Roots and Suffixes A suffix is one or more syllables attached to the end of a word to make a new word. The word it is attached to is known as the root. When a suffix is added to a root, the new word has a new meaning. The meaning of the suffix is added to the meaning of the root.

Some common suffixes are listed below, along with their meanings and examples. Notice that some have more than one meaning. Learning to identify suffixes, and knowing what they mean, will help you understand what you read.

Suffix	Meaning	Example
-ern	of or related to	eastern
-ing	an action; result of an action	dancing; drawing
-ism	act or practice of; teaching	terrorism; socialism
-less	without	treeless
-ly	in a certain manner; like	seriously; manly
-ness	state or quality	happiness

Section 3 Summary

Buddhists believe that a young Hindu prince once lived a life of luxury in northern India. He had never seen old age, sickness, or death. Then, he traveled outside the palace walls. He saw an old man. He saw a man who was very sick. He saw a dead body being carried to a funeral.

The young man gave up his life of ease. He wanted to find the causes of human suffering. The young man was Siddhartha Gautama (sih DAHR tuh GOW tuh muh). What he learned after seven years of wandering led to the start of Buddhism.

The Buddha and His Teachings

Gautama travelled in the 500s B.C. and looked for the meaning of life. At first, he studied with Hindu thinkers. But their ideas did not satisfy him.

Gautama decided to look inside himself for understanding. He began to **meditate**. Meditation was an ancient Hindu practice. After 49 days, he found the answers he had been looking for. He traveled across India and shared what he had learned. His followers called him the Buddha (BOO duh), or "Enlightened One." His teachings became known as Buddhism.

Buddhism teaches people to follow the Eightfold Path, also called the Middle Way. By doing this, a person avoids extreme pleasure or extreme unhappiness.

Buddha taught that selfish desires cause humans to suffer. To end suffering, people must give up these selfish desires for wealth, power, and pleasure. Instead, they must follow the Eightfold Path. Buddhists must learn to be wise, to behave correctly, and to develop their minds.

Key Term

meditate (MED uh tayt) *v.* to focus the mind inward in order to find spiritual awareness or relaxation

Vocabulary Strategy

Mark the Text

The word *northern* appears in the paragraph to the left. Find the word as you read and underline the suffix. Then, on the line below, write a definition of the word using the information in the chart on the previous page.

Northern means ______________

____

____

Target Reading Skill

Circle the factors in the bracketed paragraph that affect a Buddhist trying to reach nirvana.

Mark the Text

✓ Reading Check

Why do Buddhists try to follow the Middle Way?

____

____

____

✓ Reading Check

What other countries has Buddhism spread to?

____

____

____

To find this Middle Way, people must act unselfishly. They must treat people fairly. They must tell the truth at all times. They should also avoid violence and the killing of any living thing. By following the Buddha's path, their sufferings would end. They would find **nirvana**. They would not be reincarnated. ✓

Buddhism taught that all people are equal. Anyone could follow the path to nirvana. This idea appealed to many people. Like other religions, Buddhism has priests. People of any social class can be a priest or monk. The Buddha encouraged his followers to establish monasteries. There they would learn, meditate, and teach. He urged monks to become **missionaries**.

Buddhism Inside and Outside India

For many years, Buddhism and Hinduism lived side by side in India. Both share a number of basic ideas. Both believe that it is wrong to harm living things. Both value nonviolence. However, Buddhists do not accept the sacred texts of Hinduism.

Buddhism spread all over Asia. It took root in China and grew there. Buddhist monasteries were centers of religious thought in China. From China, Buddhism spread to Korea and Japan. Today, it is part of the cultures of countries such as Japan, China, and Vietnam. ✓

Review Questions

1. How did Siddhartha Gautama look for the cause of human suffering?

____

____

2. What are some of the similarities between Hinduism and Buddhism?

____

____

Key Terms

nirvana (nur VAH nuh) *n.* the lasting peace that Buddhists seek by giving up selfish desires

missionary (MISH un ehr ee) *n.* a person who spreads his or her religious beliefs to others

Prepare to Read

Section 4 The Maurya Empire

Objectives

1. Learn about the rise of the Maurya Empire.
2. Understand the effects of Asoka's leadership on the Maurya Empire.

Target Reading Skill

Understand Effects Remember that a cause makes something happen. The effect is what happens as a result of the cause. Just as an effect can have more than one cause, a cause can have more than one effect. You can find effects by answering the question, "What happened?" If there are several answers to that question, the cause had more than one effect.

Look at the last paragraph under the heading "The Rise of the Maurya Empire" on the next page. What were the effects of wealth on the Maurya Empire?

Vocabulary Strategy

Using Word Parts Sometimes when you come across a new word, you can figure out what it means if you break it down into parts. If a word contains a prefix or suffix, look for the root. The root is the word that the prefix or suffix is attached to. Take the meanings of the root and prefix or suffix and add them together. Then you will have found the meaning of the new word.

Often, when a prefix or a suffix is added to a root, the root's spelling is changed.

A final vowel, such as *a* or *e*, may be dropped: *Buddha* + *-ism* = *Buddhism*

A final *y* may change to *i*: *happy* + *-ly* = *happily*

A final consonant may be doubled: *war* + *-ing* = *warring*

Some words have more than one prefix or suffix. Some words have both prefixes and suffixes. In those cases, strip off the prefix or suffix one at a time until you can figure out what the word means.

Section 4 Summary

Around 321 B.C., Chandragupta (chun druh GOOP tuh) Maurya began his rule in northeastern India. His small kingdom grew into the huge **Maurya Empire**.

The Rise of the Maurya Empire

Before Chandragupta came to power, India was made up of a number of states. These states fought each other. Chandragupta's armies overthrew kingdoms along the Ganges River. Then they turned west, to the Indus River valley. Within a few years, he controlled most of north and central India.

Chandragupta thought that a ruler must have absolute power. According to legend, one of his advisors gave him a book of advice called *Arthasastra*. The book urged kings to control their people. It said kings should keep an army of spies to watch the people.

Chandragupta commanded a huge army. Under him, the empire became wealthy. Much of its wealth came from farming. But the Maurya Empire also traded with faraway lands. Some of these lands were Greece, Rome, and China.

[As his rule continued, Chandragupta began to fear that he would be killed. According to one story, near the end of his life, he left the throne to his son. He became a monk and starved himself to death fasting and praying.]

His rule was harsh. But Chandragupta used his wealth to improve his empire. New irrigation systems brought water to farmers. Trees were cut down, and more food was grown. Government officials promoted crafts and mining. New roads made trade with foreign lands easier. Chandragupta brought order and peace to his people. ✓

Asoka's Leadership

Chandragupta's grandson, Asoka, built the greatest empire India had ever seen.

Key Term

Maurya Empire (MOWR yuh EM pyr) *n.* Indian empire founded by Chandragupta, that included most of northern and central India

Vocabulary Strategy

Some words with suffixes are in the bracketed paragraph. Circle each word in the paragraph that has a suffix.

Mark the Text

✓ Reading Check

What kind of ruler was Chandragupta?

____

____

____

Asoka ruled for more than 35 years until 232 B.C. His empire included much of India. At first, he was as warlike as his grandfather. In about 261 B.C., he won a fight in Kalinga. Thousands of people died there. He was very sad about the deaths. He gave up war. He freed his prisoners. Later, he **converted** to Buddhism. ✓

Asoka practiced and preached the Buddha's teachings. He thought of his people as his children. He cared about them. He had hospitals built throughout the land. He had wells dug along roads so that travelers and animals would have water.

Asoka wanted to share the Buddha's message with all people in his empire. He gave moral advice. He urged **tolerance**. He also created laws that said people must be treated humanely. His advice and laws were carved on pillars of stone.

Asoka was tolerant of Hindus. Many of the Buddha's teachings became part of Hinduism during Asoka's rule. Buddhism grew under Asoka. His missionaries spread Buddhism to China. He even sent teachers to Egypt, Greece, and North Africa.

When Asoka died, India was united as never before. However, the Maurya Empire soon grew weak. It fell apart without his strong rule. Small states began to fight one another. Several centuries of invasion followed. There was much disorder.

Review Questions

1. How did Chandragupta build the Maurya Empire?

2. What were some of Asoka's accomplishments?

Key Terms

convert (kun VURT) *v.* to change one's beliefs

tolerance (TAHL ur uns) *n.* freedom from prejudice

Target Reading Skill

What effects did the Battle of Kalinga have on Asoka's life?

✓ Reading Check

What event caused Asoka to become a Buddhist?

Chapter 4 Assessment

1. India is separated from the rest of Asia by the Himalayas and
   - **A.** the Ganges River.
   - **B.** the Indus River.
   - **C.** the Hindu Kush mountain range.
   - **D.** the Great Wall of China.

2. As Aryans migrated into the northern Indus Valley, local people adopted their
   - **A.** children.
   - **B.** language and domesticated dogs.
   - **C.** language and beliefs.
   - **D.** beliefs and citadel style buildings.

3. Which of the following is true of Hindu gods and goddesses?
   - **A.** They stand for different parts of the same spirit.
   - **B.** They can take many different forms.
   - **C.** They have their own families.
   - **D.** All of the above

4. Buddhism teaches that all people should
   - **A.** pursue pleasure.
   - **B.** follow The Twelvefold Path.
   - **C.** be part of a caste system.
   - **D.** regard themselves as equal.

5. Which of the following happened under Chandragupta's rule?
   - **A.** Buddhism was carried throughout the empire.
   - **B.** Government officials promoted crafts and mining.
   - **C.** Hospitals were built throughout the empire.
   - **D.** Wells were dug along roads so that travelers and animals would not go thirsty.

Short Answer Question

What are some ways in which Hinduism and Buddhism differed from each other?

____

____

____

____

____

Prepare to Read

Section 1 The Geography of China's River Valleys

Objectives

1. Examine the geography of ancient China.
2. Find out about early civilization in China.
3. Learn about the importance of family ties in early China.

Target Reading Skill

Identify Main Ideas It is hard to remember every detail that you read. Good readers are able to find the main ideas of what they read. The main idea is the most important point. It includes all the other points, or details.

To find the main idea of a paragraph, read it through once. Then ask yourself what is the paragraph about. Do all the sentences center on the same point? If so, you've found your main idea. Sometimes it is stated in the first sentence or two.

The main idea of the paragraph below is underlined:

<u>The family was the center of early Chinese society.</u> It was more important than each person or the nation. The family came first.

As you read, look for the main ideas of paragraphs.

Vocabulary Strategy

Recognizing Signal Words Signal words are words or phrases that prepare you for what is coming next.

There are different kinds of signal words. Often signal words tell you when things happen. Some of these signal words are:

then	*later*
when	*around* (followed by a date)
in time	*in* (followed by a date)
earlier	*as early as* (followed by a date)

Section 1 Summary

The Geography of Ancient China

Ancient China covered a large area. The climate, soil, landforms, and waterways were different in each region.

The North China Plain is in East Asia. It is made of soil deposits from the Huang (hwahng) River. Northern China has only a brief summer monsoon. There is not much rain at other times. The climate is very dry. People here depend on rivers to survive.

The climate in southern China is warm and wet. Monsoons bring heavy rains from March to September. Light rain falls the rest of the year.

Mountains and seas separated China from other lands. The Chinese had little contact with other civilizations. The Chinese thought that they lived at the center of the world, so they called themselves the Middle Kingdom.

China's rivers flooded each spring. This brought fresh, fertile topsoil to the land. China's first farming villages developed along its rivers. Civilization began along the Huang. It later spread to the wetter south, along the Chang, China's longest river.

The Huang is China's second-longest river. It is also the muddiest river in the world. It is called the "Yellow River" because of the **loess** that it carries. When it floods, it deposits loess on the surrounding plain. Here, the Chinese grow a grain called millet.

The Chinese people also call the Huang "China's Sorrow." Its floods could be very destructive. Early Chinese people built **dikes** to help control flooding. ✓

Early Civilization in China

China's first farming settlements were in the Huang Valley. They may have began as early as 5000 B.C. Later on, they grew into civilizations.

Key Terms

loess (LOH es) *n.* yellow-brown soil
dike (dyk) *n.* a wall that controls or holds back water

Vocabulary Strategy

As you read this section's summary, look for the following signal words that indicate when something happened. Circle the signal words when you find them.

Mark the Text

when

as early as

later on

around 1760 B.C.

much later

✓ Reading Check

What did the Chinese do to control flooding?

____

____

____

The Shang dynasty was the first civilization in China. It arose around 1760 B.C. The Shang people built China's first cities. They created some fine bronze work. The Shang also created the first Chinese alphabet.

About 600 years after the founding of the Shang dynasty, a new group emerged. The Zhou dynasty ruled lands that bordered Shang lands. They conquered the Shang and ruled from about 1122 B.C. Much later, there was a time known as the Warring States. Small kingdoms fought for control of ancient China.

[The Chinese thought that rulers came to power because of fate. This idea was called the Mandate of Heaven. A mandate is a law. The Mandate of Heaven was used to support a king's right to rule his people. It also gave a father power over his family.] ✓

Importance of the Family

The family was the center of early Chinese society. It was much more important than each person or the nation. The family came first.

A home in ancient China might contain up to five generations. A person's status in the **extended family** depended on age and sex. As a rule, the oldest man had the most rights and power. Women were expected to obey the men. When a woman married, she became part of her husband's family. ✓

The Chinese were the first people known to use two names. One was for the family and the other was for the person. In Chinese society, the family name comes first.

Review Questions

1. What was the first known civilization in China?

____

2. Describe the importance of the family in early Chinese society.

____

Key Term

extended family (ek STEN did FAM uh lee) *n.* several generations of closely related people

Target Reading Skill

Which sentence states the main idea of the bracketed paragraph?

____

✓ Reading Check

What was the Mandate of Heaven?

____

✓ Reading Check

What factors did a person's status depend on in early Chinese families?

1. _______________
2. _______________

Prepare to Read

Section 2 Confucius and His Teachings

Objectives

1. Learn about the life of Confucius.
2. Find out about the teachings of Confucius.
3. Understand the impact of Confucianism on Chinese society.

Target Reading Skill

Identify Supporting Details The main idea of a paragraph or section is its most important point. The main idea is supported by details. Details give more information about the main idea. They may explain the main idea. They may give additional facts or examples. They tell you *what*, *where*, *why*, *how much*, or *how many*.

The main idea of the section titled "The Life of Confucius" is stated in this sentence: "Confucius was the most important early Chinese thinker."

As you read, notice how the details tell you more about the life of Confucius and why he was important.

Vocabulary Strategy

Recognizing Signal Words Signal words are words or phrases that give you clues. They help you understand what you read. They prepare you for what is coming next.

There are different kinds of signal words. Signal words may be used to sequence relationships. Sequence is the order in which things occur. It relates events in terms of when they happen.

Some signal words that may show sequence are:

first	*then*	*before*	*afterward*
next	*finally*	*earlier*	*later*

Section 2 Summary

The Life of Confucius

Confucius was the most important early Chinese thinker. The Chinese considered him to be a great teacher.

Confucius was born in 551 B.C. He came from a poor but noble family of the North China Plain. He loved learning and mostly taught himself. He hoped to get an important government office. He never succeeded. Instead, he decided to teach.

Confucius may have been China's first professional teacher. He charged students a fee to take classes. He taught his students his views of life and government. He was willing to teach poor students. But his students had to be very eager to learn. ✓

Later in his life, Confucius looked for a ruler who would follow his teachings. He could not find one. He died in 479 B.C. at the age of 73. He thought his life had been a failure. But his teachings would be followed in China for many centuries.

The Teachings of Confucius

Confucius was not an original thinker. Instead, he passed on the wise teachings of thinkers who lived before him. Many of his teachings were meant to make rulers reform. He wanted to bring peace, stability, and wealth to China.

Confucius's teachings make up a **philosophy** known as Confucianism. It was one of several philosophies in ancient China.

Confucius lived when there were many wars in China. Rulers wanted to get more power. They did not care about ruling wisely. Confucius hoped to persuade them to change their ways. His goal was to bring order to society. He thought there would be order if people behaved properly to each other. Society would prosper.

Key Terms

Confucius (kun FYOO shus) *n.* (551–479 B.C.) Chinese philosopher and teacher whose beliefs had a great influence on Chinese life

philosophy (fih LAHS uh fee) *n.* system of beliefs and values

✓ Reading Check

What kind of students did Confucius like to teach?

____

____

____

Target Reading Skill

Mark the Text

Underline the detail in the bracketed paragraph that supports the main idea that Confucius was an important Chinese thinker.

✓ Reading Check

Describe the religious traditions of ancient China.

Vocabulary Strategy

Look at the first three sentences in the bracketed paragraph. The events they describe are out of order. However, signal words show how the events are related to each other. List the events in the proper sequence.

1. __________
2. __________
3. __________

✓ Reading Check

Why was it difficult for poor men to work in the civil service?

Confucius said that the people in power must set a good example. Confucianism is a philosophy, but also served as a religion for many people. It helped guide them. It told them how to behave. Some people practiced it alongside other religions.

There were many religions in ancient China. They included worship of ancestors and a belief in spirits. Most Chinese believed that they would be happy if they led a balanced life. These ideas were supported by Taoism (DOW iz um). Taoism followed the writings of Laozi (LOW dzuh). He was a Chinese thinker who lived in the 500s B.C. Taoists believe they should live simply. They should not be selfish. On the whole, Confucianism was more widely studied than Taoism. ✓

The Influence of Confucius

Members of the Chinese **civil service** had to learn the teachings of Confucianism. Before Confucius, government posts were often given to the sons of important people. Afterward, they were based on merit. The men had to pass official tests. These tests were based on the teachings of Confucius.

The exams brought more able young men into government work. But candidates had to know how to read. This made it hard for a poor man to advance. But it was not impossible. ✓

Review Questions

1. Why did Confucius think it was important to teach rulers how to behave?

2. How did the ideas of Confucius change the way civil servants were chosen in ancient China?

Key Term

civil service (SIV ul SUR vis) *n.* the group of people who carry out the work of the government

Prepare to Read

Section 3 Warring Kingdoms Unite

Objectives

1. Learn about the rise of the Qin dynasty.
2. Find out how Emperor Shi Huangdi tried to unify the economy and culture of China.
3. Look at the actions of the Han dynasty's leaders.

Target Reading Skill

Identify Implied Main Ideas The main idea of a paragraph or section is its most important point. Sometimes the main idea is not stated directly. Instead, all the details in a paragraph or section add up to a main idea. In this case, we say the main idea is implied. It is up to you to put the details together.

For example, let's say you are studying the details on the next page following the heading "The Qin Dynasty." You could then state the main idea this way: "China was unified and strengthened by its first emperor, Shi Huangdi."

Vocabulary Strategy

Recognizing Signal Words Signal words are words or phrases that give you clues. They help you understand what you read. They prepare you for what is coming next.

There are different kinds of signal words. Signal words may be used to show different kinds of relationships, such as contrast. Contrasts are the differences between things or ideas.

Some signal words that show contrast include:

but	*however*	*on the other hand*	*yet*
not	*despite*	*even though*	

Section 3 Summary

The Qin Dynasty

China's first emperor was **Shi Huangdi**. At first, he ruled the Qin (chin) people. They lived on China's western edge. By 221 B.C., he controlled most of the land that makes up modern-day China. His dynasty is called the Qin dynasty. The name China comes from *Chin*, another way to spell *Qin*.

Shi Huangdi's rule was strong and harsh. For a long time, nomads had attacked the northern border of China. To stop this, Shi Huangdi ordered the largest building project in Chinese history. Earlier rulers had built walls to protect the border. He decided to link them. The wall took about ten years to build. It is now called the Great Wall of China. Later emperors repaired and added to the wall, making it even longer. ✓

Shi Huangdi built roads to let his armies rush to the scene of any uprisings. He killed or imprisoned local rulers who opposed him. He divided all of China into districts run by his most trusted officials.

Unifying Economy and Culture

Shi Huangdi wanted his dynasty to have one culture and one economy. He ordered that one **currency** be used in China. This made it easier for one region of China to trade with another. He also said there should be a standard system of weights and measures. He ordered an improved system of writing and a law code.

In 213 B.C., Shi Huangdi outlawed Confucianism and other beliefs. He replaced them with the Qin philosophy of legalism. Legalism states that people should be punished for bad behavior and rewarded for good behavior. Legalists thought people should serve the emperor. Shi Huangdi burned almost all the books. Only books on medicine, technology, and farming were spared. When scholars protested, he killed them. ✓

Shi Huangdi's empire did not last long after his death in 210 B.C. His dynasty lasted only 15 years.

Key Terms

Shi Huangdi (shur hwahng DEE) *n.* China's first emperor
currency (KUR un see) *n.* money used by a group or a nation

Target Reading Skill

State what all the details in the bracketed paragraph are about. Use only one sentence.

____

____

____

✓ Reading Check

How was China's Great Wall built?

____

____

____

✓ Reading Check

How did Shi Huangdi try to control his people's freedoms?

____

____

____

The Han Dynasty

Liu Bang helped defeat the Qin dynasty. By 202 B.C., he started the Han (hahn) dynasty. His government was stable. His rule was less harsh than Shi Huangdi's.

Stable governments were a mark of the Han dynasty. Han rulers wanted educated workers. They based the civil service system on Confucianism.

In 140 B.C. **Wudi** came to power. He was Liu Bang's great-grandson. He was about 15 years old. Wudi ruled for more than 50 years. He was mainly interested in war and the military. The Great Wall was improved. He made the army stronger and expanded China's land.

Wudi died in 87 B.C. China was still well-off under later Han emperors. Many new ideas and technologies were developed. But the empire was weaker. Several emperors were very young. Others fought for power. The empire began to fall apart.

As a result, **warlords** gained power. The last Han emperor was kept in power by a warlord. In A.D. 220, he replaced the Han dynasty with his own. This was the Wei dynasty. The Wei dynasty only controlled parts of northern China. It ended about 50 years later. China broke up into several smaller kingdoms. ✓

Review Questions

1. What did Shi Huangdi do to unite the economy and culture of China?

2. What was government like in China under the Han dynasty?

Key Terms

Liu Bang (LYOH bahng) *n.* founder of the Han dynasty
Wudi (woo dee) *n.* Chinese emperor who brought the Han dynasty to its peak
warlord (WAWR lawrd) *n.* a local leader of an armed group

Vocabulary Strategy

Mark the Text

In the bracketed paragraph, a signal word is used to show contrast. Find the signal word and circle it. What is being contrasted here?

✓ Reading Check

What happened in A.D. 220?

Prepare to Read

Section 4 Achievements of Ancient China

Objectives

1. Learn about the Silk Road.
2. Find out about the Han dynasty's respect for tradition and learning.
3. Discover what important advances in technology were made in China during the Han dynasty.

Target Reading Skill

Identify Supporting Details Each section of text has a main idea. The main idea is supported by details. The details give more information about the main idea.

On the next page, the main idea for the text under the heading "The Silk Road" is implied. It is not stated dirctly. But it can be determined by adding up the details and seeing what they are about. The main idea can be stated this way: "Both ideas and goods were exchanged along the Silk Road. It connected China to the Mediterranean."

As you read, note the supporting details under each heading.

Vocabulary Strategy

Recognizing Signal Words Signal words are words or phrases that give you clues. They prepare you for what is coming next.

There are different kinds of signal words. Signal words may show how things are related, such as cause and effect. As you will recall, a cause is what makes something happens. An effect is the result of the cause. Some signal words that may show cause and effect include:

Cause	Effect
because	*as a result*
if	*consequently*
on account of	*so*
since	*then*
	therefore

Section 4 Summary

The Silk Road

Wudi's conquests brought the Chinese into contact with the people of Central Asia. The Chinese exchanged goods with these people. A major trade route developed. It was called the **Silk Road**.

The Silk Road was a series of routes that covered more than 4,000 miles (6,400 kilometers). It crossed mountains and deserts. It ended in what is now Turkey. From there, traders shipped goods across the Mediterranean.

Few travelers went the entire length of the Silk Road. Instead, goods were passed from trader to trader as they crossed Asia. With each trade, the price went up. At the end, the goods were very expensive.

The Silk Road got its name from **silk**. Han farmers had developed new ways for raising silkworms, the caterpillars that made the silk. Wealthy Romans would pay high prices for Chinese silk. Wealthy Chinese would pay well for items from Rome. ✓

New ideas also traveled along the Silk Road. For example, missionaries from India traveled to China along the road. They brought Buddhism with them. By the end of the Han dynasty, Buddhism was a major religion in China.

Tradition and Learning

Tradition and learning flourished during the Han dynasty.

Tradition	Learning
• Rulers wanted to bring back respect for tradition • Returned to the teachings of Confucius • Civil service required study of Confucianism	• Poetry flourished • Scholars created first dictionary • Sima Qian wrote the a history of China ✓

Key Terms

Silk Road (silk rohd) *n.* an ancient trade route between China and Europe

silk (silk) *n.* a valuable cloth, made by silkworms

Target Reading Skill

The main idea of the section titled "The Silk Road" is "Both goods and ideas were exchanged along the Silk Road."

In the bracketed paragraphs find one example of each.

Goods: ____________________

Ideas: ____________________

✓ Reading Check

What are silkworms?

____

____

____

✓ Reading Check

What contribution to learning did Sima Qian make?

____

____

____

Vocabulary Strategy

In the bracketed paragraph, a signal word is used to show cause and effect. Find the signal word and circle it. Then write the cause and effect below.

Cause: ____________________

____

Effect: ____________________

____

✓ Reading Check

What did the Chinese write on before they invented paper?

____

____

____

Han Technology

Because the Han government was stable, the Chinese worked on improving their society. At this time, China was the most advanced civilization in the world. Farming tools were improved. The Chinese invented many devices. These things did not reach Europe for many centuries.

The Chinese made advances in the arts, in bronze-working, building temples and palaces, and in jade carvings. They also made discoveries in the field of medicine. They learned about herbal remedies and acupunture. Besides improving farm tools, they also invented the compass and the rudder, a device used to steer ships.

One of the most important Chinese inventions was paper. At first, the Chinese used wood scrolls and bones to keep records. Later, they wrote messages and even whole books on silk. Then, around A.D. 105, they invented paper. Paper helped learning and the arts in China. After several centuries, the use of paper spread across Asia and into Europe. Paper replaced papyrus from Egypt as the material for scrolls and books. ✓

The Han dynasty ended in the A.D. 200s. But its deeds were not forgotten. People in China still call themselves "the children of Han."

Review Questions

1. How did the Silk Road get its name?

____

____

____

2. In what ways did the Han dynasty show a respect for Chinese traditions?

____

____

____

Key Term

Sima Qian (sih MAH chen) *n.* (c. 145–85 B.C.) a Chinese scholar who wrote the most important history of ancient China, *Historical Records*

Chapter 5 Assessment

1. The Chinese called the Huang River "China's Sorrow" because
   A. it was so long.
   B. it was the muddiest river in the world.
   C. its floods could be very destructive.
   D. its water was poisonous to both people and crops.

2. What is the Mandate of Heaven?
   A. a Chinese religion based on the ideas of Confucius
   B. the idea used to support a king's right to rule his people
   C. the belief that soldiers killed in battle will go directly to heaven
   D. none of the above

3. The main goal of Confucianism was to
   A. serve as a religion that would unify the people of China.
   B. live in harmony with nature.
   C. provide training for members of the Chinese civil service.
   D. bring order to society.

4. How did Shi Huangdi try to control people's thoughts?
   A. He replaced Confucianism with legalism.
   B. He ordered books to be burned.
   C. He had scholars killed when they protested.
   D. all of the above

5. During which dynasty was paper invented?
   A. the Shang dynasty
   B. the Zhou dynasty
   C. the Qin dynasty
   D. the Han dynasty

Short Answer Question

Why was the Silk Road important?

____

____

____

____

____

Prepare to Read

Section 1
The Rise of Greek Civilization

Objectives

1. Understand how Greece's geographic setting influenced Greek civilization.
2. Examine early Greek history.
3. Examine the development of democracy in Greece.

Target Reading Skill

Identify Sequence A sequence is the order in which events occur. You can keep track of the order of events by making a sequence chart like the one below. In the first box, write the first event. Then write each additional event in the following boxes. The arrows show how one event leads to the next.

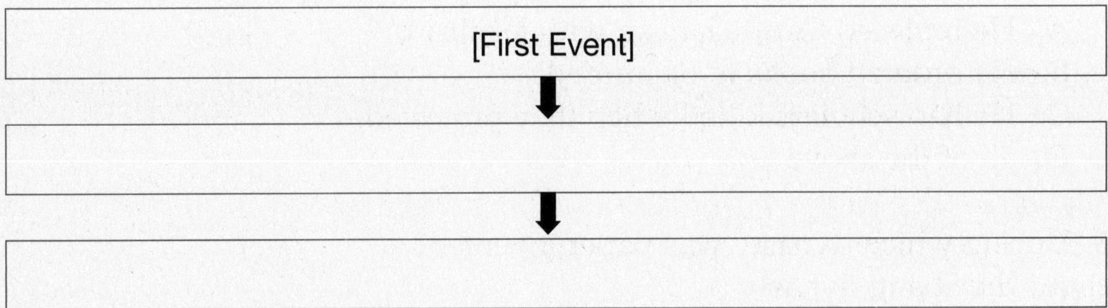

Vocabulary Strategy

Use Context to Clarify Meaning When you come across new words in your text, they are often defined for you. Sometimes there may be a brief definition in the same sentence. Sometimes the definition appears in a separate sentence. The word *or* can be used to introduce the definition. Look at the following examples.

epic, or *a long poem that tells a story*

Democracy is *a form of government in which citizens govern themselves.*

The underlined words are defined in context. In these examples, brief definitions appear in italics.

Section 1 Summary

Greece's Geographic Setting

Greece is a land of **peninsulas** and small, rocky islands. Mountains are the major landform. Only about one fifth of Greece is good for growing crops, so it's no wonder the Greeks became traders and sailors.

Some Greeks lived on real islands. Others lived in villages separated by mountains. Each community developed its own customs and beliefs. The Greeks fought each other, but they still shared the same heritage, language, and gods. ✓

Greek Beginnings

From about 3000 to about 1100 B.C., the Minoans (mi NOH unz) lived on the island of Crete. At one time, they controlled the Aegean (ee JEE un) Sea. The Minoans left writings on clay tablets. In the middle of the 1400s B.C., their civilization declined.

The Mycenaeans (my suh NEE unz) lived on the mainland. They were at the height of their power around 1400 B.C. They controlled the Aegean Sea and parts of the Mediterranean. They spread their power through conquest. They also traded widely. ✓

Greek myth tells the story of the Trojan War. It was a war between Greece and Troy. Two **epics** tell of the Trojan War. They are the *Iliad* (IL ee ud) and the *Odyssey* (AHD ih see). The poet Homer is credited for both of them. The poems explained what Greek gods were like and how Greek heroes behaved.

The Dark Ages of Greece

After the Trojan War, Greek civilization fell apart. No one knows why. Poverty was everywhere. People no longer traded beyond Greece. They forgot the art of writing. People kept history alive by word of mouth.

These years have been called Greece's Dark Ages. People settled where they could farm. Farms were built

Key Terms

peninsula (puh NIN suh luh) *n.* an area of land nearly surrounded by water

epic (EP ik) *n.* a long poem that tells a story

✓ Reading Check

What two landforms separated ancient Greek villages?

1. ______________________

2. ______________________

✓ Reading Check

Contrast how Minoans and Mycenaeans spread their power.

____

____

____

Vocabulary Strategy

The term *acropolis* is defined in context. Circle its definition.

✓ Reading Check

What were three effects of Greece's Dark Ages?

1. ______________________

2. ______________________

3. ______________________

Target Reading Skill

What important changes led to the development of city-states in Greece?

____

____

____

✓ Reading Check

What kind of ruler often replaced aristocratic governments? Who supported these rulers?

____

____

____

✓ Reading Check

Who could vote in Athens?

____

____

____

near hills for protection. They fortified or strengthened them to protect them from attack. A fortified hill was called an **acropolis.** ✓

City-States Develop

Sometime around 750 B.C., villages joined to form **city-states**. Each city-state was near an acropolis and had its own government and laws.

By the end of the Dark Ages, most city-states were ruled by **aristocrats**. They controlled most of the good land and could afford the best weapons.

The city-states became richer through trade. A middle class of merchants and artisans formed. They wanted a say in government. Aristocratic governments were often replaced by rulers called **tyrants**. They were supported by the middle and working classes. ✓

Democracy in Greece

In time, the people of some cities got rid of tyrants and adopted a form of government called **democracy**. One of them was Athens. Athens gave citizens aged 18 or older a say in discussing laws.

Not all Athenians were citizens. Only men could be citizens and they had to have both an Athenian father and mother. Slaves, women, and foreigners were not citizens. ✓

Review Questions

1. Describe the geographic setting of ancient Greece.

____

____

2. What two kinds of government developed in the Greek city-states?

____

____

Key Terms

acropolis (uh KRAH puh lis) *n.* a high, rocky hill where early people built cities
city-state (SIH tee stayt) *n.* a city with its own government
aristocrat (uh RIS tuh krat) *n.* a member of a rich and powerful family
tyrant (TY runt) *n.* a ruler who takes power with the support of the middle and working classes
democracy (dih MAHK ruh see) *n.* a form of government in which citizens govern themselves

Prepare to Read

Section 2
Religion, Philosophy, and the Arts

Objectives

1. Identify the religious beliefs of the ancient Greeks.
2. Explore how the Greeks searched for knowledge about the world.
3. Describe the relationship between democracy and new ideas in Greek city-states.

Target Reading Skill

Recognize Sequence Signal Words Signal words or phrases give you clues when reading. They help you understand what you are reading and prepare you for what's coming next.

There are different kinds of signal words. Some show time, place, or direction. Signal words point out how ideas or events are related. As you read, look for words like *first, during that time,* and *in [date]* that signal order.

Vocabulary Strategy

Use Context to Clarify Meaning Sometimes you can pick up clues from the words, phrases, and sentences around an unfamiliar word to help you understand it. The underlined words in the passage below give clues to the meaning of the word *oracle.*

> The Greeks visited **oracles**. At these shrines, they would ask the gods to give them advice or to reveal the future.

An oracle was a shrine where gods could be asked for advice or to reveal the future.

Section 2 Summary

The Golden Age of Athens

The Golden Age of Athens lasted from 479 B.C. to 431 B.C. Athens grew rich from trade and silver mined by slaves. Its allies paid **tribute**, which added to the city's wealth.

During that time, philosophy, the arts, and democracy thrived. For about 30 years, Pericles was the most powerful man in Athenian politics. The city began to pay officials a salary, so poor citizens could hold office. ✓

Ancient Greek Religious Beliefs

Greeks worshiped a family of twelve gods. Each ruled a different area of human life and the natural world. The gods had human characteristics, but were **immortal**.

The gods were led by their king, Zeus. He ruled from Mt. Olympus, Greece's highest mountain. Each city-state honored one of the twelve gods by building a temple to that god. Athena (uh THEE nuh) was the patron goddess of Athens.

The Greeks also honored their gods at festivals. Every four years, the city-states came together to honor Zeus at Olympus. The modern Olympic Games are based on this tradition. ✓

The Greeks visited **oracles** to ask the gods for advice or to see into the future.

The Search for Knowledge

During the Golden Age, several important **philosophers** taught in Athens. One of them was Socrates (SAHK ruh teez). He asked questions that made people think about their beliefs.

Key Terms

tribute (TRIB yoot) *n.* payment made by a less powerful state or nation to a more powerful one
immortal (ih MAWR tul) *n.* someone or something that lives forever
oracle (OR uh kul) *n.* a sacred site used to consult a god or goddess; any priest or priestess who spoke for the gods
philosopher (fih LAHS uh fur) *n.* someone who used reason to understand the world; in Greece the earliest philosophers used reason to explain natural events

Target Reading Skill

What words signal when philosophy and the arts flourished in Athens?

____

____

✓ Reading Check

How did Pericles strengthen democracy?

____

____

____

✓ Reading Check

How did the Greeks honor their gods?

____

____

____

Socrates was put on trial and accused of dishonoring the gods and leading young people astray. He was sentenced to death. ✓

Plato (PLAY toh) was a friend of Socrates who wrote *The Republic*. It describes an ideal society.

Visual and Dramatic Arts

The Greeks used architecture and sculpture to honor their gods. The Acropolis was the religious center of Athens, but was destroyed during a war. Pericles rebuilt it.

With the new Acropolis, Greek architecture reached its peak. The greatest building was a temple to the goddess Athena. Its sculptures are arranged to show balance and order. The goal of Greek art was to show images of perfection.

Athenians were the first to write plays. Tragedies told of people who were destroyed when they were forced to make impossible choices. Between scenes, a chorus sang poems. The chorus often gave background information, commented on events, or praised the gods. ✓

Poets also wrote comedies. They made fun of well-known citizens and jokes about the customs of the day.

Many City-States, One People

The Greeks valued free thinking. They developed new ideas in philosophy, religion, government, and the arts. The spread of education and wealth from trade allowed them to explore new ideas. ✓

The city-states competed against each other, but their citizens spoke the same language.

Review Questions

1. What was the Golden Age of Athens?

____

____

2. What characteristic did people in city-states throughout Greece share?

____

____

Key Term

tragedy (TRAJ uh dee) *n.* a serious drama that ends in disaster

✓ Reading Check

Why was Socrates put on trial?

____

____

____

Vocabulary Strategy

Look at the word *Tragedies* in the underlined sentence. Although it is defined below, there are clues to what it means. Circle the words or phrases that help you learn its meaning.

Mark the Text

✓ Reading Check

What three things did the chorus in a Greek drama do?

1. ______________________________

2. ______________________________

3. ______________________________

✓ Reading Check

What areas did ancient Greeks spend time thinking about?

____

____

____

Chapter 6 Assessment

1. Why did ancient Greeks think of their communities as separate countries?
   A. A different language was spoken in each community.
   B. Each community's people came from a different country.
   C. Each community practiced a different religion.
   D. Geographical features cut communities off from one another.

2. What early cultural group lived on the island of Crete?
   A. the Athenians
   B. the Minoans
   C. the Mycenaeans
   D. the Spartans

3. Who could be a citizen in ancient Athens?
   A. men and women aged 18 and over who were born in Athens
   B. men aged 18 and over who were born in Athens
   C. men aged 21 and over who had an Athenian father
   D. men aged 18 and over whose parents were both Athenians

4. Who was the most powerful man in Athenian politics during the Golden Age?
   A. Aristotle
   B. Pericles
   C. Plato
   D. Socrates

5. What was the function of the chorus in a Greek tragedy?
   A. to provide background information
   B. to comment on events
   C. to praise the gods
   D. all of the above

Short Answer Question

How did city-states arise in ancient Greece?

____

____

____

____

____

Prepare to Read

Section 1 Daily Life in Athens

Objectives

1. Learn about public life in Athens.
2. Find out how Athenians spent their time when they were home.
3. Understand how slavery operated in ancient Greece.

Target Reading Skill

Compare and Contrast When you compare, you look at similarities between things. Similarities are things that are like other things. For example, people in two different city-states may have the same language and religion.

When you contrast, you look at the differences between things. For example, the way men lived differed from the way women lived.

Comparing and contrasting can help you sort out information. As you read, compare and contrast what you're reading with what you already know. As you read this section, compare and contrast the daily life of Athenians.

Vocabulary Strategy

Word Origins Many English words come from ancient Greek. Often, Greek words combine more than one root. The same roots may be used in a number of combinations.

The Greek word *agora* appears in the English word *agoraphobia.* The word *phobia* is also from Greek. It means "abnormal fear or dread." Thus, agoraphobia is an abnormal fear of being in open places. Can you see how this word is related to *agora*? Other English words that contain Greek roots include *acrobat, acrophobia,* and *metropolis.*

Section 1 Summary

Public Life

The Acropolis was the center of religious life in **Athens**, but the **Agora** was the center of public life. The Acropolis rose above the nearby Agora.

In the morning, many Athenian men went to the Agora, where they talked of politics, philosophy, and local events. Around them, buyers and **vendors** bargained for good prices. Farmers and artisans sold their wares from stands under trees. ✓

Temples and government buildings lined the Agora. The Greek classical style still influences how buildings are built.

At Home in Athens

Throughout Greece, homes were built of mud bricks. Rooms were set around an open courtyard that was hidden from the street. The courtyard was the center of the household. Other rooms might include a kitchen, storerooms, a dining room, and bedrooms.

The ancient Greeks ate simple foods. Breakfast might be just bread. Midday meals might add cheese or olives to the bread. Dinner would be a hot meal. It might consist of fish and vegetables, followed by cheese, fruit, and cakes. Most Athenians ate little meat. Even wealthy families ate meat only during religious festivals. ✓

Most of the people in the Agora were men. Athenian women spent their days at home. Men thought women needed to be protected. They thought that keeping them out of public was the best way to protect them.

Key Terms

Athens (ATH unz) *n.* a city-state in ancient Greece; the capital of modern-day Greece
agora (AG uh ruh) *n.* a public market and meeting place in an ancient Greek city; the Agora, spelled with a capital *A*, refers to the agora of Athens
vendor (VEN dur) *n.* a seller of goods

Vocabulary Strategy

Philosophy comes from Greek words for "love" (*philos*) and "wisdom" (*sophia*). Based on this knowledge, what do you think it means?

____

____

✓ Reading Check

What business did Athenians conduct in the Agora?

____

____

____

✓ Reading Check

What kinds of foods did Athenians eat?

____

____

Target Reading Skill

Where did Athenian men spend their time? Where did Athenian women spend their time? What was similar about their daily lives?

____

____

____

Most Greeks thought women should be guided by men. Women could not take part in politics or vote. However, they could be priestesses in religious groups.

Women ran the home. Wealthy women were in charge of the spinning and weaving. They looked after food and wine supplies. They cared for young children. Slaves were also the woman's responsibility.

Poor women often worked outside of the home. They found jobs making pottery, tending sheep, or making cloth.

Slavery in Ancient Greece

The work of slaves gave men time to go to the Agora and time to take part in government.

Slavery was common in Athens. There may have been 100,000 slaves in Athens. That's almost one third of the population.

Many free people were enslaved when they were captured during war. Others were captured by pirates. The children of slaves were also slaves. Many slaves were foreigners.

Slaves were not citizens and had no rights. They could only become free by buying their freedom, or if their master freed them.

Slaves did many kinds of work. Some worked on farms or in mines. Others helped artisans make pottery, construct buildings, or forge weapons and armor. Most Greek households could not run without slaves. Slaves served food, tended children, and wove cloth. ✓

✓ Reading Check

What kinds of labor did slaves perform?

____

____

____

Review Questions

1. What activities took place in the Agora?

____

____

2. What were the responsibilities of men compared to those of women in ancient Athens?

____

____

Key Term

slavery (SLAY vur ee) *n.* condition of being owned by someone else

CHAPTER 7

Prepare to Read

Section 2 Athens and Sparta

Objectives

1. Learn how people lived in ancient Sparta.
2. Discover results of the Persian invasion of Greece.
3. Understand the conflicts the Athenian empire faced.

Target Reading Skill

Identify Contrasts When you contrast, you look at the differences between two things or events. When you read, contrasting will help you understand why things are different. Contrasting is a way of sorting out what you read.

Sometimes the contrasting information is contained in a single sentence or paragraph. Sometimes it is given in different paragraphs under a single heading. Contrasts may be signaled by words or phrases, such as *although*, *yet*, *as opposed to*, *however*, or *on the other hand*.

In this section, you will read about the Spartan people. They had many of the same elements of Greek culture as the Athenians. But they differed in other ways. As you read, list the differences between Athens and Sparta.

Vocabulary Strategy

Word Origins Many English words come from ancient Greek. Most of the Greek words used in English are spelled differently. They may also have different meanings from the original words. Some English words are based on Greek words that were originally the names of people or places. The table below lists a few.

Greek name	English word	Meaning
marathon	marathon	a long-distance foot race
Olympus	Olympic	relating to the modern Olympic games
solon	solon	a lawmaker, especially a wise one
Sparta	Spartan	like the Spartans; plain

Section 2 Summary

Living in Sparta

Life in **Sparta** was harsh and cruel. The Spartans were tough, silent, and grim. Sparta's army equaled Athens' in the 400s B.C., but Sparta never came close to matching Athens' other achievements. ✓

In its early days, Sparta was much like other Greek cities. There were wars inside and outside of the city. That turned Sparta into a powerful war machine. There was one basic rule: Always put the city's needs above your own.

The Spartans conquered the land around their city. They turned the conquered people into **helots**. Helots did all the farm work on land owned by Spartan citizens. This left the Spartans free to wage war.

Growing up in Sparta

The government controlled Spartans from birth. Only healthy children were raised. At age seven, boys began military training, which continued for 13 years.

When he was 20, a young man officially became a soldier. At age 30, he could take his place in the assembly. Only nonslave males born in Sparta were citizens.

Girls trained and competed in wrestling and spear throwing. They were not expected to be soldiers, but Spartans believed strong, healthy girls would have strong, healthy children.

Spartan women had a somewhat better life than women in other Greek city-states. They were allowed to own land and even took part in business. But they had to obey men. ✓

Key Terms

Sparta (SPAHR tuh) *n.* a city-state in ancient Greece
helots (HEL uts) *n.* in ancient Sparta, the term for slaves who were owned by the state

✓ Reading Check

What type of people were the Spartans?

Vocabulary Strategy

Helot is a Greek term. It was originally the name of a town whose inhabitants were enslaved by the Spartans. One meaning of the suffix *-ism* is "the condition of being." What does the word *helotism* mean?

Target Reading Skill

Contrast the life of Spartan women to that of Athenian women.

✓ Reading Check

What was life like for the women of Sparta?

The Persians Invade

Near the beginning of the 400s B.C., Persia posed a threat to Greece. It had already gained control of the Greek colonies on the west coast of Asia Minor.

In the fall of 490 B.C., the Persians landed in Greece. They gathered at Marathon (MAR uh thahn), about 25 miles (40 km) north of Athens. The Persians outnumbered the Athenian army by at least two to one.

A surprise attack by the Athenians overwhelmed the Persians. ✓

✓ Reading Check

What happened during the battle at Marathon?

____

____

____

Conflict and the Athenian Empire

More battles followed. After the Persians' defeat, Athens forced other city-states to bow to its will. It supported democratic groups in other city-states, but focused on freedom for its own people.

Sparta and Athens at War

Athens began to act unfairly toward other city-states, which paid Athens tribute for protection.

Some of the city-states looked to Sparta for protection. In 431 B.C., allies of Sparta and Athens started the **Peloponnesian War**. Early in the war, Athens was struck by a **plague**, which lasted five years. It killed about one third of Athens' people.

Sparta and Persia became allies and staged a **blockade**. They closed the harbor where Athens received food shipments. Athens surrendered and never again dominated the Greek world. ✓

✓ Reading Check

How did Sparta and other city-states defeat Athens?

____

____

____

Review Questions

1. Describe what life was like for boys living in Sparta.

____

____

2. How did the Greeks overcome the Persian invasion?

____

____

Key Terms

Peloponnesian War (pel uh puh NEE shun wawr) *n.* (431–404 B.C.), war fought between Athens and Sparta

plague (playg) *n.* a widespread disease

blockade (blah KAYD) *n.* an action taken to isolate the enemy and cut off its supplies

Prepare to Read

Section 3
The Spread of Greek Culture

Objectives

1. Learn how King Philip of Macedonia came to power and how Alexander the Great built his empire.
2. Understand what role the conquests of Alexander the Great played in spreading Greek culture.

Target Reading Skill

Making Comparisons Comparing two or more situations lets you see how they are alike. It's easier to understand new facts by comparing them with facts you already know. For example, which of the following facts is easier to picture?

> Alexandria's harbor was dominated by a huge lighthouse that rose about 350 feet (106 m) in the air.
>
> Alexandria's lighthouse was somewhat taller than a football field is long.

Most people would choose the second statement.

As you read this section, compare the ideas of Alexander the Great to those of the people who came before him.

Vocabulary Strategy

Word Origins Often, words of Greek origin combine more than one root. The roots may be used in a number of different combinations. Often a Greek word is the root of many other words in English.

Many words dealing with science and mathematics are of Greek origin, or have Greek roots. You can see this from the following list:

geo ("earth") + *metria* ("measurement") = *geometry*
geo ("earth") + *graphos* ("writing") = *geography*
geo ("earth") + *logos* ("word" or "science") = *geology*
bio ("life") + *logos* ("word" or "science") = *biology*
mathematikos ("mathematical") = *mathematics*

Section 3 Summary

Target Reading Skill

How were Philip's attitudes about Greece similar to those of his predecessors? Circle the clue word that helps you recognize similarities.

Mark the Text

Alexander, the son of King Philip of Macedonia (mas uh DOH nee uh), thought of himself as Greek. But people who lived to the south thought the Macedonians were **barbarians**.

Alexander's tutor was the Greek philosopher Aristotle. He taught the boy Greek literature, philosophy, and science. He also passed along his feelings that the Greeks deserved to rule.

Philip Comes to Power

Like his predecessors, King Philip had Greek ancestors and thought of himself as Greek. When he came to power, he dreamed of conquering the Greek city-states.

When King Philip seized power in 359 B.C., he united Macedonia and formed alliances with many Greek city-states. He built an army stronger than Sparta's. Then he captured one city-state after another. ✓

✓ Reading Check

How did King Philip conquer Greece?

____

____

____

Alexander Builds an Empire
Death of a King

After he conquered Greece, Philip planned to attack Persia. But he was **assassinated**. At age 20, his son Alexander became king.

Alexander invaded the Persian Empire, winning battle after battle. His territories stretched beyond the Indus River in India.

Within 11 years, he earned the right to be called **Alexander the Great**. Wherever he went, he established cities. He named many of them after himself. ✓

✓ Reading Check

How did Alexander come to be known as Alexander the Great?

____

____

____

At last, his troops refused to go any farther. In Babylon, he came down with a fever and died. He held the throne for only 13 years, but his conquests had spread Greek culture throughout a large area.

Key Terms

barbarian (bahr BEHR eeun) *n.* a person who belongs to a group that others consider wild, or uncivilized

assassinate (uh SAS uh nayt) *v.* to murder for political reasons

Alexander the Great (al ig ZAN dur thuh grayt) *n.* king of Macedonia (336–323 B.C.); conquered Persia and Egypt and invaded India

Greek Culture Spreads

After 50 years, Alexander's empire split into three kingdoms ruled by his former commanders.

Many Greek soldiers remained in the new kingdoms. Greek traders and artisans followed. They kept Greek culture alive in these **Hellenistic** kingdoms.

Alexander tried not to destroy the cultures of the people he defeated. He hoped the local cultures would mix with Greek culture. This did not happen in the Hellenistic kingdoms. Their cities were modeled after Greek cities and Greek kings ruled. Greeks held the most important jobs.

The greatest Hellenistic city was Alexandria in Egypt. It became a famous trading center.

The important Hellenistic cities were centers of learning. Alexandria had the largest library in the world, and scholars from all over came to use the library. ✓

Math and Science

Mathematics and science flourished in Alexandria. A mathematician named Euclid (YOO klid) developed a system of geometry still used today.

Many scientists in Hellenistic times knew that Earth was round. Eratosthenes (ehr uh TAHS thuh neez) calculated the distance around the Earth.

Probably the greatest scientist of the time was Archimedes (ar kuh MEE deez). He discovered the use of pulleys and levers to lift very heavy objects.

Review Questions

1. How did Alexander's upbringing affect his attitudes about Greek culture?

____

____

2. What features of Greek culture were carried over into the Hellenistic kingdoms?

____

____

Key Term

Hellenistic (hel uh NIS tik) *adj.* describing Greek history or culture after the death of Alexander the Great

Vocabulary Strategy

What branch of mathematics has a name that begins with the same Greek root as *geography*?

____

____

✓ Reading Check

Why was Alexandria in Egypt such an important city?

____

____

Chapter 7 Assessment

1. What was the role of women in ancient Greece?
   A. They sat on the councils that made all the decisions.
   B. They worked like slaves.
   C. They had to obey the men in their lives.
   D. They went to war along with the men.

2. Most of the work in ancient Greece was performed by
   A. slaves.
   B. philosophers.
   C. women.
   D. boys.

3. The Spartans were well known for their
   A. art and architecture.
   B. war skills.
   C. philosophy.
   D. open society.

4. What country finally succeeded in uniting the Greek city-states?
   A. Athens
   B. Sparta
   C. Persia
   D. Macedonia

5. Which of the following describes the three Hellenistic kingdoms?
   A. Their cities were modeled after Greek cities.
   B. Greeks held the most important jobs.
   C. They were set up by Alexander's former commanders.
   D. all of the above

Short Answer Question

How did Athens lose its dominance over the rest of Greece?

___

___

___

___

___

Chapter 8 Prepare to Read

Section 1 The Roman Republic

Objectives

1. Learn about the geography and early settlement of Rome.
2. Understand how Romans formed a republic.
3. Identify the reasons why the Roman Republic went into decline.

Target Reading Skill

Use Word Parts When you see an unfamiliar word, try to break it into parts. This will help you pronounce it. You may find roots, prefixes, or suffixes.

A root is a word that is used to make other words. A prefix is a group of letters added in front of the root. A suffix is a group of letters that are attached at the end of a root. Prefixes and suffixes change the word's meaning.

In this section you will read the word *reorganized*. Break it into a prefix and root to learn its meaning. The prefix re- means "again." The root "organize" means "to put in order."

Vocabulary Strategy

Recognize Signal Words Signal words or phrases give you clues. They help you understand what you read and prepare you for what's coming next. Often signal words show time, place, or direction.

> Some signal words that show time are *then*, *when*, *in time*, *around* (followed by a date), *in* (followed by a date), *as early as* (followed by a date), *earlier*, and *later*.

Section 1 Summary

Rome's Geography and Early Settlement

Rome was at the center of a peninsula, now called Italy, that juts out into the Mediterranean Sea. The Mediterranean was the center of the known world.

The first settlements date from the 900s B.C. Rome grew slowly. About 600 B.C., the Etruscans (ih TRUS kunz) took power. Eventually, the Romans drove the Etruscans from power, but they kept many Etruscan ideas, including many of their gods, the Greek alphabet, and the toga. ✓

✓ Reading Check

What parts of the Etruscan culture did the Romans keep?

____

____

____

Romans Form a Republic

The Romans did not want to rely on one ruler. They created a new form of government called a **republic**. The leaders ruled in the name of the people.

The senate was the government's most powerful part. It was made up of 300 upper-class men called **patricians**. Ordinary citizens were called **plebeians**. In the early republic, they could not hold office.

The government was led by two **consuls** that enforced the laws and policies. Both had to agree before the government could take action. Either consul could say, "**Veto**." Then the matter would be dropped. If the consuls were not able to agree during an emergency, a **dictator** could be appointed.

As Rome expanded, troubles arose between patricians and plebeians. Patricians thought of themselves as leaders. Plebeians thought the senate was unfair to them.

Key Terms

republic (rih PUB lik) *n.* a type of government in which citizens select their leaders
patrician (puh TRISH un) *n.* a member of a wealthy family in the ancient Roman Republic
plebeian (plih BEE un) *n.* an ordinary citizen in the ancient Roman Republic
consul (KAHN sul) *n.* an elected official who led the Roman Republic
veto (VEE toh) *n.* the power of one branch of government to reject bills or proposals passed by another branch of government
dictator (DIK tay tur) *n.* a person in the ancient Roman Republic appointed to rule in times of emergency, with all the powers of a king

Patricians bought small farms they combined to make huge farms that were worked by slaves. Many plebeian farmers became jobless.

In time, plebeians refused to fight in the Roman army. The patricians gave in to one of their demands. It was a written code called the Laws of the Twelve Tables. It applied equally to all citizens. ✓

Meanwhile, Roman armies invaded lands ruled by Carthage. They destroyed Carthage and conquered Greece by 146 B.C. Then they turned their attention to Gaul, most of which is now France.

The Decline of the Republic

By 120 B.C., Rome was in trouble. For the next 75 years, generals with private armies fought for power. Rome was about to break up when Julius Caesar became leader.

Caesar was eager for power. He led the army that conquered Gaul. War broke out between Caesar and the senate, and Caesar won and became dictator in 48 B.C. Four years later he became dictator for life and reorganized the government. Many senators hated the idea Rome seemed to have a king. On March 15, 44 B.C., Caesar attended a senate meeting. Afterward, he was assassinated by a group of senators. ✓

Thirteen years of civil war followed. At the end, Caesar's adopted son, Octavian (ahk TAY vee un), took power. The senate gave him the title Augustus (aw GUS tus), which means "highly respected." He was the first emperor of Rome. The Roman Republic lasted nearly 500 years.

Review Questions

1. Describe the geography and early settlement of Rome.

____

____

2. What were the important features of the Roman Republic?

____

____

✓ Reading Check

What complaints did the plebeians have against the patricians?

____

____

____

Vocabulary Strategy

Mark the Text: As you read this section, circle the words that signal when events took place.

✓ Reading Check

What did Julius Caesar do to become dictator of Rome?

____

____

____

Target Reading Skill

What is the meaning of *reorganize*?

____

____

____

Prepare to Read

Section 2 The Roman Empire

Objectives

1. Learn how Rome ruled an empire.
2. Understand the Greek influence on Rome.
3. Identify aspects of Roman architecture and technology.
4. Learn about Roman law.

Target Reading Skill

Recognize Word Origins The origin of a word is where the word comes from. The English language is full of words from other languages, such as Greek and Latin. Often, these words have changed over time. Sometimes, a foreign word or root is joined with English prefixes or suffixes to make a new word.

In this section, you will read the key term *aqueduct*. You may not know what it means, but you can uncover its meaning if you know that it comes from two Latin words: The word *aqua* means "water;" the word *ductus* means "the act of leading."

What other words can you think of that contain one or the other of these Latin roots?

Vocabulary Strategy

Recognize Signal Words Signal words are words or phrases that give you clues to help you understand what you read and prepare you for what is coming next. There are different kinds of signal words. Signal words may show relationships such as sequence. Sequence is the order in which things occur. It shows how events are related to each other.

> Some signal words that may show sequence include *first*, *next*, *then*, *finally*, *before*, *earlier*, and *later*.

Section 2 Summary

Ruling an Empire

Rome gained more territory and the Roman Empire stretched from Britain to Egypt.

Augustus often ignored the senate, but he was careful not to act like a king. In return, Romans gave him as much power as he wanted.

The empire was divided into **provinces**. The Romans did not force their culture on conquered peoples. They wanted peaceful provinces that would provide raw materials. They wanted people to provide a market for Roman goods and pay taxes.

After Augustus died, there were good, bad, and terrible emperors. In A.D. 96, Rome entered the age of the five "good emperors." The greatest of them may have been Hadrian (HAY dree un). He issued a code of laws, reorganized the army, and encouraged learning. The last of the good emperors was Marcus Aurelius (MAHR kus aw REE lee us). His son was a terrible leader who brought an end to Rome's age of peace. ✓

The Greek Influence on Rome

Many Romans visited Greece to study art, architecture, and ideas about government. Like the Greeks, the Romans practiced **polytheism**. Many Roman gods and goddesses had Greek counterparts.

The Greeks and the Romans valued learning, but in different ways. The Greeks were interested in ideas and the Romans were interested in using their studies to build things. Under the Romans, architecture and engineering blossomed. ✓

Architecture and Technology

Early Roman art and architecture copied the Etruscans. Then the Romans copied Greek sculpture and architecture. Later, they developed their own style.

Key Terms

province (PRAH vins) *n.* a unit of an empire

polytheism (PAHL ih thee iz um) *n.* a belief in more than one god

Target Reading Skill

The word *polytheism* comes from the Greek words *poly* and *theos*. If *theos* means "god," what does *poly* mean?

____

____

✓ Reading Check

List three reasons Hadrian was considered to be one of the five "good emperors."

____

____

____

✓ Reading Check

In what ways did the Greeks and Romans value learning?

Greeks: ______________________

____

Romans: ______________________

____

Vocabulary Strategy

Circle the sequence signal words in the first paragraph.

Mark the Text

✓ Reading Check

What are some characteristics of Roman buildings?

____

____

____

✓ Reading Check

List two features of Justinian's code and explain their meaning.

1. ______________________

____

2. ______________________

____

Roman buildings were heavier and stronger than those of the Greeks. The Romans used **arches** to build larger structures and arched ceilings to create large open spaces inside.

Earlier, most large buildings were built of bricks covered with thin slabs of white marble. The Romans developed concrete. It helped them build taller buildings.

The **Colosseum** may have been the greatest Roman building. It was a giant arena that held 50,000 spectators. The floor could be flooded for mock naval battles. ✓

Roman engineers built roads throughout the empire. The Romans also built **aqueducts** that were often many miles long. A channel along the top carried water from the countryside to the cities.

Roman Law

Roman law spread throughout the empire. The ruler Justinian (juh STIN ee uhn) created a famous code of justice. It includes these laws:

> "No one suffers a penalty for what he thinks. No one may be forcibly removed from his own house. The burden of proof is upon the person who accuses." ✓

Roman law was passed down to other cultures, including our own.

Review Questions

1. How did Rome handle the difficulties of governing its large empire?

____

____

2. What did the Romans learn from the Greeks?

____

____

Key Terms

arch (ahrch) *n.* a curved structure used for support
Colosseum (kahl uh SEE um) *n.* a large amphitheater built in Rome
aqueduct (AK wuh dukt) *n.* a structure that carries water over long distances

Chapter 8 Assessment

1. Which of the following is a key feature of a republican government?
   A. rule by a king
   B. dictatorship
   C. polytheism
   D. elected officials

2. In the Roman Republic, what happened if the two consuls disagreed during an emergency?
   A. A dictator was appointed.
   B. A third consul was appointed.
   C. The senate made the final decision.
   D. All citizens voted.

3. How did the Romans rule their empire?
   A. Conquered peoples were forced to become soldiers in the Roman army.
   B. They forced the conquered peoples to adopt Roman ways.
   C. They destroyed the cultures of conquered peoples.
   D. They did not force their way of life on the conquered peoples.

4. Many Romans visited Greece to study
   A. art and architecture.
   B. ideas about government.
   C. both A and B
   D. none of the above

5. The Romans were heavily influenced by
   A. the Greeks.
   B. the Gauls.
   C. the Persians.
   D. the Carthaginians.

Short Answer Question

What were the main differences between the patricians and the plebeians?

____

____

____

____

____

Prepare to Read

Section 1 Roman Daily Life

Objectives

1. Discover who could be a Roman citizen.
2. Find out how different social classes lived.
3. Understand the importance of family life.
4. Learn about slavery in ancient Rome.

Target Reading Skill

Identify Main Ideas It's hard to remember every detail you read. But it helps to know the main idea, or the most important point.

To help you find the main ideas, look first at each heading. The headings will give you clues. Then, read the text that comes after each heading. As you read, ask yourself what each paragraph is about.

On the next page, the main idea for the text under the heading "Roman Citizens" is stated in one sentence: "In the early days, only people who lived in the city of Rome could be citizens."

As you read, look for the main idea in each section and write it down.

Vocabulary Strategy

Word Origins Many English words come from Latin, but most are spelled differently. They may also have different meanings from the original words.

Below are terms that deal with everyday life in ancient Rome. They are all from Latin.

villa (*villa*), *estate* (*status*), *colosseum* (*colloseus*), *circus* (*circus*), *gladiator* (*gladius*), *slave* (*sclavus*)

Latin word	English word
villa	villa
status	estate
colloseus	colosseum
circus	circus
gladius	gladiator
sclavus	slave

Section 1 Summary

Roman Citizens

In the early days, only people who lived in the city of Rome could be citizens. Every five years, Roman men registered for the **census**, which was the only way to claim citizenship. They declared their families, slaves, and wealth. If a man did not register, he could lose his property, or even be sold into slavery. ✓

As the Roman Empire expanded, people beyond Rome were made citizens, but residents of Rome felt a special love for their city.

Roman Social Classes

Roman society had a few rich people and many poor people and slaves. Most poor Romans were either slaves or jobless and relied on government support.

The rich often had elegant homes in the cities and country estates called **villas**. Some wealthy families had huge estates in the provinces, where much of the empire's food was grown.

Most Romans lived in poorly built housing. Houses were made of wood, so fires were frequent. One fire, in A.D. 64, destroyed most of the city.

Poor citizens needed wheat for bread to survive. Sometimes harvests were bad or grain shipments were late. Then, the poor often rioted. To prevent this, the emperors provided free grain. They also provided shows at the Colosseum or in arenas called **circuses**. ✓

These shows could be violent. They included fights between animals, between animals and humans, and between humans. The highlights were the fights between **gladiators**, who fought to the death. Most gladiators were slaves, who had been captured in battle.

Key Terms

census (SEN sus) *n.* an official count of people living in a place
villa (VIL uh) *n.* a country estate
circus (SUR kus) *n.* an arena in ancient Rome or the show held there
gladiator (GLAD ee ay tur) *n.* a person who fought to the death as entertainment for the Roman public

✓ Reading Check

How did a person become a Roman citizen?

____

____

Target Reading Skill

Which sentence states the main idea in the section "Roman Social Classes"? **Mark the Text** Underline it.

✓ Reading Check

What conditions often led the poor people of ancient Rome to riot?

____

____

____

Vocabulary Strategy

In Latin, the word *circus* means "circle." What does this tell you about the shape of the arenas used for the Roman circuses?

____

____

Roman Family Life

Romans valued family life. The government rewarded upper-class families for having more children. There were penalties for unmarried men over 20 and childless couples.

The head of a Roman household was the *paterfamilias* (pay tur fuh MIL ee us), which means "father of the family." Under Roman law, the *paterfamilias* had absolute power over the household. He owned his wife, children, slaves, and furniture. In the early days, he could sell his children into slavery.

A woman's place depended on the type of marriage she made. She might keep ties with her own family. The only role she had in her husband's family was to produce children.

The amount of freedom a woman had depended on her husband's wealth and status. Wealthy women had a great deal of freedom. Some women trained to be doctors. Others became involved in business. Lower-class women took on various kinds of work. ☑

✓ Reading Check

What rights did men and women have in ancient Rome?

____

____

____

Slavery in Rome

Slavery was common in ancient Rome. Almost every wealthy family owned slaves, who had almost no rights. They helped raise children and served as companions. Sometimes they rose to important positions in their owners' households.

Household slaves were treated the best. Slaves on farms sometimes worked chained together. Gladiator slaves risked death every time they fought. Roman warships were powered by slaves trained as rowers.

Some slaves were able buy their freedom. These might be slaves with special skills, such as gladiators or chariot racers. ☑

✓ Reading Check

Who owned slaves in ancient Rome?

____

____

____

Review Questions

1. Who could claim Roman citizenship?

____

____

2. Why did the Roman government feed and entertain its people?

____

____

Prepare to Read

Section 2
Christianity and the Roman Empire

Objectives

1. Learn about the rise of Christianity in the Roman Empire.
2. Discover how Christianity spread throughout the empire.
3. Understand the government's reaction to Christianity.

Target Reading Skill

Identify Supporting Details The main idea of a paragraph or section is its most important point, which is supported by details. Details give more information. They may explain the main idea or give additional facts or examples. They tell you what, where, why, how much, or how many.

The heading at the top of the next page is "The Rise of Christianity." As you read, notice how the facts tell you more about how Christianity grew. These are the details that support the main idea.

As you read, write the main idea of each section on a sheet of paper. Below it, write the details that support the main ideas.

Vocabulary Strategy

Word Origins Many English words dealing with Christianity come from Greek or Latin. Latin became the language of the Roman Catholic Church. The table below gives some English words dealing with religion, along with their Latin or Greek origins. Watch for these words as you read this section.

English Word	Latin Word	Greek Word
Bible	*biblia*, "book"	*biblos*, "papyrus"
Christ	*Christus*	*christos*, "the anointed"
epistle	*epistola*	*epistole*, "letter"
Messiah	*Messias*	*Messias*, "anointed"

Section 2 Summary

Vocabulary Strategy

The word *disciple* comes from the Latin word *discipulus*, which means "learner." If Jesus' disciples were learners, what does this make Jesus?

The Rise of Christianity

Christianity was one of many religions in the Roman Empire. The Romans allowed conquered people to keep their own religions, but they had to be loyal to Roman gods and the emperor.

When the Romans conquered Judaea (joo DEE uh), they let the Jews worship their God. But many Jews resented foreign rule. Some believed a **messiah** would free them. Opposition to Roman rule grew. As punishment, the Romans appointed a new ruler of Judaea. His name was Herod (HEHR ud). **Jesus** was born during Herod's reign.

Stories about Jesus are found in the New Testament. It is part of the Christian Bible. After Jesus died, his **disciples** told stories about his life and teachings. Four stories of his life were written down. These writings are known as the Gospels.

Jesus spent three years traveling and preaching. Much of what he taught was part of Jewish tradition. He said there was only one God and that people were to love their neighbors as themselves. He promised people who followed his teachings would have everlasting life. His followers believed he was their messiah.

The Romans feared Jesus would lead an armed revolt so they condemned him to death. Jesus was crucified (KROO suh fyd), or put to death by being nailed to a large wooden cross. According to the Gospels, Jesus rose from the dead and spoke to his disciples, telling them to spread his teachings. ✓

✓ Reading Check

Why did the Romans fear Jesus?

Key Terms

messiah (muh SY uh) *n.* a savior in Judaism and Christianity
Jesus (JEE zus) *n.* founder of Christianity; believed by Christians to be the Messiah
disciple (dih SY pul) *n.* a follower of a person or a belief

Christianity Spreads

The Greek word for *messiah* was *christos* (KRIS tohs). As educated people accepted Jesus' teachings, they began calling him Christ. After his death, his followers were called Christians. The new religion spread from Jerusalem to Antioch, Syria. Finally, it spread to Rome.

One of Jesus' most devoted disciples was named Paul. He accepted Christianity after a vision in which Jesus spoke to him. Paul traveled to share the word of Jesus. Paul's writings helped turn the Christian faith into an organized religion. He wrote **epistles** to Christian groups in distant cities. Some of them became a part of the Christian Bible.

The new religion gained followers. Many poor city dwellers welcomed its message as good news. ✓

Rome Reacts

Christians refused to worship Roman gods or the emperor, so many Roman officials saw them as enemies. When Rome burned in A.D. 64, the emperor blamed the Christians, who were arrested and sent to their deaths.

Over the next 250 years, the Roman Empire began to decline, and some Romans blamed the Christians. Still, Christianity spread throughout the empire.

The emperor Diocletian (dy uh KLEE shuhn) outlawed Christian services. He jailed Christian priests and put many believers to death. But many Romans saw Christians as **martyrs** and heroes. ✓

Review Questions

1. What ideas did Jesus teach?

2. To what new groups did Paul want to spread the teachings of Jesus?

Key Terms

epistle (ee PIS ul) *n.* in the Bible, letters written by disciples
martyr (MAHR tur) *n.* a person who dies for a cause

Target Reading Skill

What details in the paragraphs under the heading "Christianity Spreads" tell about the growth of Christianity?

✓ Reading Check

Why did Christianity find many followers in the cities?

✓ Reading Check

How did the Romans persecute Christians?

Prepare to Read

Section 3 The Fall of Rome

Objectives

1. Explore how bad government contributed to the decline of the empire.
2. Understand the fall of the Roman Empire.
3. Discuss Constantine's role in support for Christianity.
4. Learn how invaders brought about the collapse of the empire.

Target Reading Skill

Identify Implied Main Ideas The main idea of a paragraph or section is its most important point. Sometimes the main idea is not stated directly. All the details in a paragraph or section add up to a main idea. In a case like this, the main idea is implied. It is up to you to put the details together.

As you read, study the details in each section. Then write the section's main idea on a sheet of paper. Under the main idea, write the details that support it.

Vocabulary Strategy

Word Origins Many English words come from names of people or places. For example, people who follow the teachings of Jesus are called *Christians*. As you will recall, Christ was the name many of Jesus' followers called him.

The word *Byzantine* comes from *Byzantium*. That was the name of the city that became the capital of the Byzantine Empire. *Byzantine* is used to refer to things associated with the Byzantine Empire. But the word has also come to mean "characterized by complexity or intrigue." That definition could describe the government of the Byzantine Empire.

Section 3 Summary

From Good Rule to Bad

Commodus came to power when Marcus Aurelius died. Because he was only 18, he allowed others to help run the empire. He let others destroy the senate's power. ✓

The Empire Crumbles

The decline of the Roman Empire began under Commodus. The emperors who followed were almost always successful generals, and not politicians. They often stole money to enrich themselves. The government and the economy grew weak. The senate lost power, and would-be rulers gained the throne by violence.

Once, the Roman army had been made up of citizen soldiers. Now, it was filled with **mercenaries**. Mercenaries are motivated by money, not by loyalty to a cause. They often switch sides if it's to their advantage. ✓

The Roman Empire was too big to be ruled from one place. Many conquered territories broke away.

Rome stopped conquering new lands, so there were no new sources of wealth and the empire struggled to pay its army. Food was also scarce, so prices went up. To pay for it, the government made more coins. They had less silver in them, which led to **inflation**. Money soon became worthless.

The emperor Diocletian tried to save Rome. He divided the empire into two parts to make it easier to control. He ruled the wealthier East and a co-emperor ruled the West.

Key Terms

mercenary (MUR suh neh ree) *n.* a soldier who serves for pay in a foreign army

inflation (in FLAY shun) *n.* an economic situation in which the government issues more money with lower value

Target Reading Skill

In one sentence, state the main idea that all the details in the bracketed paragraph support.

____

____

✓ Reading Check

What problems did having a mercenary army cause for the empire?

____

____

Constantine and Christianity

When Diocletian and his co-emperor retired, generals fought for power. The winner, **Constantine**, believed the Christian God had helped him win. He became sole ruler of the Roman Empire in the West. In the East, the Roman Empire was shared. In 313, Licinius (ly SIN ee us) took complete control of the eastern empire.

Constantine and Licinius both allowed people freedom to worship. Soon, Christianity became the religion accepted by the government of the Roman Empire.

Constantine won several battles against Licinius and became emperor of both the East and West. Constantine moved the capital to the city of Byzantium (bih ZAM tee um). Constantine called the city New Rome, but it came to be known as Constantinople (kahn stan tuh NOH pul), "the city of Constantine." ✓

✓ Reading Check

What city became the new capital of the Roman Empire?

____

____

____

Invasions and Collapse

Constantine struggled to keep the empire together. After his death, invaders from the north swept in. Today, we call them Germanic tribes. One tribe, the Vandals (VAN dulz), took Rome in 455. The Roman emperor was almost powerless.

Vocabulary Strategy

Originally, a *Vandal* was a member of a Germanic tribe. A vandal is a person who destroys property. How do you think the word *vandal* got the meaning?

____

____

____

The last Roman emperor was a 14-year-old named Romulus Augustulus (RAHM yuh lus oh GUS chuh lus). In 476, a German general took power and sent the emperor to work on a farm. The eastern part of the empire remained strong and became the Byzantine Empire. ✓

✓ Reading Check

Who was Romulus Augustulus, and what was his fate?

____

____

Review Questions

1. What factors contributed to the Roman Empire's decline?

____

____

2. What did Constantine do to show he accepted Christianity?

____

____

Key Terms

Constantine (KAHN stun teen) *n.* emperor of Rome from A.D. 312 to 337

Chapter 9 Assessment

1. What could happen to a Roman citizen who failed to register for the census?
   A. He could be sent to prison.
   B. He could be forced to leave the city.
   C. He could be sold into slavery.
   D. He could be thrown to the lions.

2. Which of the following was a Roman social class?
   A. patricians
   B. plebeians
   C. slaves
   D. all of the above

3. The letters written by the disciple Paul, called epistles, became part of
   A. the Roman code of law.
   B. the Christian Bible.
   C. Justinian's laws.
   D. the Jewish Torah.

4. What did Constantine call his new capital?
   A. Byzantium
   B. Constantinople
   C. New Rome
   D. New Jerusalem

5. The last Roman emperor was
   A. Marcus Aurelius.
   B. Commodus.
   C. Constantine.
   D. Romulus Augustulus.

Short Answer Question

How did the lives of the rich and poor differ in ancient Rome?

____

____

____

____

____

Prepare to Read

Section 1
The Byzantine Empire

Objectives

1. Find out how Constantinople and the Byzantine Empire became powerful.
2. Discover the achievements of the Age of Justinian.
3. Learn about the later years of the Byzantine Empire.

Target Reading Skill

Preview and Set a Purpose Reading a textbook is different from reading other books. There is a special way to read a textbook. To make your reading powerful, preview and set a purpose for your reading.

Before you read this section, take a minute to preview it. Look at the title, "The Byzantine Empire," and the three objectives. Now flip through the next two pages. Read each heading. They tell you what the section is about. As you preview, use this information to give yourself a reason to read. What makes you curious about the section? Are you curious about the emperor of this empire? Read to satisfy that curiosity—that's your purpose for reading.

Vocabulary Strategy

Use Context Clues to Determine Meaning Words work together like a team to explain meaning. The meaning of a word may depend on its **context**. A word's context is the other words and sentences that surround it.

Try this example. Say that you did not know the meaning of the word *icons* in this sentence:

"Many Christians prayed to <u>icons</u> that showed saints."

You could ask yourself: "What information can I use from the sentence?" Answer: "It tells me that icons show saints." Then ask: "What kinds of things can show other things?" Answer: "Pictures or paintings can show something."

In this case, icons are paintings that show saints.

Section 1 Summary

Constantinople at a Crossroads

At its peak, the Roman Empire ruled many lands. The emperor **Constantine** began to rule in A.D. 306. He made two big changes. He became a Christian, and he moved the empire's capital.

Constantine chose Byzantium, an ancient Greek city in the east. Constantine renamed the city after himself— **Constantinople**. By the early 500s, it was a busy city of half a million people. The people who lived there still were called Byzantines. Over time, the Roman Empire split in two. The eastern half was stronger. It had the strongest army in the world. Trade also made it strong.

Constantinople was at a major crossroads of land and sea trade routes. The Byzantines charged taxes on all goods that went through the city. Trade made the empire grow rich. ✓

The western Roman Empire however, was weak. In 476, a Germanic leader took over. This event is known as the fall of the Roman Empire.

The Age of Justinian

Although Rome fell, a strong army and good laws protected Constantinople. The Byzantine Empire had many wise rulers. One of the greatest was **Justinian**. He had a team organize all the old Roman laws. The result was **Justinian's Code**. The legal systems of most modern European countries are based on Justinian's Code.

Byzantine experts also copied the works of the ancient Greeks. At its peak, Byzantine civilization blended Greek, Roman, and Christian culture. Later, scholars took this knowledge to Italy. ✓

Key Terms

Constantine (KAHN stun teen) *n.* a Roman emperor
Constantinople (kahn stan tuh NOH pul) *n.* the capital of the eastern Roman Empire and later of the Byzantine Empire
Justinian (jus TIN ee un) *n.* a great Byzantine emperor
Justinian's Code (jus TIN ee unz kohd) *n.* an organized collection and explanation of Roman laws for use by the Byzantine Empire

✓ Reading Check

Mark the Text: Circle two reasons why Constantinople became rich and powerful.

✓ Reading Check

Which cultures influenced Byzantine civilization?

____

____

____

The Empire's Later Years

After Justinian died, the Byzantine Empire began to get weak. It shrank in size and power. The empire was weakened from inside problems and outside forces.

Most Byzantines were Christians. But they did not practice Christianity the same way that people in Western Europe did. In Europe, the pope had a lot of power. Byzantines did not accept the pope. Instead, the Byzantine emperor chose the patriarch. The patriarch was the highest church official in Constantinople. Greek was the language of the Byzantine church. Latin was used by the Roman church. The two branches of Christianity grew apart.

At that time, many Christians prayed to icons. These were paintings of saints, or holy people. A Byzantine emperor decided that icons broke God's rules. The pope, however, disagreed. He banished the emperor from the church.

Byzantines did not think the pope had the right to do this. This led to a **schism** in the Christian church in 1054. Now there were two forms of Christianity. In the west was the Roman Catholic Church. In the east was the Eastern (Greek) Orthodox Church.

During the 1000s, Muslim peoples were gaining power. By the late 1100s, Turks had taken parts of Asia Minor from the Byzantine Empire. Europeans were also a threat. In 1171, problems with trade led to a war with Venice. And in the early 1200s, Constantinople was attacked by Christian crusaders.

In 1453, Turks overpowered Constantinople. The new rulers renamed the city Istanbul. It became the capital of the Ottoman Empire. ✓

Review Questions

1. Why was Justinian's Code so important?

____

____

2. What caused the schism in the Christian church?

____

____

Key Term

schism (SIZ um) *n.* a split, particularly in a church or religion

Target Reading Skill

If your purpose was to learn more about the empire's later years, list one fact from the bracketed paragraph that helps you meet your purpose.

Purpose: Learn more about the empire's later years

Fact: ______________________________

____

Vocabulary Strategy

What does the word *patriarch* mean in the underlined sentence above? What clues can you find in the surrounding words, phrases, or sentences? Circle the words in the paragraph that help you learn what *patriarch* means, then write a definition below.

Mark the Text

____

____

____

✓ Reading Check

Underline the events that led to Constantinople's fall.

How many events did you find?

Mark the Text

____

____

____

Prepare to Read

Section 2
The Beginnings of Islam

Objectives

1. Learn about the Arabian Peninsula, its nomadic people, and its centers of trade.
2. Find out about the life and mission of the Muslim prophet Muhammad.
3. Learn about Muslim beliefs.

Target Reading Skill

Preview and Predict Making predictions before you read the text helps you set a purpose. It also helps you remember what you have read. First, preview the section. Look at the section title, objectives, and headings. Then predict what the section will tell you. Based on your preview, you will probably predict that this section tells how Islam, Muhammad, and the Muslims are connected.

List two facts that you expect to learn about the beginning of Islam.

Prediction 1: ____

Prediction 2: ____

As you read, check your predictions. How right were they? If they were not accurate, pay closer attention while you preview.

Vocabulary Strategy

Use Context to Determine Meaning Sometimes you can pick up clues about the meaning of an unfamiliar word from the words and sentences around the word. Sometimes the definition appears near the word. Look at the following examples.

caravans, or *groups of traders traveling together for safety*

Muslim or *person who follows the teachings of Muhammad*

hijra, an Arabic word that means "*the migration*"

Do you see how the definition of the underlined word follows the word? Look for definitions of unfamiliar words as you read.

Section 2 Summary

The Arabian Peninsula

Most of the Arabian Peninsula is desert. It has no major rivers and gets little rain. Yet many groups of Bedouins lived in the desert.

The Bedouins were **nomads**. They knew how find a desert oasis. An oasis is a green area within a desert. It gets its water from below the ground. Oases supplied water for the nomads and their animals.

Vocabulary Strategy

The word *oasis* is defined in context. Circle its definition.

Mark the Text

The Bedouins also worked as guides for traders in **caravans**. Desert caravans relied on camels to carry both people and goods. Camels are well-known for being able to store water for long periods. ✓

✓ Reading Check

Why did Bedouins make good guides for traders?

____

____

____

The Arabian oases became busy trading centers. One of the most important was Mecca.

The Prophet Muhammad

Muhammad was born in **Mecca**. It is said that when he was 40 years old, God spoke to him. God told him that people should agree to obey the one true God. A person who accepted Muhammad's teachings was known as a **Muslim**. The religion of Muslims is called Islam.

Most people of Mecca thought Muhammad's teachings were a threat to their old gods. They also feared that Muhammad might gain political power.

In 622, Muhammad and his followers were invited to a city north of Mecca. The people there believed in Muhammad. This journey is known as the hijra (hih JY ruh), or "the migration." The year of the hijra became year 1 on the Muslim calendar. ✓

✓ Reading Check

Why did Muhammad leave Mecca in 622?

____

____

____

In 630, Muhammad returned in triumph to Mecca. He died two years later. By then, Islam had spread all across the Arabian Peninsula.

Key Terms

nomads (NOH madz) *n.* people with no permanent home, who move from place to place in search of food, water, or pasture
caravan (KA ruh van) *n.* a group of traders traveling together
Muhammad (muh HAM ud) *n.* the prophet and founder of Islam
Mecca (MEK uh) *n.* a trading center and Muhammad's birthplace
Muslim (MUZ lum) *n.* a follower of Islam

Muslim Belief

A muezzin (myoo EZ in) calls Muslims to worship five times a day. Some Muslims gather in a **mosque**. Others kneel outside. Wherever they are, Muslims kneel facing toward Mecca.

Basic Muslim beliefs are stated in the Five Pillars of Islam. Their holy book is the **Quran**. It contains God's messages to Muhammad. Many converts to Islam learn Arabic to read the Quran. The Arabic word for God is *Allah.*

Like Jews and Christians, Muslims believe in one God. Muhammad saw himself as the last prophet following Abraham and Moses. He respected Jews and Christians. He called them "people of the Book."

The Quran taught that men and women were spiritually equal. It gave women rights under the law. They could inherit property and get an education. Muslim women could not be forced to marry. They could get a divorce.

In 656, the Muslim leader was assassinated. His death split the Muslim world in two. Muslims disagreed about who should be their new leader. Over time, two main groups were formed. ☑

The smaller group was called the Shiites (SHEE yts). They thought the leader should be from Muhammad's family. The larger group were the Sunnis (SOO neez). They thought any truly religious man could rule. Today, about 85 percent of all Muslims are Sunnis.

Review Questions

1. What is written in the Quran?

____

____

2. What do Jews, Christians, and Muslims have in common?

____

____

Key Terms

mosque (mahsk) *n.* a Muslim house of worship
Quran (koo RAHN) *n.* the holy book of Islam

Target Reading Skill

Based on what you have read so far, are your predictions on target? If not, revise or change your predictions now.

New predictions: ______________________

____

____

____

✓ Reading Check

What is the difference between the Shiites and Sunnis?

____

____

____

Prepare to Read

Section 3 The Golden Age of Muslim Civilization

Objectives

1. Find out how the religion of Islam spread.
2. Learn about the golden age of Islam under the rule of the caliphs.

Preview and Ask Questions Begin this section by previewing the title, headings, and objectives. What do you predict will be the most important ideas in the section? How can you tell?

Now write two questions that will help you understand or remember important ideas or facts. For example, you might ask yourself the following questions:

- How did Islam spread to other places?
- What were some achievements of Islamic culture?

Find the answers to your questions as you read.

Keep asking questions about what you think will come next. Does the text answer your questions? Were you able to predict what would be covered under each heading?

Vocabulary Strategy

Use Context Clues to Determine Meaning English words have more than one meaning. To help figure out the meaning of these words, use context clues. For example, the word *back* is used in two different ways in the sentences below.

He wrote his answers on the **back** of the worksheet.

You can figure out that *back* means "other side" from the word "worksheet."

She asked her friends to **back** her plan.

By using context clues, you can figure out that *back* means "support."

Section 3 Summary

The Spread of Islam

Muhammad died in 632. Within 150 years, Islam had spread west into North Africa and what is now Spain. It spread north into Persia. It also spread east to India and China.

How did Islam spread? Arab merchants often traveled west, north, and east. They also traveled along the Mediterranean coast. Many of these traders were Muslims who spread the religion of Islam. Also, Arab armies conquered nearby regions.

In the 700s and 800s, most Christians living along parts of the Mediterranean converted to Islam. But, Arab forces were defeated in 732 in present-day France. This stopped the Muslim advance into Christian Europe.

Muhammad and Islam united the Arabs and made them strong. At the same time, other empires near them were defeated or weak. These two reasons made the Arabs successful conquerors.

The Byzantine rulers nearby did not accept different religions. The Muslims did. Muslim rulers allowed Christians and Jews to practice their own religions. Non-Muslims however, had fewer rights than Muslims. And they had to pay a special tax. ✓

The Golden Age

Muslim culture had its golden age from about 800 to 1100. Under the **caliphs**, the empire grew and became rich. It got wealth from the many lands it ruled and from trade. The capital was Baghdad. The caliph was believed to be Muhammad's successor, or the next person who had the right to rule.

Key Term

caliph (KAY lif) *n.* a Muslim ruler

Target Reading Skill

Choose one of the questions you asked earlier. Now answer your question based on what you have read.

Answer: ______________________

Vocabulary Strategy

The word *practice* has several meanings. You may already know one of its meanings. What is its meaning in the underlined sentence?

____

✓ Reading Check

Compare Muslim rulers and Byzantine rulers.

____

Harun ar-Rashid (hah ROON ar rah SHEED) became caliph of Baghdad in 786. For 23 years, he ruled an exciting and glamorous court. Guests drank from cups decorated with jewels. He also paid many musicians, dancers, and artists to live in Baghdad.

Arabs studied history and ideas from other cultures. They studied Greek and Indian mathematics. A Muslim helped develop algebra. The famous scientist Ibn Sina (IB un SEE nah) put together the medical knowledge of the Greeks and Arabs in the *Canon of Medicine*.

Muslims loved their poetry. Poets were treated like today's rock or rap stars. **Omar Khayyam** lived almost one thousand years ago. He wrote poems in the Persian language that are still read today.

One group, the **Sufis**, used poetry to teach their ideas. They believed the world would reveal its mysteries to careful observers. Sufi missionaries also helped spread Islam to Central Asia, India, and Africa south of the Sahara. ✓

The most famous Sufi poet was Rumi (ROO mee). He founded a religious group that Europeans know as the Whirling Dervishes. They talked to God with music and dance.

✓ Reading Check

What did the Sufis teach?

____

____

____

Review Questions

1. Describe two ways that Islam spread beyond the Arabian Peninsula.

____

____

2. What did Arab scholars contribute to mathematics and science?

____

____

Key Terms

Omar Khayyam (OH mahr ky AHM) *n.* a Muslim poet, mathematician, and astronomer

Sufis (SOO feez) *n.* a mystical Muslim group

Chapter 10 Assessment

1. The Byzantine emperor who organized the old Roman laws was
   A. Constantine.
   B. Justinian.
   C. Harun ar-Rashid.
   D. Ibn Sina.

2. The highest church official in Constantinople was known as the
   A. pope.
   B. prophet.
   C. patriarch.
   D. muezzin.

3. The Bedouins were
   A. people who lived in Constantinople.
   B. nomads who lived in the Arabian desert.
   C. traders who traveled between Europe, Asia, and Africa.
   D. a Muslim group that used poetry to teach their ideas.

4. Muslims are called to worship
   A. once a day.
   B. twice a day.
   C. five times a day.
   D. once a week.

5. During the golden age of Muslim culture, the capital of the Muslim empire was at
   A. Constantinople.
   B. Mecca.
   C. Medina.
   D. Baghdad.

Short Answer Question

What religious beliefs do Muslims, Jews, and Christians share?

____

____

____

____

____

Prepare to Read

Section 1
Africa and the Bantu

Objectives

1. Learn about the physical geography of Africa.
2. Find out about the Bantu and their movement across the continent.

Target Reading Skill

Reread or Read Ahead Rereading is an easy skill that can make you a better reader. Rereading means to read something again. Sometimes you may not understand a word or idea the first time you read it. There may be words you do not recognize.

When this happens, reread. It's okay to reread two or more times. Look for specific information as you reread. Look for connections among the words and sentences. Put together what you do understand with what you don't understand.

Vocabulary Strategy

Use Context to Clarify Meaning When you see a word that you do not know, you may not need to look it up in a dictionary. In this workbook, key terms appear in **blue**. The definitions are in a box at the bottom of the page. Stopping to look at the definition can break up your reading. Instead, continue to read to the end of the paragraph. See if you can figure out what the word means from its context. Clues can include examples and explanations. Then look at the definition on the bottom of the page to see if you were right. Finally, reread the paragraph to make sure you understood what you read.

Section 1 Summary

Over 4,000 years ago, many **Bantu** families left their homes in West Africa, and never returned. No one knows why they first moved. Over time, their **migration** took them across most of Africa south of the Equator. Today, the Bantu population is more than 200 million.

Africa's Physical Geography

On both sides of the Equator are tropical rain forests. They have hot, moist climates. Surrounding these forests are **savanna**. Much of Africa is savanna. Africa's lions, zebras, and elephants live mainly on the savannas. North and south of the savannas are deserts. The **Sahara** is the world's largest desert. Along the eastern edge of Africa runs a band of lakes, deep valleys, and rugged mountains.

Africa's physical geography affects the way people live. There is little farming in the deserts, since there is too little water. People herd cattle on the savannas. But cattle cannot survive in the rain forests. ✓

Groups that live in the same surroundings may live differently. The Mbooti (em BOO tee) people survive in the rain forest by hunting animals and gathering plants. But other people in the forest are farmers.

The Bantu Migrations

Geography did not stop the Bantus from moving across Africa. Their migrations went on for more than 1,000 years. This was the largest migration in history.

Historians know little about the history of Africa south of the Sahara. That area is called sub-Saharan Africa. The Sahara separated this part of Africa from Europe for years. Today, people are trying to put together the history of this area. It is like solving a puzzle.

Key Terms

Bantu (BAN too) *n.* a large group of central and southern Africans who speak related languages
migration (my GRAY shun) *n.* the movement from one country or region to settle in another
savanna (suh VAN uh) *n.* grassland with few trees and bushes
Sahara (suh HA ruh) *n.* a huge desert across North Africa

Target Reading Skill

Reread the paragraphs under the heading "Africa's Physical Geography." Underline the physical features that make it hard to migrate.

Mark the Text

✓ Reading Check

How do Africa's physical features affect how people live?

Vocabulary Strategy

Use context clues to write a definition of the word *disintegrated*. Circle words or phrases in the text that helped you write your definition.

Some clues to the puzzle have disappeared. Old wooden and clay buildings have disintegrated. Even iron tools and weapons have rusted. Scientists use new methods to find information about the past. **Oral histories** told by traditional African storytellers have also helped.

Clues tell us that most Bantu peoples were fishers, farmers, and herders. Villages were made up of families from the same **clan**. Many clans traced their relatives from their mother's side. The mother's side of the family passed down power and property.

The Bantu peoples moved slowly from their traditional homes. New generations also moved a short distance looking for better farmland and better grazing. As they moved, the environment changed. In many places, they had to change the way they lived. The Bantu peoples learned to raise new crops or new kinds of animals.

Often, Bantu people moved to places where other people lived. Sometimes they joined the groups already living there. Sometimes the Bantu and other groups shared their cultures. At other times, they forced the people who were already there to leave.

The Bantu knew how to work with metal. Iron axes helped them to cut down trees and clear land. They also had iron weapons for hunting and for warfare. ✓

✓ Reading Check

Which skills did the Bantu bring with them?

Bantu migrations went on for many generations. When an area got crowded, groups moved. In time, the Bantu had settled all over Central and Southern Africa.

Review Questions

1. Describe the important physical features of Africa.

2. Over how many years did the Bantu migrations occur?

Key Terms

oral history (OR ul HIS tuh ree) *n.* accounts of the past that people pass down by word of mouth

clan (klan) *n.* a group of families who trace their roots to the same ancestor

CHAPTER
11

Prepare to Read

Section 2
Kingdoms of West Africa

Objectives

1. Learn about trading kingdoms of the West African savanna.
2. Investigate the kingdoms of the West African rain forests.

Target Reading Skill

Paraphrase Paraphrasing is putting what you read into your own words. It is another skill that can help you understand what you read.

Look at the first paragraph under the heading "Kingdoms of the Savanna." It could be paraphrased like this: "The kingdoms of the savanna grew rich through the taxes they charged traders who traveled through their land."

As you read, paraphrase the information following each heading.

Vocabulary Strategy

Use Context to Understand Words Social studies textbooks often have words that you may not know. There is one good way to figure out the meaning of a word. Look for clues in the words and sentences just before and after the word. Clues in a word's context can include examples, explanations, or even a definition. Also, you may happen to know something about the topic that gives a clue. As you read, use the graphic organizer as a guide.

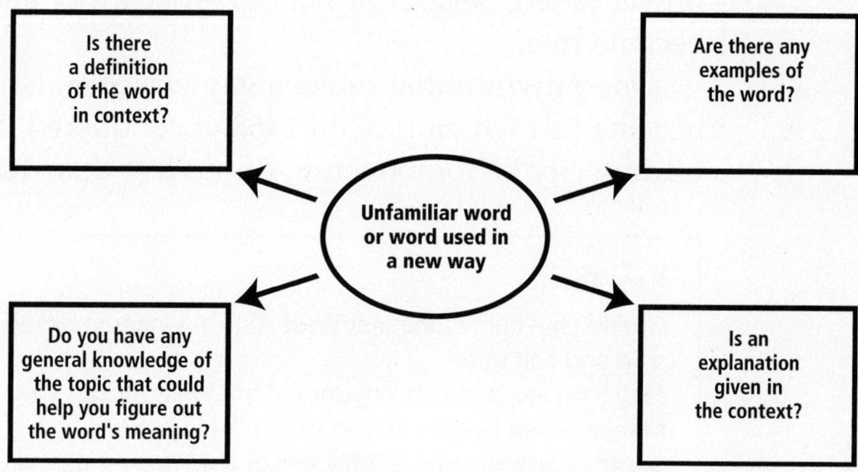
Is there a definition of the word in context?
Are there any examples of the word?
Unfamiliar word or word used in a new way
Do you have any general knowledge of the topic that could help you figure out the word's meaning?
Is an explanation given in the context?

Section 2 Summary

Kingdoms of the Savanna

The kingdoms of the savanna controlled important trade routes across the Sahara. The Niger River was another important route. Traders on these routes had to pay taxes to the kingdoms. This made the kingdoms rich. In return, the rulers kept peace and order. Traders could then travel safely.

Salt and gold were the two most popular items of West African trade. People needed salt to flavor food, preserve meat, and stay healthy. But, it was scarce in the rain forest region. People there, however, had gold. They traded gold for salt. ✓

Ghana was in the perfect place to take control of the Sahara trade routes. Ghana was just north of the rich gold fields. By about A.D. 800, it was a major trading kingdom. By about A.D. 1000, though, invaders overran Ghana. By the 1200s, it had broken up.

Soon, a powerful new kingdom, **Mali** controlled the gold and salt trade. It was centered in the Upper Niger Valley. Mali's ruler Sundiata (sun JAH tah), conquered surrounding areas. By 1255, when Sundiata died, Mali was the most powerful kingdom in West Africa.

In 1312, **Mansa Musa** became ruler of Mali and expanded his kingdom. Traders from North Africa had brought a new religion, Islam, to West Africa. Mansa Musa made Islam the official religion. He also made Mali a center of learning. In the late 1300s, Mali's power faded. Several provinces broke away and became free.

One province that broke away was **Songhai**. It became its own empire. In 1468, it conquered the rich trading city of Tombouctou. But in less than 100 years,

Key Terms

Ghana (GAH nuh) *n.* the first West African kingdom based on the gold and salt trade
Mali (MAH lee) *n.* a rich kingdom of the West African savanna
Mansa Musa (MAHN sah MOO sah) *n.* a king of Mali
Songhai (SAWNG hy) *n.* a kingdom of the West African savanna

Vocabulary Strategy

Look for at least one word in this section that is unfamiliar to you. Use the graphic organizer on the previous page and the word's context to write a brief definition below. (Choose a word **other than** the Key Terms in blue.)

____

____

____

✓ Reading Check

Name the two most important trade items in West Africa.

1. ______________________________

2. ______________________________

Target Reading Skill

Paraphrase the bracketed paragraph. Write your paraphrase on the lines below. Try to use less than 30 words!

____

____

____

Songhai began to lose power. By the late 1500s, it fell to Morocco, in North Africa. This was the end of the rich trading empires of West Africa.

Kingdoms of the Forest

At the time of the savanna kingdoms, other kingdoms began in the south. The peoples of the rain forests there were not Muslim. They had religions with hundreds of gods.

Two important forest kingdoms were **Ile-Ife** and **Benin**. They were both located in what is now Nigeria. Trade made them rich. They also had more people than other rain forest regions.

About A.D 1000, Ile-Ife became a major trading center. The kingdom's leaders were called onis (OH neez). We know little about Ile-Ife because the present-day town of Ife was built on top of it. Also, dampness has rusted iron and rotted wood and fabrics. Many life-like sculptures have been found in the last 100 years. They date from between the 1100s and the 1300s. Some of the sculptures may be portraits of the onis.

The city of Benin dates to the 1200s. At that time, workers mined copper, iron, and gold. Benin's leaders, called obas (OH buz) sold slaves to African traders. By the 1500s, Benin had become very rich. It stayed strong until the late 1600s. Benin spent its riches on art. The obas hired artists to make beautiful objects from bronze, brass, ivory, and copper. ✓

Review Questions

1. What were the names of the three major kingdoms of the West African savanna?

____

____

2. Describe some of the art objects that the people of Ile-Ife and Benin created.

____

____

Key Terms

Ile-Ife (EE lay EE fay) *n.* the capital of a kingdom of the West African rain forest

Benin (beh NEEN) *n.* a kingdom of the West African rain forest

✓ Reading Check

What were the leaders of Ile-Ife and Benin called?

Ile-Ife's leaders: _______________

____

Benin's leaders: _______________

____

Prepare to Read

Section 3
East Africa's Great Trading Centers

Objectives

1. Learn about the powerful cities of Aksum and Lalibela.
2. Find out why the coastal cities of East Africa were important.

Target Reading Skill

Summarize When you summarize, you write a short statement of what you have read. You focus on the main points. You leave out less important details. A summary is shorter than the original text. It is helpful to keep the main ideas and facts in the correct order.

Look at the example:

> The merchants of Aksum traded as far away as India. As they traded goods with foreign merchants, they also exchanged ideas with them.

You could summarize it this way: "The merchants of Aksum exchanged ideas along with goods."

Vocabulary Strategy

Use Context to Understand Words Sometimes you can pick up clues from the words, phrases, and sentences around an unfamiliar word. The clues help you understand what the word means. Say you didn't know what *Swahili* means. Read the example below.

> Contact between Africans and Arabs <u>in the city-states of East Africa</u> led to a new <u>culture and language</u>. It was called **Swahili**. It was a <u>Bantu language with words borrowed from Arabic</u>.

Did you notice that the underlined words are clues? Read the sample again. Now you know that *Swahili* is the name of a Bantu language with words borrowed from Arabic, spoken in East Africa.

Section 3 Summary

Ancient Ethiopia

The city of **Aksum** was built in the mountains far from the coast. But, it had a trading port at Adulis (AD oo lis) on the Red Sea. Over time, Aksum conquered much of modern Ethiopia and southwestern Arabia. Aksum grew in strength and wealth.

Aksum merchants traded as far away as India. One of the main goods they controlled was ivory. Ivory is the white material from elephant tusks. It was valued for carving. As the Aksums traded goods with foreign merchants, they also exchanged ideas with them.

During the A.D. 300s, King Ezana (ay ZAH nuh) of Aksum learned about Christianity. Soon, he became a Christian. Then, he made Christianity the official religion of Aksum. Over time, most of Aksum's people became Christians.

For hundreds of years, Aksum controlled the major trade routes linking Africa with Europe and Asia. In the A.D. 600s, Muslims fought for control of the Red Sea routes. The Muslims ended up conquering the coast. This ended the trade that had given Aksum its power.

Many of the lands around Ethiopia converted to Islam. But Ethiopia stayed Christian. The Ethiopians had little contact with other Christians. Because of this, unique customs and traditions began.

One unique feature is a group of churches built about A.D. 1200, under King Lalibela. They were carved underground in the solid red rock. Their flat rooftops are level with the surrounding land. These churches are in a town named Lalibela in honor of the king. Ethiopian Christians still use them. ✓

Rich Centers of Trade

Muslims gained control of Indian Ocean trade. Trade centers developed along the east coast of Africa. By 1400, there were about 30 **city-states**, including a

Key Terms

Aksum (AHK soom) *n.* an important East African center of trade
city-state (SIH tee stayt) *n.* a city that is also a separate, independent state

Vocabulary Strategy

Look at the word *ivory* in the underlined sentence. You may know what it means. If you don't, there are clues to what it means. Circle the words or phrases that help you learn its meaning.

Mark the Text

✓ Reading Check

Describe the churches of Lalibela.

Target Reading Skill

Summarize the bracketed paragraph. Give two ways that Arabs influenced the East African coast.

1. ______________________

2. ______________________

✓ Reading Check

What were two possible causes for the collapse of Great Zimbabwe?

1. ______________________

2. ______________________

beautiful city called Kilwa. Trade thrived because the region had gold and ivory.

The merchants of **Kilwa** traded goods from inland for goods brought in by sea. Contact between Africans and Arabs in Kilwa and other city-states led to a new culture and language called Swahili. Swahili was spoken all along the East African coast. Most people on the coast also converted to Islam.

In the 1500s, Portuguese troops captured and looted Kilwa and the other coastal city-states. Portugal took over the trade routes. The influence of Swahili, however, remained. Today, Swahili is still used in East Africa. Islam is still an important religion.

Much of the gold traded at Kilwa came from an inland area to the south ruled by **Great Zimbabwe**. It grew rich and powerful through trade. Historians believe that Great Zimbabwe was founded by about 1100. Its people were Bantu speakers and most were poor farmers. The leaders who ran the gold trade were very rich.

By 1500, Great Zimbabwe had fallen. Trade routes may have moved. Farmers may have worn out the soil. But its glory was not completely lost. Its stone ruins still stand. ✓

Review Questions

1. What change did King Ezana of Aksum make?

____

____

2. What connection was there between Great Zimbabwe and Kilwa?

____

____

Key Terms

Kilwa (KEEL wah) *n.* a trading city on the East African coast
Swahili (swah HEE lee) *n.* a Bantu language with Arabic words
Great Zimbabwe (grayt zim BAHB way) *n.* a powerful Southeast African city

Chapter 11 Assessment

1. What special skill did the Bantu have that they carried with them in their migrations?
   A. speaking Arabic
   B. reading and writing
   C. working with metals
   D. leading caravans across the desert

2. Which king of Mali made Islam the official religion there?
   A. Sundiata
   B. Mansa Musa
   C. Ezana
   D. Lalibela

3. Ile-Ife and Benin were kingdoms in the
   A. savanna.
   B. rain forest.
   C. coast of East Africa.
   D. Sahara.

4. What was the new language that developed from contact between Africans and Arabs in East Africa?
   A. Arabic
   B. Bantu
   C. Swahili
   D. Afro-Arabic

5. Much of the gold traded at Kilwa came from an area known as
   A. Ghana.
   B. Mali.
   C. Ethiopia.
   D. Great Zimbabwe.

Short Answer Question

Why did most kingdoms grow rich?

____

____

____

____

____

Prepare to Read

Section 1
South America and the Incas

Objectives

1. Find out about the geography of the Americas.
2. Learn about the Incan Empire in South America.

Target Reading Skill

Identify Main Ideas Good readers look for the main ideas of what they read. The main idea is the most important point. It includes all the other points, or details.

To help you find the main idea of a paragraph, read it through once. Then ask yourself what the paragraph is about. Do all the sentences center on the same subject? If so, you've found the main idea. Sometimes it is written in the first sentence or two.

The main idea of the paragraph below is underlined:

> <u>The Incas ruled a powerful empire</u>. At its peak, it stretched 2,500 miles (4,020 kilometers). This empire grew from small beginnings.

As you read, find the main ideas of paragraphs.

Vocabulary Strategy

Recognize Roots Often, a word has a few letters attached to the beginning or the end to make another word. For example, the letters *un-* may be at the beginning of a word. Or the letters *-ing* may be at the end of a word. If you remove those added letters, you are left with the root word. A root is a word that is used to make other words. The word *well* is the root of the word *unwell*. The word *carry* is the root for *carrying*. Notice how adding a few letters to the beginning or end of each word changes its meaning.

When you see a new word, look at it closely. Look for a root word that you already know. If you know the root, you can use it to figure out the meaning of the new word.

Section 1 Summary

Geography of the Americas

Many groups of people have lived in the Americas for thousands of years. Each group developed different ways of life to fit their geographic settings.

Temperatures in North America are very cold in the far north. They are hot and tropical in the region called Middle America. In South America, the mountain areas are cold. Areas near the Equator are hot. They are much cooler in the far south. Two of the largest rivers in the world, the Mississippi and the Amazon, are located in the Americas. ✓

The Mountain Empire of the Incas

The **Incas** ruled a huge empire in South America. At its peak, it stretched 2,500 miles (4,020 kilometers). This empire grew from small beginnings.

About the year A.D. 1200, the Incas settled in a small village in the rugged, steep **Andes**. The village, **Cuzco**, became the Incas' capital.

The Incas took control of nearby lands. They conquered other peoples. Many groups came under Incan rule. By the 1400s, the Incan Empire had as many as 12 million people. The Incan ruler had an amazing system of getting information about the empire.

The Incan ruler was called Sapa Inca, or "the emperor." The people believed he was related to the sun-god. Sapa Inca owned all the land. He relied on officials to help him run his empire.

Officials used a **census** to keep track of people. It helped to make sure that everyone paid taxes. Farmers gave part of their crops. In return, the empire took care of the poor, the sick, and the elderly.

Key Terms

Incas (ING kuhz) *n.* people of a powerful South American empire
Andes (AN deez) *n.* a mountain chain of western South America
Cuzco (KOOZ koh) *n.* the capital city of the Incan Empire
census (SEN sus) *n.* an official count of people

Vocabulary Strategy

Each of the underlined words to the left contains another word that is its root. Circle the roots you find in these words. The root of the first word, *different*, is *differ*.

✓ Reading Check

Name the largest two river systems in the world, which are found in the Americas.

1. ______________________

2. ______________________

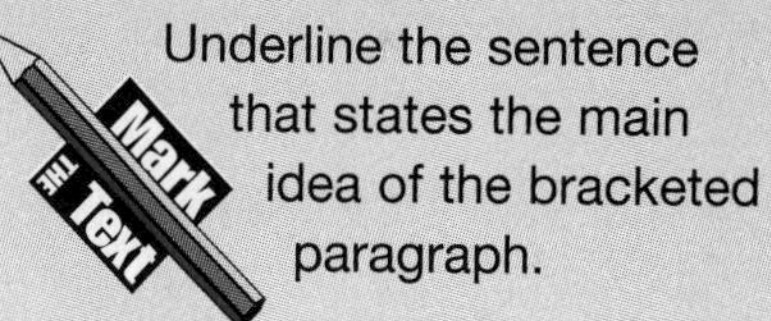

Target Reading Skill

Underline the sentence that states the main idea of the bracketed paragraph.

The official spoken language of the Incas was Quechua (KECH wuh). They had no written language. Instead, they kept records on a **quipu**.

Sapa Inca used relay runners to get information about his huge empire. These runners carried quipus across miles of roads and bridges. The Incan armies and trade caravans also used these roads. Runners, armies, and caravans helped unify the empire.

The Incas were amazing builders. They built paved roads, huge walls, and buildings on top of high mountains. They did this using simple stone tools. Much of what the Incas built is made of stone and still standing.

When the Incas made a wall, they made sure its stones fit together perfectly. They did not use mortar or cement so that stones could move and resettle during earthquakes. This kept the walls from cracking.

The Andes are steep, dry, and rocky. There is little farmland. The Incas built **terraces** so that they could farm on mountain slopes. Terraces held the soil in place so rain would not wash it away. Stone-lined channels carried water to these farms.

In the 1530s, a Spanish conquistador (kahn KEES tuh dawr), or conqueror, named Francisco Pizarro arrived in South America. He wanted to conquer its peoples. Pizarro captured the emperor and killed his men. ✓

The Spanish had better weapons. They carried diseases that the Incas had never been exposed to. These diseases killed many of the Incas. The Spanish soon gained control of the Incan Empire.

✓ Reading Check

Underline the name of the Spanish conquistador who conquered the Incas.

Mark THE Text

Review Questions

1. How far did the Incan Empire stretch at its peak?

2. How did Sapa Inca keep his empire unified?

Key Terms

quipu (KEE poo) *n.* knotted strings used to record information
terraces (TEHR us iz) *n.* steplike ledges cut into mountains

Prepare to Read

Section 2
Cultures of Middle America

Objectives

1. Learn about the Mayan culture of Middle America.
2. Find out about the powerful Aztec Empire.

Target Reading Skill

Identify Supporting Details The main idea of a paragraph or a section is its most important point. The main idea is supported by details. Details give more information. They tell you *what, where, why, how much,* or *how many* about the main idea.

This is the main idea of the paragraphs under the heading "The Culture of the Mayas": Mayan culture was based on farming. Farming supported cities in the Yucatan Peninsula.

When you read, notice how the details tell you more about the Mayan culture, such as how the people lived.

Vocabulary Strategy

Find Roots Often, syllables or groups of syllables are added at the beginning or end of a word to make a new word. The meaning of the new word is related to the original word. But it is changed in some way. For example, we can add the syllable *un-* at the beginning of *well. Un-* means "not" or "no," so the new word, *unwell,* means the opposite of the original word, *well.* It is still related to the original word because it uses the original word as its root.

When you come across a new word, look at it closely. See if it contains any other words that you already know. Often, you can use a new word's root to help you figure out what it means.

Section 2 Summary

The Culture of the Mayas

The culture of the **Mayas** grew up in the part of Middle America called Central America on the Yucatan Peninsula. Their way of life lasted hundreds of years. The greatest period was from about A.D. 250 until 900.

Mayan life was based on farming. They used **slash-and-burn agriculture**. After a few years, the soil would be worn out. Farmers would then have to start somewhere new.

Mayan farmers grew beans, squash, and peppers. But the most important crop was **maize**. It was so important that they had a god of corn. Corn needs sun and rain to grow. The Mayas also worshiped a rain god and a sun god.

Mayan cities were built for government and religion. Different rulers ruled different cities. Important priests and nobles lived in large palaces in the city. But, ordinary people lived on the edges of the city. Events to honor gods were held at large pyramids. Some events used human sacrifice.

Mayan priests were skilled mathematicians. They made a calendar to plan when to hold religious festivals. Other Mayans created **hieroglyphics** to keep track of information. ✓

Around A.D. 900, the Mayas left their cities. No one knows why they left. It may have been because of crop failures, war, or disease. Or people may have rebelled against their leaders. Today, descendants of the Mayas still live in Middle America and follow the old traditions.

Key Terms

Mayas (MAH yuhz) *n.* a people who established a great civilization in Middle America

slash-and-burn agriculture (slash and burn AG rih kul chur) *n.* a farming technique in which trees are cut down and burned

maize (mayz) *n.* corn

hieroglyphics (hy ur oh GLIF iks) *n.* the signs and symbols that made up the Mayan writing system

Vocabulary Strategy

Each of the underlined words to the right contains another word that is its root. Circle the roots you find in these words. The root of the first word, *greatest*, is *great*.

Mark the Text

Target Reading Skill

Which two details in the bracketed paragraph support the main idea that the Mayas had a strong culture?

Detail 1: ______________________

Detail 2: ______________________

✓ Reading Check

What did Mayan priests do?

____

____

____

The Aztec Empire

The **Aztecs** first settled in the 1100s. By the 1470s, their empire stretched from the Gulf of Mexico to the Pacific Ocean. The Aztec emperor, Moctexuma, ruled these lands. He forced the people he conquered to pay heavy taxes. People could pay using food, gold, or slaves.

Tenochtitlán was a grand capital. At its center were a plaza and pyramid-temples. There were schools for the sons of nobles and large stone palaces. Raised streets, or causeways, crossed the lake to the mainland. Aqueducts brought fresh water to the city.

The Aztecs built island gardens for farming in the lake around the capital. They also built boat canals to take produce to market.

Aztec religion included human sacrifices. Priests used a calendar based on the Mayan calendar. Aztecs also kept records using hieroglyphs similar to those used by the Mayas.

The chart shows the Aztec society class system.

1. Emperor
2. Royal family, nobles, priests, military leaders
3. Soldiers
4. Artisans and merchants
5. Farmers
6. Slaves ✓

In 1519, Spanish conquistadors invaded the Aztec Empire. Many Aztecs were killed in fierce battles and by diseases carried by the Spanish. In 1521, the Aztecs surrendered.

Review Questions

1. What was Mayan life based on?

____

____

2. How did the Aztec Empire make new farmland?

____

____

Key Terms

Aztecs (AZ teks) *n.* a people who lived in the Valley of Mexico
Tenochtitlán (teh nawch tee TLAHN) *n.* capital city of the Aztecs

✓ Reading Check

List the five levels of Aztec society from most important to least important.

1. ______________
2. ______________
3. ______________
4. ______________
5. ______________

Prepare to Read

Section 3
Cultures of North America

Objectives

1. Find out about the Mound Builders of eastern North America.
2. Learn about the cultures of the Southwest and the Great Plains.
3. Find out about the Woodland peoples of North America.

Target Reading Skill

Identify Implied Main Ideas Sometimes the main idea is not stated directly. Instead, all the details in a paragraph or section add up to a main idea. In this case, we say the main idea is implied. It is up to you to add up the details. You will then be able to find the main idea.

For example, let's say you are studying the details on the next page following the heading "The Eastern Mound Builders." You could state the main idea this way:

> The Mound Builders were hunters and gatherers who relied on the land's resources. They became settled farmers who built small mounds.

Vocabulary Strategy

Recognize Compound Words When you come across a new word, you may be able to figure out what it means if you break it into parts. For example, if you did not know what the word *snowball* means, you could break it into: *snow* and *ball*. A snowball is a ball of snow. Many words in English are made by combining two or more words. Such words are referred to as *compound* words. As you read, use what you know about compound words.

Here are some common words that are made up of two words:

sometimes	*highway*	*farmland*	*worldwide*
Woodland	*earthquake*	*mainland*	*countryside*
Northwest	*underline*	*mountaintop*	*waterway*
Southwest	*everyone*	*landform*	

Section 3 Summary

The Eastern Mound Builders

The **Mound Builders** lived along rivers in eastern North America. Rivers provided fish and fresh water. Mound Builders hunted wild animals and gathered nuts. When they began to grow their own food, they began to form settlements.

The Adena group of Mound Builders lived in the Ohio Valley around 600 B.C. They built mounds less than 20 feet high. Some of their mounds were tombs. The Adena culture seems to have declined about 100 B.C.

The Hopewell culture lived along the Ohio and upper Mississippi rivers. Their mounds were larger than the Adena's. The Hopewell lived in many small villages with local leaders. They also grew more crops than the Adena. In about A.D. 400, the Hopewell stopped building new mounds and their culture declined.

[By about A.D. 700, the Mississippian (mis uh SIP ee un) culture started. These peoples lived in both small and large communities. They lived along rivers and built mounds. Mississippians also grew new kinds of crops. Maize and beans were important in their diet.] ✓

Some Mississippian centers grew into cities. The largest was Cahokia (kuh HOH kee uh) in what is now Illinois. One of its mounds was 100 feet tall. Cahokia had as many as 20,000 to 30,000 people. By 1250, the number of people had dropped. Then this culture also disappeared.

Peoples of the Southwest and the Great Plains

Anasazi culture began in the Southwest about A.D. 100. Their trading center may have been in Chaco Canyon, in present-day New Mexico.

Key Terms

Mound Builders (mownd BIL durz) *n.* Native American groups who built earthen mounds
Anasazi (ah nuh SAH zee) *n.* one of the ancient Native American peoples of the Southwest

Vocabulary Strategy

One of the words below is a compound word. Circle it. Draw a vertical line through the compound word to separate the two words.

eastern
Midwest
Southwest
Mound Builders

Target Reading Skill

Read the bracketed paragraph. Circle the letter of the sentence below that best states the main idea of the paragraph.

a. The Mississippians were nomadic Mound Builders.

b. The Mississippians were Mound Builders who farmed near rivers.

✓ Reading Check

How did the Mississippians live?

____

____

____

Harsh winters and hot, dry summers make farming hard in the Southwest. The Anasazi, however, built canals and dams to water their fields. They grew maize, beans, and squash for food, and cotton for cloth.

The Anasazi were smart home builders. Their **pueblos** kept people warm in the winter and cool in the summer. Special rooms called **kivas** were used for religious ceremonies. Between 1275 and 1300, very little rain fell. The Anasazi left and never came back.

For years, the Plains Indians lived in the **Great Plains**. Each group had its own language and traditions. Some were farmers. They lived in lodges made of earth and wood. Others followed herds of bison. They lived in tipis (TEE peaz). ✓

✓ Reading Check

How did the Plains Indians live?

____

____

____

After the Europeans arrived, the Native Americans' lives changed. Many suffered from diseases brought by Europeans. They lost their land to European settlement. Many native cultures began to break down. Today, people work to save the traditional cultures.

Peoples of the Woodlands

The peoples of the Northwest Coast hunted in the forests and fished for salmon. They lived in villages of wooden homes.

The Iroquois (IHR uh kwoy) lived in the eastern woodlands. They hunted and farmed. In the 1500s, five Iroquois nations formed a peace group. It was called the Iroquois League. At that time, it was the best-organized political system in the Americas. ✓

✓ Reading Check

What was the Iroquois League?

____

____

____

Review Questions

1. List the three groups of Mound Builders.

____

____

2. What is the climate of the Southwest like?

____

____

Key Terms

pueblo (PWEB loh) *n.* a Native American stone or adobe dwelling
kiva (KEE vah) *n.* a round room used for religious ceremonies
Great Plains (grayt playnz) *n.* a mostly flat and grassy region of western North America

Chapter 12 Assessment

1. To be able to farm on steep mountain slopes, the Incas built
   A. aqueducts.
   B. fences.
   C. bridges
   D. terraces.

2. Mayan life was based on
   A. farming.
   B. hunting and gathering.
   C. fishing.
   D. trade with the Spanish.

3. The Aztecs built floating gardens because
   A. they wanted to make their city more beautiful.
   B. they wanted to please the rain god.
   C. they needed more farmland.
   D. they were experimenting with new building techniques.

4. What did the Adena, the Hopewell, and the Mississippians have in common?
   A. They all worshiped the same god.
   B. They formed a group called the Iroquois League.
   C. They were all Mound Builders.
   D. They all lived in Middle America.

5. How did the Anasazi deal with the harsh winters and hot, dry summers?
   A. They bathed in the rivers.
   B. They made clothing and blankets out of animal skins.
   C. They migrated north in the summer and south in the winter.
   D. They built pueblos that kept them warm in the winter and cool in the summer.

Short Answer Question

How did the arrival of Europeans affect the Native Americans?

Prepare to Read

Section 1
Golden Ages of China

Objectives

1. Learn about the Golden Age of the Tang dynasty.
2. Discover the achievements of the Song dynasty, which ruled China after the Tang.
3. Find out about Mongol rule of China.

Identify Causes and Effects When something happens in history, it's the result of something else. The event that happens first is called the cause. What happens because of that event is called the effect.

This section is about three important time periods in Chinese history. Use a chart like the one below to keep track of causes and effects during each of these time periods.

Cause	Effect
Song dynasty brings order	Expands merit system in hiring

Vocabulary Strategy

Use Roots and Suffixes A suffix is one or more syllables attached to the end of a word to make a new word. The word it is attached to is the root. When a suffix is added to a root, the new word has a new meaning.

Some common suffixes are listed below, along with their meanings and examples. Notice that some have more than one meaning. Learning to identify suffixes, and knowing what they mean, will help you understand what you read.

Suffix	Meaning	Example
-al	of or like	coastal
-en	made of; to become or cause to be	wooden; darken
-ern	of or related to	eastern
-ful	full of, characterized by, having	joyful; beautiful
-ing	an action; result of an action	dancing; drawing
-ish	of or belonging to; like; tending to be	boyish; selfish

Section 1 Summary

The **Silk Road** was not a single road. It was a chain of linked trade routes. Its name came from one of the most valuable goods carried on it—silk.

The Tang Dynasty

China has been ruled by many different dynasties. In 618, the Tang **dynasty** came to power. The Tang dynasty brought a golden age of politics and culture. China grew in area and population.

Tang leaders finished the Grand Canal, a project that an earlier dynasty had started. The huge shipping waterway linked the Huang and Chang rivers. The Grand Canal joined northern and southern China.

The greatest Tang ruler was Tang Taizong (tang ty ZAWNG). He was a successful general, scholar, and historian. Late in life, he tired of war. He studied the teachings of Confucius (kun FYOO shus), an ancient Chinese teacher. Confucius taught that a peaceful society was possible if people treated each other with respect.

Tang Taizong used Confucius's ideas to change the government. He hired officials trained in Confucius's ideas and gave land to peasants. ✓

The Song Dynasty

After 850, fighting among groups within China ended the Tang dynasty. The **Song** restored order. The Song dynasty ruled China from 960 to 1279.

The Song rulers expanded the **merit system** of hiring officials. Before the Song, officials came from powerful families. Hiring people for their ability to do a job well improved the Chinese government.

Key Terms

Silk Road (silk rohd) *n.* a chain of trade routes stretching from China to the Mediterranean Sea
dynasty (DY nus tee) *n.* a series of rulers from the same family
Tang (tahng) *n.* a dynasty that ruled China for almost 300 years
Song (sawng) *n.* a dynasty that ruled China after the Tang
merit system (MEHR it SIS tum) *n.* a system of hiring people based on their abilities

Vocabulary Strategy

The words below appear in the section titled "The Tang Dynasty". Each of these words contains a suffix. Find the meaning of the suffix from the chart on the previous page and write it next to the word below.

golden: ____________________

northern: ____________________

successful: ____________________

Underline the suffix in each word when you come across it in your reading. Did knowing what the suffix meant help you determine what each word means?

✓ Reading Check

List two achievements of Tang Taizong.

1. ____________________

____

2. ____________________

____

Target Reading Skill

What made it easier for people to buy books? List that as a cause. What resulted from more people having books? List three effects.

Cause: ______________________

Effect 1: ______________________

Effect 2: ______________________

Effect 3: ______________________

✓ Reading Check

What were some of the achievements of the Song dynasty?

____

✓ Reading Check

Describe Mongol rule of China.

____

Chinese rulers supported many forms of art. During the Song dynasty, artists created the first Chinese landscape paintings. Song rulers also prized art objects made of porcelain (PAWR suh lin), a type of clay.

The Song invented a new way to print books. For years, the Chinese had printed books using a carved wooden block for each page. Around 1045, they came up with movable type. Separate characters could be set to make a page, then rearranged to make a new page.

Books became less expensive. Before, only the rich could buy them. Now, more people could afford them. The number and kinds of books increased. More people learned to read and write. Books helped spread knowledge throughout China. ✓

The Mongols Conquer China

The Mongols were nomads and fierce warriors from Central Asia north of China. Under Genghis Khan, they built an empire that stretched from Korea to Eastern Europe and included northern China.

Kublai Khan was Genghis Khan's grandson. He came to power in 1259. Within 20 years, he had conquered the rest of China. He called his dynasty Yuan.

The Mongols centralized government. They did not let the old Chinese ruling class govern. The Mongols kept their own language and customs. ✓

Visitors from all over the world were welcome at Kublai Khan's court. One of them was Marco Polo from Italy. He wrote about what he saw at the Khan's court. Polo's writing caused trade between Europe and China to grow.

Mongol rule in China came to an end in 1368 when a Chinese peasant led an uprising against the Mongols.

Review Questions

1. What is the Grand Canal?

____

2. What did the Song do to improve government?

____

Key Term

Kublai Khan (KOO bly kahn) *n.* a Mongol emperor of China

Prepare to Read

Section 2 Medieval Japan

Objectives

1. Learn about the geography of Japan.
2. Discover the changes that occurred during the Heian period of Japanese history.
3. Find out about feudalism and the rule of the shoguns in Japan.

Target Reading Skill

Understand Effects Remember that a cause makes something happen. The effect is what happens as a result of the cause. Just as an effect can have more than one cause, a cause can have more than one effect. You can find effects by answering the question, "What happened?" If there are several answers to that question, the cause had more than one effect.

Look at the second paragraph under the heading "A Country of Islands" on the next page. What were the effects of Japan's geography?

Vocabulary Strategy

Use Roots and Suffixes As you learned in the last section, a suffix is one or more syllables attached to the end of a word to make a new word. The new word combines the meaning of the suffix with the meaning of the original word.

You learned some common suffixes in the last section. Below are more suffixes, along with their meanings and examples. Notice that some have more than one meaning. Learning to identify suffixes, and knowing what they mean, will help you understand what you read.

Suffix	Meaning	Example
-ate	office, function, group of officials	shogunate
-ese	of a country or place	Japanese
-ion	act or condition	isolation, invasion
-ism	act or practice of; teaching of	feudalism; socialism
-less	without	treeless
-ment	act or result of; condition of being	improvement; disappointment

Section 2 Summary

A Country of Islands

Japan is an **archipelago** in the Pacific Ocean off the coast of Asia's mainland. The islands of Japan were formed by volcanoes. Earthquakes are common in the area.

[Japan has many mountains, which makes it hard to travel by land. The Japanese used the sea for travel instead. The sea also protected Japan from invaders. This isolation helped the Japanese develop a unique way of life.] ✓

The Heian Empire

The Heian (HAY ahn) period in Japan lasted from 794 to 1185. Before this period, Japan's culture was similar to China's. During the 800s, Japan began to have its own traditions.

Heian emperors ruled from the capital, **Kyoto**. It had mansions for the nobles, two markets, and a palace for the emperor.

The Heian period was mostly peaceful. Japanese culture thrived. Nobles enjoyed fine architecture, literature, and beautiful gardens. The nobles felt that their importance set them apart from others. But most people were poor and worked hard. ✓

Feudalism in Japan

During the 1000s, the Japanese emperor ruled the capital. But he had less control over the rest of Japan. At the same time, the nobles gained power. They owned huge estates where peasants were legally bound to work. This system is known as **feudalism**.

Rich estate owners often disobeyed the emperor. They hired armies of **samurai** to defend their estates. Samurai warriors believed that honor meant more than wealth or even life.

Key Terms

archipelago (ahr kuh PEL uh goh) *n.* a group of islands
Kyoto (KEE oh toh) *n.* the capital city of medieval Japan
feudalism (FYOOD ul iz um) *n.* a system in which poor people are legally bound to work for wealthy landowners
samurai (SAM uh ry) *n.* Japanese warriors

Vocabulary Strategy

The words *Japanese* and *isolation* appear in the bracketed paragraph below. Each word contains a suffix. As you read the paragraph determine each word's root. Then find the meaning of the suffix from the chart on the previous page. Finally, write the meaning of the new word created by adding the suffix to the root.

Mark the Text

Japanese ______________________

____

isolation ______________________

____

✓ Reading Check

Describe Japan's geography.

____

____

____

✓ Reading Check

How did nobles live during the Heian period?

____

____

____

Over time, there were more and more samurai warriors. They formed their own clans. Each clan pledged loyalty to a warlord, or daimyo (DY myoh). Small wars broke out between different warlords. In time, the Minamoto clan became the most powerful. ✓

In 1192, the emperor gave the title of **shogun** to the leader of the Minamoto clan. He became the supreme ruler of all Japan. He set up a shogunate, or military dynasty.

Japan and the Outside World

In the 1200s, the Mongols under Kublai Khan tried to invade Japan twice. They failed both times. For the next 300 years, few foreigners came to Japan. Then, in 1543, several Portuguese ships landed on Japan's coast. Trade grew between East and West. Thousands of Japanese became Christians.

In 1603, Tokugawa Ieyasu (to koo GAH wah ee yay AH soo) became shogun. To end fighting among samurai bands, he divided Japan into 250 regions. The daimyo of each region swore loyalty to him. A time of peace and prosperity began.

[At the same time, the Tokugawas got rid of foreign influences. They feared that Europeans might try to conquer Japan. They outlawed Christianity and forced Europeans to leave. By 1638, they had closed Japan's ports. Japan was cut off from the outside world for the next 200 years.] ✓

Review Questions

1. Why did Japan develop a unique way of life?

____

____

2. What happened to the emperor and the nobles during the 1000s?

____

____

Key Term

shogun (SHOH gun) *n.* the supreme military commander of Japan

✓ Reading Check

List two reasons the samurai became powerful.

1. ______________________________

____

2. ______________________________

____

Target Reading Skill

Read the bracketed paragraph again. Look for two effects of the Tokugawas' fear that Europe might try to conquer Japan.

Effect 1: ______________________________

____

Effect 2: ______________________________

____

✓ Reading Check

How did the Tokugawas change Japan?

____

____

____

Prepare to Read

Section 3
The Great Mughal Empire in India

Objectives

1. Find out about the geography of the Indian subcontinent.
2. Learn about the Delhi Sultanate, a period of Muslim rule.
3. Learn about the founding and achievements of the Mughal Empire.

Target Reading Skill

Recognize Cause-and-Effect Signal Words As you read, watch for clues that show cause and effect. Often, a word will give you a signal that what is being described is either a cause or an effect. Words such as *because*, *affect*, *as a result*, *so*, *therefore*, and *from* signal a cause or effect.

In the following example, *from* signals a cause: "From this blend of ideas and beliefs came one of the world's oldest religions, Hinduism."

The cause: a blend of beliefs and ideas

The effect: Hinduism

Vocabulary Strategy

Using Prefixes and Roots A prefix is one or more syllables attached in front of the root to make a new word. The new word combines the meaning of the prefix with the meaning of the original word.

Some common prefixes are listed below, along with their meanings and examples. Notice that some of them have more than one meaning. Learning to identify prefixes, and knowing what they mean, will help you understand what you read.

Prefix	Meaning	Example
non-	not	nontoxic
pre-	before	prehistory
re-	again	reread
sub-	under, beneath, below; lower in rank	subsoil, subhead
un-	not; the opposite of	unused

Section 3 Summary

India's Geography

The Indian subcontinent is the southernmost part of Central Asia. A mountain range called the Himalayas stretches across the north of India. The Himalayas have helped isolate India from the lands to the north.

South of the Himalayas is a large plain. There are major river systems there. They include the Indus and Ganges rivers. The land here is good for farming. Farther south are highlands and plains. ✓

The Delhi Sultanate

Muslim invaders began to raid India around A.D. 1000. From 1206 to 1526, a series of **sultans**, or Muslim rulers, ruled northern India. This period is called the Delhi Sultanate.

A Hindu revival had started about A.D. 600. Hindus accept many gods. But they believe these gods are all part of one supreme being. They also believe that social classes are part of the natural order of the universe.

The Hindu **caste system** ruled everyday life. A person's job and status depended on caste.

The Muslims of the Delhi Sultanate did not become part of Hindu society. Muslim culture is based on very different beliefs. Hindus and Muslims were split by religious conflicts.

In 1526, a Mongol prince named Babur (BAH bur) invaded the weakened Delhi Sultanate. The sultan's army was larger than Babur's army. But because the Mongols had cannons and were better fighters, they defeated the sultan's army. As a result, Babur gained control of Delhi, the capital city. ✓

The Mughal Empire

Babur founded the **Mughal Empire**. This empire controlled India until the 1700s. About 25 years after

Key Terms

sultan (SUL tun) *n.* a Muslim ruler
caste system (kast SIS tum) *n.* the Hindu social class system
Mughal Empire (MOO gul EM pyr) *n.* Muslim rule of India

Vocabulary Strategy

The word below appears in the first bracketed paragraph. How does the prefix *sub-* tell you that a subcontinent is different than a continent? *Hint:* Use the chart on the previous page.

subcontinent

✓ Reading Check

Describe India's geography.

Target Reading Skill

Circle the signal word(s) in the bracketed paragraph below that helped you understand why the Delhi Sultanate fell to the Mongols.
Then write the signal words on the lines below.

✓ Reading Check

How was the Delhi Sultanate defeated?

Babur's death, his grandson, **Akbar**, became emperor. Akbar became India's greatest Mughal leader.

Akbar was a talented soldier. He made the Mughal Empire much larger through conquest, and treaties.

Akbar set up studios for painters and supported poets. He brought together scholars from different religions. He talked to Muslims, Hindus, Buddhists, and Christians about their beliefs.

Even though Akbar was a Muslim, he let his subjects practice their religion freely. He also ended unfair taxation of non-Muslims. He gave government jobs to the best people, whatever their religion. His policies helped Hindus and Muslims live together in peace. They also helped build Mughal power in India.

When Akbar died in 1605, most of northern India was under his control. He earned the nickname "the Great." His government was so stable it allowed the empire to go on growing for the next 100 years.

In 1628, Akbar's grandson, Shah Jahan (shah juh HAHN), became emperor. He spent a fortune on buildings. The most famous is the Taj Mahal.

His son, Aurangzeb (AWR ung zeb), spent still more money on expensive wars. He tried to force Hindus to convert to the Muslim faith. He also began to tax them again. Many Hindus rebelled. Fighting the rebels cost still more money. Aurangzeb died in 1707, and the empire split into small kingdoms. ✓

✓ Reading Check

How did Aurangzeb create problems for the Mughal Empire?

____

____

____

Review Questions

1. What was the Delhi Sultanate?

____

____

2. Why was Akbar called "the Great"?

____

____

Key Term

Akbar (AK bahr) *n.* the greatest Mughal leader of India

Taj Mahal (tahzh muh HAHL) *n.* a tomb built by Shah Jahan for his wife

Chapter 13 Assessment

1. Why was the Grand Canal important to China?
   A. It allowed ships to travel between the Pacific and Atlantic oceans.
   B. It allowed ships to travel more quickly between China and the Mediterranean Sea.
   C. It linked the Huang and Chiang rivers, joining northern and southern China.
   D. It provided a water route through the Himalayas to India.

2. What was the result of the invention of movable type?
   A. Books became common and most people forgot about them.
   B. Books became more expensive and only the rich could buy them.
   C. There were more books, but only scholars bought them.
   D. There were more books, and more people learned to read and write.

3. In Japan, which group was called the shogunate?
   A. the military dynasty
   B. the Mongol invaders
   C. the Portuguese traders
   D. the merchant class

4. In Hindu society, a person's job and status depended on
   A. money.
   B. religion.
   C. race.
   D. caste.

5. The greatest Mughal leader in India was
   A. Akbar.
   B. Aurangzeb.
   C. Babur.
   D. Shah Jahan.

Short Answer Question

How did shoguns gain power in Japan?

____

____

____

____

____

Prepare to Read

Section 1
Feudalism and the Manor System

Objectives

1. Learn about the Middle Ages.
2. Find out how land and power were divided under feudalism.
3. Learn how the manor system worked.
4. Discover what life was like for peasants and serfs.

Target Reading Skill

Recognize Sequence Signal Words Signal words are words or phrases that prepare you for what is coming next. They are like road signs that tell drivers when to exit or what is coming next.

Some important signal words tell about the sequence of events. Some common signal words include *when, first, then, began*, and *in* (followed by a date). They signal the order in which events took place. This section talks about the Middle Ages. To help keep the order of events clear, look for signal words and phrases.

Vocabulary Strategy

Using Word Origins Almost half of the words in English used to be Latin words. During the Middle Ages many people spoke French. Many French words used to be Latin words. The chart below shows three French and English words that came from Latin.

English Word	French Word	Latin Word
manor	*manoir*	*manere*, "to dwell"
vassal	*vassal*	*vassallus*, "servant,"
serf	*serf*	*servus*, "slave"

The English word *serve* also comes from the Latin word *servus*. Other words that are related include *server* and *service.* Can you think of any other words that begin with *serv-* ? *Hint:* What is the name for someone who serves others?

Section 1 Summary

The Middle Ages

The **Middle Ages** are the period of time between ancient and modern times. The Middle Ages began about A.D. 500 and ended around 1500.

When the Roman Empire broke up, invading groups created many small kingdoms. Most of the invaders could not read or write. Soon, very few people in Europe could read or write.

One of the invading groups was the Franks. Charlemagne (SHAHR luh mayn) became king of the Franks in 768. Soon, he ruled an empire that stretched across most of Western Europe.

Charlemagne ruled for nearly 50 years. He opened schools so people could learn to read and write. He also spread the Christian religion and improved the economy. When Charlemagne died, his sons fought over the empire. This made the empire weak. Many groups came in to attack. ✓

The Vikings came from the far north of Europe. They burned and looted European towns. Charlemagne's empire was gone.

Feudalism: A Kind of Government

Slowly a new way of life came about. It was called **feudalism**. By about 1000, it was the way of life for Western Europe.

Nobles, or lords, who owned the land had the most power. They gave land to their vassals. A vassal was someone who promised to follow the lord's laws and fight for him.

Vassals who rode horses and led men into battle were called **knights**. Vassals helped pay for armies that would fight for the lord. In exchange, lords promised to protect their vassals and their lands. ✓

Key Terms

Middle Ages (MID ul AY juz) *n.* the years between ancient and modern times
feudalism (FYOOD ul iz um) *n.* a system in which land was owned by kings or lords but held by vassals in return for their loyalty
knight (nyt) *n.* a man who received land for serving a lord

Target Reading Skill

Circle the words in the bracketed paragraphs that signal sequence.

✓ Reading Check

Why did Charlemagne's empire fall apart?

____

____

____

✓ Reading Check

What did lords give vassals in exchange for the vassals' loyalty?

____

____

____

The Manor System

Feudalism was a way for people to protect themselves and share power. Manorialism was a way for people to receive food, clothing, and shelter. The **manor** included fields, houses, animals, and peasants who worked there. Most manors were far from towns. So, they had to be able to supply everything they needed. ✓

✓ Reading Check

Why did a manor need to supply everything?

A lord ruled over the poor people who lived on his manor. He made the rules and acted as judge. And he collected taxes from the peasants who lived there.

Peasants and Serfs

Most of the people of **medieval** Europe were not lords, ladies, or knights. They were peasants.

Vocabulary Strategy

The word *medieval* comes from two Latin words, *medium*, which means "middle," and *aevum*, which means "ages." What does *medieval* mean?

Peasants were often very poor. They did all the work on manors. Most peasants were also **serfs**. When a noble was given a manor, its serfs became his property. Serfs could not leave the manor or get married without the noble's permission.

A serf is not the same as a slave. A serf could save enough money to buy land and become a free peasant. Sometimes, a serf escaped to a city to become free. But most serfs were serfs their whole lives.

Medieval peasants worked very hard. Even the children worked. Peasants lived in dark, one-room huts. For heating and cooking, they built a fire on the dirt floor. Smoke filled their huts. They ate simple food such as bread and cabbage. ✓

✓ Reading Check

What was life like for medieval peasants?

Review Questions

1. Why is this period of time called the Middle Ages?

2. What was feudalism?

Key Terms

manor (MAN ur) *n.* a large estate, ruled by a lord
medieval (mee dee EE vul) *adj.* referring to the Middle Ages
serf (surf) *n.* a farm worker considered part of the manor

Prepare to Read

Section 2
The Church and the Rise of Cities

Objectives

1. Learn about the Roman Catholic Church during the Middle Ages.
2. Discover the connection between growing trade and growing towns.
3. Find out what life was like in a medieval town.
4. Learn about culture and learning in the Middle Ages.

Target Reading Skill

Identify Sequence A sequence is the order in which a group of events occurs. For example, in order to get ready for school, you go through several steps. Is your before school sequence like this one: Get up, brush teeth, get dressed, have breakfast? What would happen next?

As you read, study the sequence of important events. To help, make a chart like the one below. The first event is filled in for you. As you read, fill in the next event that happened when you come across it.

1. As manors got crowded, lords let serfs buy freedom and move to towns.
2.

Vocabulary Strategy

Using Word Origins Latin was once the language of the Roman Catholic Church. As a result, many English words about Christianity come from Latin. The table below gives some English words about religion, along with their Latin origins. Watch for these words as you read this section.

English Words	Latin Words
bishop	*episcopus*
pope	*papa*
priest	*presbyter*
monastery	*monasterium*
convent	*conventus*

Section 2 Summary

The Church in the Middle Ages

During the Middle Ages, nearly everyone in Western Europe was a Roman Catholic. The Roman Catholic Church was so powerful that it was known simply as "the Church."

The Church offered hope in the belief of heaven after death. The Church had great wealth from the taxes it collected. It took land from lords when the **clergy** provided services for the lord. And it used the threat of **excommunication** to make people obey.

Almost every village had a priest. Priests served bishops. An archbishop was served by several bishops. And the pope was served by all.

The clergy were part of every major event in peoples lives—birth, illness, marriage, or death. The clergy helped people follow Church rules about how to live. They also forgave people's sins.

Some religious men, or monks lived together in religious communities called monasteries. Religious women, or nuns, lived in convents. ✓

✓ Reading Check

What are monasteries and convents?

____

____

____

Monks and nuns looked after the sick and set up schools. Monks copied ancient books, saving knowledge that otherwise would have been lost.

Trade Revives and Towns Grow

Feudalism and the Church made Europe a safer place. The population grew. Merchants traveled to far away places to buy and sell goods.

As trade grew, so did local markets. Some local markets grew into large market towns. Sometimes traders would get together at places where they knew they would find travelers, such as river crossings. Towns grew in these places, too. ✓

✓ Reading Check

Underline the three reasons that caused towns to grow.

Mark THE Text

At this time, many manors were getting overcrowded. Many lords were glad to let peasants buy freedom and move to towns.

Key Terms

clergy (KLUR jee) *n.* persons who perform religious services
excommunication (eks kuh myoo ni KAY shun) *n.* expelling someone from the Church

Life in Towns and Cities

By about 1300, many towns in Western Europe were growing into cities. Town life was much different than manor life. Towns and cities could not raise everything they needed. Instead, people bought goods. A new class of people began. It was made up of merchants and crafts workers. It was called the *middle class*. These people were between the noble and peasant classes.

Many merchants and crafts workers started groups called **guilds**. Guilds decided how much to charge and made sure the items were made well.

It took time to become a member of a guild. Between the ages of 8 and 14, a boy who wanted to learn a trade became an **apprentice**. He lived and worked with a master of that trade for up to seven years. Then he could become a journeyman, or paid worker. If his work was good, he could join the guild.

Medieval towns and cities were dirty and crowded. Diseases spread quickly. The bubonic plague, called the Black Death, began in 1347. It killed one out every three people in Europe! ✓

Medieval Culture

The new cities attracted people who enjoyed learning and teaching. Talented artists created beautiful art-work. ✓

Stories, poems, and songs about **chivalry** were popular. Throughout the land, **troubadours** went from place to place. They sang about brave deeds done by knights to win the love of a worthy woman.

Review Questions

1. How was the Church important in everyday life?

____

____

2. What were the guilds?

____

____

Key Terms

guild (gild) *n.* an organization of crafts workers or tradespeople
apprentice (uh PREN tis) *n.* an unpaid person training in a trade
chivalry (SHIV ul ree) *n.* the code of honorable conduct for knights
troubadour (TROO bu dawr) *n.* a traveling poet and musician

Vocabulary Strategy

The word *apprentice*, used below, comes from the French word *apprendre*, "to learn." Why do you think this word was used to describe apprentices?

____

____

Target Reading Skill

What were the steps that an apprentice followed in order to become a member of a guild?

1. ______________________

2. ______________________

3. ______________________

✓ Reading Check

What was the Black Death?

____

____

____

✓ Reading Check

What was good about living in a medieval city?

____

____

____

Prepare to Read

Section 3 The Crusades

Objectives

1. Learn about what caused the Crusades.
2. Find out about the different Crusades.
3. Discover the effects the Crusades had on life in Europe.

Target Reading Skill

Recognize Sequence Signal Words Drivers need signs to tell them about the road. Readers also need signs. Signal words prepare you for what is coming next.

There are different kinds of signal words. One of the most common uses of signal words is to show the passing of time. Signal words show how events link together.

This section is about the Crusades, which took place over many years. To help keep the order of events clear, look for words such as *first*, *then*, *finally*, and *in [date]*. They signal the order in which the events took place.

Vocabulary Strategy

Using Word Origins English is a language that likes to borrow words. Often, words change their meaning over time.

The word *crusade* comes from the Latin word for cross, *crux*. Knights wore the sign of the cross on their armor, which gave them the name crusader. Today, a *crusade* means taking action for a cause. You could say that someone is a crusader for the environment. If you heard that a group in your school was crusading for a school recycling program, what would that tell you about the group?

Section 3 Summary

In 1095, Pope Urban II had a message for the people of Europe. He wanted them to capture the Holy Land. The **Holy Land** had fallen to an enemy, he said. Christians must win it back. This began 200 years of **Crusades**.

Causes of the Crusades

For almost 900 years, European Christians had been going to **Jerusalem** as **pilgrims**. Nobles and peasants wanted to visit places written about in the Bible.

Jerusalem had been controlled by Arab Muslims for hundreds of years. They usually welcomed Christian pilgrims. But, when Turkish invaders took control in the 1000s, things changed. First, they attacked Christian pilgrims. Then they closed the roads to Jerusalem.

Pope Urban II wanted the Holy Land to be under Christian control. He wanted Christian pilgrims to be able to visit religious sites there. The pope had other reasons, too. He believed a crusade would bring Europe together. Then Europeans would stop fighting among themselves. He also wanted power for himself and the Church. ✓

Some Europeans had other reasons for wanting the Crusades. They wanted to control the Holy Land, too. And they also wanted to control trade routes between Africa, Asia, and Europe.

A Series of Crusades

[The best way to recapture the Holy Land was by using a strong army of lords and knights. But first, a small group of common people went to fight.]

Key Terms

Holy Land (HOH lee land) *n.* Jerusalem and parts of the surrounding area where Jesus lived and taught

Crusades (kroo SAYDZ) *n.* a series of military expeditions launched by Europeans to win the Holy Land back from Muslim control

Jerusalem (juh ROOZ uh lum) *n.* a city in the Holy Land

pilgrim (PIL grum) *n.* a person who journeys to a sacred place

Vocabulary Strategy

Pilgrim is a Latin word that means foreigner or stranger. Why was that a good word for European travelers to the Holy Land?

____

____

____

✓ Reading Check

Why did the pope want to conquer the Holy Land?

____

____

____

Target Reading Skill

What word in the bracketed paragraph signals sequence? How does this clue help you understand the paragraphs that follow?

____

____

____

____

Peter the Hermit was a small man who wore monk's robes. He led a "people's crusade" in 1096. When they got to Constantinople, the Byzantine emperor tried to get them to wait for help. Peter agreed, but his followers rebelled. They attacked the Turks, who easily defeated them. Only a small part of Peter's army survived.

The armies of the First Crusade sent by Pope Urban II finally arrived. The knights were joined by what was left of Peter's army. They captured Jerusalem in 1099. During the fighting, they killed about 10,000 of the Muslim, Christian, and Jewish people there.

The Second Crusade had little success. A strong Arab Muslim leader had come to power. He was known as Saladin (SAL uh din). By 1187, he had retaken Jerusalem. King Richard I of England tried to talk him into giving Jerusalem back to the Christians. Saladin refused, saying that it was as precious to Muslims as it was to Christians. But he agreed to reopen it to Christian pilgrims. ✓

✓ Reading Check

Why did Saladin refuse to give up Jerusalem?

____

The Results of the Crusades

The crusaders captured the Holy Land for a while. But they were unable to keep it. Still, the Crusades brought important changes to Europe.

The Crusades boosted trade. This led to the growth of towns and cities. The Crusades also encouraged the use of money in Europe. For much of the Middle Ages, most people bartered. That is, they traded goods for other goods, for land, or for protection. But far from home, the crusaders had to buy supplies. Money was easier to use. ✓

✓ Reading Check

Underline two effects of the Crusades.

Mark the Text

The crusaders also brought back new ideas and technology. Europeans learned to make better ships and maps. This would help them later to become explorers.

Review Questions

1. What was the chief goal of the crusaders?

____

2. How did the Crusades change life in Europe?

____

CHAPTER
14

Prepare to Read

Section 4 The Power of Kings

Objectives

1. Learn how nation building began in Europe.
2. Find out about nation building in England.
3. Discover how the Hundred Years' War affected England and France.

Target Reading Skill

Identify Sequence A sequence is the order in which events occur. As you read, study the sequence of important events. Paying attention to the order of events can help you understand and remember them.

A sequence chart like the one below is a good tool. Use it to track the events that led to nation building in England. The first event has been filled in for you. Write each additional event in a box. Use as many boxes as you need. Use arrows to show how one event leads to the next.

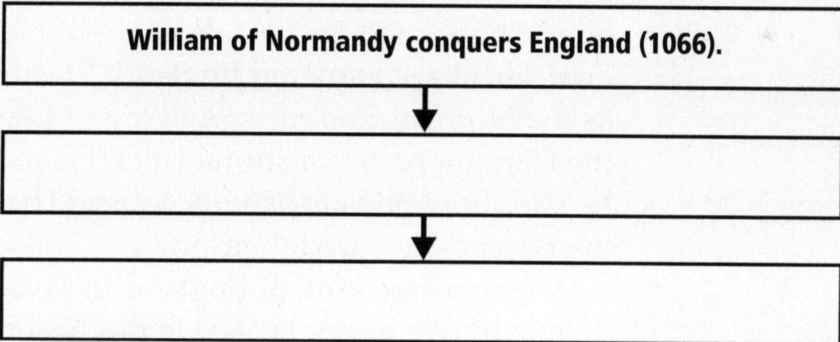
William of Normandy conquers England (1066).

Vocabulary Strategy

Using Word Origins The names of places often tell us something about them. You may know that New York is named after the city of York in England. New Jersey is named after the island of Jersey in the English Channel.

In Section 1 of this workbook, you read about the Franks. They were people who conquered Gaul. Because of that, the region became known as France. Can you see the resemblance between *France* and *Frank*? (In French, the word *Frank* is spelled *Franc*.)

England gets its name from the Old English words *Engla* and *land*, which mean "land of the Angles." The Angles were a group of people who settled in eastern England in the A.D. 500s. In time, the entire country was named for them.

Section 4 Summary

Nation Building

When the 1200s began, Europe was still a feudal society. Kings ruled kingdoms. However, some lords had more wealth than the king.

Target Reading Skill

What events in the bracketed paragraph helped the power of kings grow? List them in order below.

____

____

____

Then feudalism began to weaken and the power of kings began to grow. One reason was the growth of towns and cities. Kings agreed to protect towns in return for money paid by townspeople. With that money, kings hired armies to attack nobles who gave too much trouble.

As kings became more powerful, they united more of their kingdom. The larger kingdoms began to turn into **nations**. That happened because people began to think of themselves as English or French. Once people had been loyal to a lord or vassal. Now they were loyal to a king and his government. ✓

✓ Reading Check

What happened when kings became more powerful?

____

____

____

Changes in England

By the 1200s, England was almost a nation. Here is how it happened. In 1066, William of Normandy, a French duke, conquered England. This became known as the Norman Conquest. As king of England, William the Conqueror was a strong ruler. He made sure that he had more power than his nobles. The kings who followed him increased their power.

John became king of England in 1199. He forced people to pay heavy taxes. He put his enemies in jail unfairly. He took land from the Church.

John had angered the nobles and clergy. The pope declared that John was no longer king. English nobles and bishops gave John a list of demands. He was forced to put his royal seal on the list called the **Magna Carta**. These new laws limited the king's power. People could no longer be jailed without a reason. Taxes had to be approved by others.

Key Terms

nation (NAY shun) *n.* people that share land and government
Magna Carta (MAG nuh KAHR tuh) *n.* the "Great Charter," in which the king's power over his nobles was limited

A group of advisors to the king later became the **Model Parliament**. As it gained power, Parliament helped unify England. The Magna Carta also strengthened the king's power. Now that the nobles had a say in government, they were more willing to support the king. ✓

The Hundred Years' War

In 1328, the French king died. King Edward III of England claimed to be king of France. The French nobles did not agree. Edward III invaded France. This began the **Hundred Years' War**.

The war dragged on, fought by one king after another. England won most of the battles. But the tide turned in 1429. A peasant girl called Joan of Arc took charge of the French forces at the battle of Orléans.

Under Joan's command, the French defeated the English at Orléans. She then led her forces to other victories. In 1430, she was taken prisoner and put on trial for witchcraft. She was convicted and burned at the stake. Her death inspired the French to many victories. By 1453, the English had been driven from most of France.

During the war, new weapons such as the longbow and cannon increased the power of footsoldiers. Armored knights became less valuable in battle. Feudal castles could not stop cannonballs. Kings now needed large armies. ✓

The Hundred Years' War also led to national feeling in France and England.

Review Questions

1. Why did feudalism decline?

____

____

2. Who fought the Hundred Years' War?

____

____

Key Terms

Model Parliament (MAHD ul PAR luh munt) *n.* a council of lords, clergy, and common people that advised the English king

Hundred Years' War (HUN drud yeerz wawr) *n.* a series of conflicts between England and France, 1337–1453

✓ Reading Check

Why did nobles support the king after he signed the Magna Carta?

____

____

____

Vocabulary Strategy

An American city is named after the city of Orléans in France. Which city is this?

____

✓ Reading Check

What made foot soldiers more powerful than knights?

____

____

____

Chapter 14 Assessment

1. When did the Middle Ages begin?
   A. when the Roman Empire broke up
   B. when Charlemagne became king of the Franks
   C. when Charlemagne's empire broke up after his death
   D. when feudalism became the way of life for Western Europe

2. What type of government existed in the Middle Ages?
   A. manorialism
   B. crusades
   C. feudalism
   D. trading empires

3. During the Middle Ages, a paid worker in a trade was a(n)
   A. peasant.
   B. apprentice.
   C. journeyman.
   D. troubadour.

4. Why did Pope Urban II want to capture the Holy Land?
   A. He wanted to conquer Constantinople.
   B. He wanted to control trade routes.
   C. He wanted Muslim pilgrims to be able to visit the Holy Land.
   D. He thought a crusade would unite Europe.

5. What list of demands limited the English king's power in 1215?
   A. the List of Parliament
   B. the Magna Carta
   C. the Excommunication
   D. the Medieval Code

Short Answer Question

Who was Joan of Arc and how did she influence the outcome of the Hundred Years' War?

____

____

____

____

____

Prepare to Read

Section 1
The Renaissance Begins

Objectives

1. Find out why Italy was the birthplace of the Renaissance.
2. Understand how literature and art changed during the Renaissance.

Target Reading Skill

Identify Causes and Effects When you're reading, it's important to recognize causes and effects. A cause makes something happen, like a pebble thrown into a lake. An effect is what happens, like the ripple caused by the pebble. As you read, ask yourself what happened. The answer is the effect. Then ask yourself why it happened. That answer is the cause.

As you read this section, identify why the Renaissance started in Italy. Then identify the effects of the Renaissance. Write the causes and effects in an outline like the one below:

I. Why the Renaissance started in Italy
   A.
   B.
II. The effects of the Renaissance
   A.
   B.

Vocabulary Strategy

Use Context Clues The meaning of a word may depend on its context. The context gives you clues to a word's meaning.

Here's an example. See if the other words in this sentence tell you of the word *history*:

> History began when people started to keep written records of their experiences.

Ask yourself, "What information does the sentence give me about the word?" Answer: "I know that history began when people kept written records of their experiences. So history must be the written record of human experience."

Section 1 Summary

Target Reading Skill

List two causes that led to the birth of the Renaissance.

1. ____________________

2. ____________________

The *Mona Lisa* may be one of the most famous pieces of art in the world. It was painted by Leonardo da Vinci (lee uh NAHR doh duh VIN chee). He was a great Italian artist, but he was also a great inventor and scientist.

Da Vinci lived during an exciting time called the **Renaissance**. That's the name for the period between 1300 and 1650 in Europe, when the culture changed greatly. Artists used new skills and techniques, and scholars began to look at the world in new ways.

The Renaissance Begins in Italy

The Renaissance was a change in culture that started around the 1300s in Italy. Italy is located on the Mediterranean Sea. In the late Middle Ages, Italy's location helped it become a center of trade with the wealthy lands of the East. Although Feudalism ruled the rest of Europe, Italy's merchants were making big fortunes.

Because Italy's trade was based in its cities, these cities became centers of power and wealth. Many nobles moved to the cities to seek their fortunes. The most powerful Italian cities became independent city-states. They were not controlled by a king or by a noble. Even the Church had little power in these cities. ✓

✓ Reading Check

How did Italy differ from the rest of Europe?

____

____

____

Key Term

Renaissance (REN uh sahns) *n.* a widespread change in culture that took place in Europe beginning with the 1300s

Renaissance Art and Literature

The Renaissance was a time of great artistic achievement. Artists created stunning paintings and sculptures. During the Middle Ages, art had focused on the Church, but that began to change in the 1300s.

Life no longer centered on feudalism and the Church. Many artists and teachers rediscovered the ideas and writings of the ancient Romans and Greeks. These works explored nature, beauty, and other topics that had been ignored during the Middle Ages. This new interest in the classics is known as **humanism**.

The first great humanist was Francesco Petrarch (frahn CHES koh PEA trahrk). As a child, he loved the works of Latin writers. His own writing shows a view of love and nature very different from medieval forms.

Renaissance artists also began to focus on nature and the human form. They still created religious scenes, but they showed the human body with great accuracy.

You have read about Leonardo da Vinci. He filled more than 4,000 notebook pages with sketches and notes about the world around him. Another great artist of the time was Michelangelo (my kul AN juh loh). His greatest work may be the painted ceiling of the Sistene Chapel. It is among the best-known paintings in history.

The sculptor Donatello (doh nuh TEL oh) created life-like sculptures of the human body. He was inspired by the ancient Greeks and Romans. Some of his most famous works are a series of sculptures of the Biblical figure David. ✓

Review Questions

1. What effect did the rise of cities have on life in Italy?

____

____

2. How did the focus of Italian artists change during the Renaissance?

____

____

Key Term

humanism (HYOO muh niz um) *n.* interest in the classics

Vocabulary Strategy

Mark the Text

What does the word *classics* mean in the underlined sentence? What clues can you find in the surrounding words, phrases, or sentences? Circle the words in this paragraph that could help you learn what *classics* means.

✓ Reading Check

What was the main focus of Renaissance artists?

____

____

____

Prepare to Read

Section 2
The Renaissance Moves North

Objectives

1. Understand how the Renaissance spread from Italy to the north.
2. Identify key literary figures and ideas of the Northern Renaissance.
3. Identify key artists and artistic ideas of the Northern Renaissance.

Target Reading Skill

Recognize Multiple Causes A cause makes something happen. An effect is the result. Often, an effect can have more than one cause. Sometimes there are several factors that cause an event to happen.

Looking for more than one cause will help you better understand why something happened. As you read this section, look for the multiple reasons why the Renaissance spread to the North.

Vocabulary Strategy

Use Context to Clarify Meaning When you come across a word you do not know, you may not need to stop reading to look up its meaning. In this book, key terms appear in blue, and their definitions are at the bottom of the page. Looking at the definition breaks up your reading. Before you do that, continue to read to the end of the paragraph. See if you can figure out what the word means from its context. Clues can include examples and explanations. After you're done reading look at the definition to see how accurate you were. Finally, reread the paragraph to make sure you understood what you read.

Section 2 Summary

In the mid-1400s, Johannes Gutenberg (yoh HAHN us GOOT un burg) began work on a new project that would change the way books were made. He developed a system of **movable type**. He also invented a printing press, which was a machine that used movable type to print pages. The availability of books changed the way information and ideas spread in Europe and the world.

Renaissance Thought and Literature Spreads

Over time, the changes happening in Italy during the Renaissance began spreading northward into Europe. Industry and trade expanded. The feudal and religious base of medieval society weakened. Changes in literature, art, and culture followed. Renaissance ideas and Gutenberg's printing methods helped bring changes to the entire continent.

As in Italy, many scholars in northern and western Europe became interested in humanism. Renaissance thinkers all over applied these ideas to religious thinking. This movement is called Christian humanism. The leading figure of this movement was Desiderius Erasmus (des uh DIHR ee us ih RAZ mus).

Erasmus was a Roman Catholic priest and wrote the book *In Praise of Folly*. In it, he mocked, or disrespected, certain Church practices. He believed these practices had little to do with true faith. In fact, he thought they often covered up wrong doings. His work had a great impact on education in Europe. ✓

Key Term

movable type (MOO vuh bul typ) *n.* individual letters and marks that can be arranged and rearranged quickly

Vocabulary Strategy

Mark the Text

From context clues, write a definition of the term *printing press*. Circle words or phrases in the text that helped you write your definition.

____

____

Target Reading Skill

List some of the causes that allowed Renaissance ideas to spread northward.

____

____

____

____

✓ Reading Check

Why did Erasmus mock certain Church practices?

____

____

____

One of Erasmus's friends was England's Sir Thomas More (sur TAHM us mawr). He had also been influenced by Greek thinkers. He wrote *Utopia* (yoo TOH pea uh). It describes an ideal world based on Greek thinking. In writing about this perfect place, More pointed out problems in his own world. Among those problems were the differences between the politically weak and the politically powerful.

Art of the Northern Renaissance

Several artists in northern and western Europe made an impact during the Renaissance. Jan van Eyck (yahn van yk) was a Flemish painter and a master of realistic portraits. He was able to create rich visual effects. He is noted for his bright colors and eye for realism. His paintings show details of everyday life in a region that is now part of Belgium and the Netherlands. He was only one of several well-known Renaissance painters from the Netherlands. ✓

✓ Reading Check

From which country did Jan Van Eyck come?

____

____

Albrecht Dürer (AHL brekt DYOOR ur) was a German painter. He also made woodcuts and engravings. In the late 1400s, he visited Italy. He wanted to see for himself the work of Italian Renaissance masters.

Dürer had many interests and his work reflected events of the time. These events would shake the religious foundation of Europe. You will read about them in the next section. Together, they are known as the Reformation.

Review Questions

1. Identify two literary figures of the Renaissance in western and northern Europe.

____

____

2. Identify two artists who were part of the Northern Renaissance.

____

____

Prepare to Read

Section 3
Martin Luther and The Reformation

Objectives

1. Understand the developments that led to the Reformation.
2. Learn about Luther's criticism of the Church.
3. Understand the immediate effects of Luther's ideas in Europe.

Target Reading Skill

Understand Effects Remember, a cause makes something happen and the effect is the result. A cause can have more than one effect. You can find the effect by answering the question, "What happened?" If there are several answers, then the cause had more than one effect.

As you read this section, think of the Church's behavior as a cause. What was the effect? Write the effects in a diagram like the one below.

CAUSE:
↓
EVENT: Luther posts his 95 Theses
↓
EFFECTS:

Vocabulary Strategy

Use Context to Clarify Meaning Words are often defined in the text. Sometimes the definition appears in a separate sentence. Sometimes, the word *or* is used to introduce the definition. Look at the following examples.

indulgences, or *pardons for sins given by the pope in return for money*

judgment, or *a decision given by a judge or court*

The underlined words are defined in context.

Section 3 Summary

In the early 1500s, the Roman Catholic Church was trying to raise money to build a glorious new church in Rome. Priests like Johann Tetzel (YOH hahn Tet sul) sold **indulgences** as part of this effort. But attitudes toward this and other Church practices were changing.

The Church at the Time of Luther

During the Middle Ages, the Church had been at the heart of European life. By the time of the Renaissance, it was one of the most powerful political institutions in Europe. It waged war and made friends with other states. Its leader, the pope, had power like a king.

Erasmus and other writers of the Renaissance pointed out the changes happening in the Church. They thought Church leaders had sometimes lost sight of the Church's main purpose, which was to guide people's religious lives.

In the early 1500s, a monk named Martin Luther (MAHRT un LOO thur) became very unhappy with the Church. For several years, he had struggled with his belief in Church teachings. He was troubled by the Church's belief in good works as a way to get to heaven.

Luther heard of Tetzel's efforts to sell indulgences and he became angry. He challenged the Church. ✓

Luther Starts the Reformation

In 1517, Luther wrote a document in which he challenged the Church's use of indulgences. The document featured 95 theses, or arguments. Luther posted his 95 Theses on the church door in Wittenberg, Germany.

Luther said people could find **salvation** through faith alone. This differed from Church teachings. The Church believed that only a priest could perform certain rituals. Luther wrote that priests were nothing more than officeholders or politicians.

Key Terms

indulgence (in DUL juns) *n.* an official pardon for a sin given by the pope in return for money

salvation (sal VAY shun) *n.* to go to heaven, in religious terms

✓ Reading Check

How did the Church's great power lead to criticism of the Church during the Renaissance?

____

____

Vocabulary Strategy

The term *theses* is defined in context. Circle its definition.

Luther also challenged the pope's authority. He said the Bible was the only true authority, and the pope's teachings should follow the Bible. Otherwise, people should disobey the pope. ✓

Luther's ideas outraged Church officials. The Church succeeded in having Luther labeled an outlaw in Germany, but his popularity was growing. The judgment against him was never enforced.

The Reformation Succeeds

Luther's break from the Church was the beginning of the **Reformation**. The Reformation succeeded for many reasons. Some nobles resented the pope and the Church's power. The poor liked Luther's message of equality. In the 1520s, German peasants revolted, but Luther spoke out against them. He said people should respect authority in nonreligious matters. ✓

The movement became known as Lutheranism (LOO thur un iz um). It spread through many parts of Germany, as well as Sweden, Norway, and other parts of Europe. In 1555, the Church of Rome finally gave in. The Peace of Augsburg (peas uv AWGS burg) gave Lutherans the right to practice their religion.

But it did not end the Reformation. Reformation ideas affected other parts of Europe.

Review Questions

1. What action by Johann Tetzel upset Luther and led to his posting of the 95 Theses?

____

____

2. What happened to Luther after he was declared an outlaw in Germany?

____

____

> **Key Term**
>
> **Reformation** (ref ur MAY shun) *n.* Luther's break with the Catholic Church and the movement it inspired

✓ Reading Check

What did Luther say was the final authority in religious matters?

____

____

✓ Reading Check

Why were peasants drawn to Luther's teachings?

____

____

____

Target Reading Skill

In this section, you have read about Luther's criticisms of the Church. What effects did Luther's criticisms have on the Church? How did Church leaders respond to his criticisms?

Effects: ______________________

____

Response: ____________________

____

Prepare to Read

Section 4
Reformation Ideas Spread

Objectives

1. Learn that Luther was the first of several religious reformers.
2. Identify other religious movements of the 1500s in Europe.
3. Understand how the Catholic Church responded to the Reformation.

Target Reading Skill

Recognize Cause-and-Effect Signal Words As you read, watch for clues that show cause and effect. Causes and effects follow one another in a certain order. Often, a word will give you a signal that what's being described is either a cause or an effect. Words like *so, suddenly, finally, for this reason,* and *as a result* signal a relationship between a cause and its effects.

This section contains information about the spread of Reformation ideas. To help keep the order of events clear, look for words that signal the relationship between a cause and its effects.

Vocabulary Strategy

Use Context to Clarify Meaning Sometimes you may read a word you recognize, but it may not have the usual meaning. Many words have more than one definition. What a word means depends on its context. For example, the word *order* has many meanings. You cannot know what meaning the author had in mind unless you look at the context.

Some examples are listed below.

	Definitions	Examples
order	the way things are placed	Put it in alphabetical order.
	a peaceful condition in which people obey rules	The police will restore order.
	people with shared beliefs	He joined an order of monks.
	to ask for something that one wants to buy	I will order the pizza.

Section 4 Summary

King Henry VIII of England wanted to have a male child to inherit his throne. He and his wife Catherine had a daughter. Henry decided he needed to marry another woman, but first he needed the Church to end his marriage to Catherine. The pope refused Henry's request.

Henry had always been a strong supporter of the Church. He had even written an attack on Martin Luther's ideas. In response, the pope had given Henry the title of Defender of the Faith. But in 1534, Henry officially broke from the Catholic Church. He became head of the Church of England. Now the people of England were part of the Reformation.

The Reformation After Luther

Many people in Europe adopted Luther's ideas in the mid-1500s. Several other **Protestant** groups appeared.

John Calvin began preaching in Switzerland. He believed that faith alone could win salvation. He also believed that God had long ago decided who would be saved. This idea is known as predestination.

Ulrich Zwingli (ool rik ZWING lee) was also from Switzerland. His followers, known as Zwinglians, believed the Bible contained all religious truth.

The Anabaptists (an uh BAP tists) formed at this time. They did not believe infants should be baptized. They believed that only older people should be baptized. They thought older people were the only people who had the faith it required. ✓

Key Term

Protestant (PRAHT us tunt) *adj.* refers to Christian groups that separated from the Catholic church

✓ Reading Check

Where did the Zwinglians first appear?

____

____

____

The Protestant Reformation

Groups	Founders	Country	Beliefs
Lutherans	Martin Luther	Germany	• Salvation through faith • Challenged priests' role • True authority is Bible
Calvinists	John Calvin	Switzerland	• Salvation through faith • Predestination
Zwinglians	Ulrich Zwingli	Switzerland	Bible contains all religious truth
Anabaptists	Conrad Grebel	Switzerland	Opposed to baptism of infants

Target Reading Skill

Circle the words that signal the effect of the Reformation on the Church.

Mark the Text

____

____

The Catholic Church Reforms

The Reformation was a major challenge to the Church of Rome. As a result, the Church started its own reforms during the mid-1500s which helped it regain strength in much of Europe. The reforms of Luther and others was called the Protestant Reformation. The Catholic Church's reforms were called the Catholic Reformation.

Vocabulary Strategy

The word *order* is used in the bracketed paragraph. Find it and circle it. How is it used here? Copy the correct definition from the chart at the beginning of this section.

Mark the Text

____

____

____

[A key development of the Catholic Reformation was the founding of the Society of Jesus. This was a religious order, or group. It was led by Ignatius Loyola (ig NAY shus loy OH luh). Its members are called Jesuits (JEZH oo its). They worked to educate people and to spread the Catholic faith. They helped build the Church's strength in southern Europe.] ✓

✓ Reading Check

What was the function of the Jesuits?

____

____

____

The Catholic Church was also strengthened by Paul III. He became pope in 1534. He helped the Church focus on its abuses, which included corrupt practices among the clergy. In 1542, Paul III called for a meeting. It is known as the Council of Trent. This meeting helped steer the Church back to matters of religion and spirituality.

Review Questions

1. How did the Reformation develop following Luther's break from the Church?

____

____

2. How did the Catholic Church respond to the Reformation?

____

____

Chapter 15 Assessment

1. How did the growth of Italian cities at the beginning of the Renaissance affect the feudal system?
   - **A.** The growth of cities strengthened feudalism.
   - **B.** The growth of cities weakened feudalism.
   - **C.** The growth of cities forced nobles to fight one another.
   - **D.** The growth of cities expanded feudalism into the city environment.

2. How did Renaissance art differ from medieval art?
   - **A.** Renaissance artists only painted religious scenes.
   - **B.** Renaissance artists showed the human body with great accuracy and detail.
   - **C.** Renaissance artists did not paint religious scenes.
   - **D.** Renaissance artists did not show the human body.

3. What did Erasmus write in his book *In Praise of Folly*?
   - **A.** He broke ties with the Roman Church over indulgences.
   - **B.** He said that priests were nothing more than officeholders.
   - **C.** He defended the authority of the pope to rule on religious matters.
   - **D.** He mocked Church practices he thought had little to do with true faith.

4. Which of the following was one of Luther's central Reformation ideas?
   - **A.** The Jesuits should spread religious faith.
   - **B.** Infants should not be baptized.
   - **C.** Women should be allowed into the priesthood.
   - **D.** Faith, not good works, was the key to salvation.

5. The Society of Jesus was formed to
   - **A.** help educate people and spread the Catholic faith.
   - **B.** lead a Crusade against Protestants.
   - **C.** bring an end to the Catholic Reformation.
   - **D.** select a new pope at the Council of Trent.

Short Answer Question

What was Henry VIII's reason for breaking with the Church of Rome?

Prepare to Read

Section 1
European Exploration Begins

Objectives

1. Learn why Europeans began exploring the world in the 1400s.
2. Identify the early achievements of Portuguese exploration under Prince Henry the Navigator.
3. Understand how Portugal's efforts inspired early Spanish exploration.

Target Reading Skill

Paraphrase To paraphrase is to put a thought or idea into your own words. Paraphrasing can help you understand and remember what you read. You could paraphrase the first paragraph in this section in this way:

> Marco Polo's trip and the Crusades gave Europeans a glimpse of the East. The Italians got wealthy through trade and other European countries wanted a piece of the pie.

As you read, paraphrase or use your own words to explain the information following each heading.

Vocabulary Strategy

Use Context to Determine Meaning Sometimes you can get clues from the words, phrases, and sentences around an unfamiliar word that will help you understand it. The underlined words in the paragraph below give clues to the meaning of the word *isthmus.*

> In 1513, a Spanish explorer named Vasco Núñez de Balboa arrived on the *Isthmus* of Panama. It is a narrow strip of land that connects the continents of North and South America.

An isthmus is a narrow strip of land that connects two larger areas of land.

Section 1 Summary

Why Europe Looked to the East

You have read about Marco Polo's journey and the Crusades. These events made Europeans aware of the wonders of the East. Italian merchants made fortunes bringing spices and other goods from Asia and northern Africa. Other Europeans wanted to expand trade. ✓

Spain and Portugal are on the Iberian Peninsula. There, Christians had been fighting to remove the Moors. The Moors were Muslims who had arrived there in the 700s.

Portuguese Exploration

Prince Henry became a leader in Portuguese exploration.

As a young man, Henry helped conquer Ceuta (say OO tah) in North Africa. It was a rich trading city. For several years, he was its governor.

Henry decided to explore the African coast. He put up money for voyages of discovery. Over several decades, explorers pushed farther down Africa's western coast. By the mid-1400s, they had begun the European trade of African slaves.

In 1488, Bartolomeu Dias (bahr too loo MEE OO DEE us) sailed around the southern tip of Africa. The next year, he named it the Cape of Storms. It is now called the Cape of Good Hope. ✓

In November 1497, Vasco da Gama (VAHS koh duh GAM uh) also sailed around the Cape of Good Hope and into the Indian Ocean. Then he sailed to Calicut (KAL uh kut) in India. He was honored as a hero at home.

Columbus Sails Under Spanish Flag

Most people of the time thought the Earth was flat. But many scholars knew it was round. Christopher Columbus thought that if he sailed far enough west, he would reach Asia and the lands of the East.

He tried for several years to get support for his plan. In 1492, Queen Isabella of Spain agreed to pay for the voyage. That year, Columbus led three ships, the *Niña*, the *Pinta*, and the *Santa María*. ✓

After ten weeks, Columbus and his crew reached an island in the area now called the Caribbean. It was

✓ Reading Check

What two factors caused Europeans to look to the East during the Renaissance?

____

____

____

Target Reading Skill

Paraphrase the paragraph that begins "Henry decided to explore..."

____

____

____

✓ Reading Check

What two names were given to the Southern tip of Africa?

1. ______________________

2. ______________________

✓ Reading Check

Why did Columbus believe he could sail west from Europe and reach Asia?

____

____

____

October 12, 1492. Columbus's journey changed history. Instead of reaching Asia, he had reached the Americas.

Other Explorers Look West

By the early 1500s, Europeans knew that the Americas were not the lands of the East.

A Spanish explorer named Vasco Núñez de Balboa (VAHS koh NOO nyeth theh bal BOH uh) arrived on the **Isthmus** of Panama (IS mis uv PAN uh mah). It connects the continents of North and South America. Balboa had heard about a huge ocean and gold treasure to the west. He set off on an expedition to find both. After three weeks, they reached the shores of a great sea. It was the Pacific Ocean. Balboa called it the South Sea. Then he claimed it and all the lands it touched for Spain.

Another Portuguese navigator set out to find Asia by sailing west. His name was Ferdinand Magellan (FUR duh nand muh JEL un). Three of his ships made it to the Pacific Ocean. He kept sailing West, and he landed in the Philippines, where he was killed by natives. One of his ships made it back to Spain, marking the first **circumnavigation** of the globe.

Many Europeans looked for a shortcut through North America. <u>They called it the Northwest Passage</u>. It was not until the 1900s that a ship succeeded in traveling from the Atlantic to the Pacific by sailing north of Canada. ✓

Vocabulary Strategy

Look at the phrase *Northwest Passage* in the underlined sentence. Look in the context for clues to its meaning. Circle the words or phrases that help you learn its meaning.

Mark the Text

✓ Reading Check

In what way were Magellan's voyage and the Northwest passage similar? In what way were they different?

Similar: ____________________

____

Different: ____________________

____

Review Questions

1. Which part of Europe dominated Asian trade at the start of the Renaissance?

____

____

2. How did the conquest of Ceuta affect the Portuguese?

____

____

Key Terms

isthmus (IS mis) *n.* a strip of land connecting two areas of land

circumnavigation (sur kum nav ih GAY shun) *n.* going completely around Earth, especially by water

Prepare to Read

Section 2 Europeans in India and Southeast Asia

Objectives

1. Learn how Portugal traded in India.
2. Understand how Portuguese trade expanded into India and the Spice Islands.
3. Identify the English and the Dutch as challengers to Portugal's power in Asia.

Target Reading Skill

Summarize You will learn more from your reading if you summarize it. When you summarize, you use your own words to restate the key points. A good summary includes important events and details. It notes the order in which the events occurred. It also makes connections between the events.

Use the graphic organizer below to summarize what you have read.

The Portuguese seek to control the spice trade.
↓
↓

Vocabulary Strategy

Use Context to Determine Meaning Sometimes you can pick up clues from the words, phrases, and sentences around an unfamiliar word that will help you understand it. The underlined words in the paragraph below give clues to the meaning of the word *Calicut*.

> Portugal was the first European country to reach the rich ports of Asia. Vasco da Gama's voyage had reached *Calicut*. It was a trading center in India.

Calicut was a trading center in India.

Section 2 Summary

✓ Reading Check

Why did Vasco da Gama come home empty-handed on his first voyage to Calicut?

____

____

____

The people of Europe greatly prized spices. The spices that only cost a few dollars today were worth a small fortune hundreds of years ago.

Portugal Gains a Foothold in India

Portugal was the first European country to sail to Asia when Vasco da Gama reached Calicut, India. But da Gama left empty-handed. Calicut traders rejected the humble trade goods he brought from Europe. ✓

In 1500, Pedro Alvarez Cabral (PAY droh AL vuh rez kuh BRAHL) set out for India. On the way, he landed in an area that is now southeastern Brazil. He claimed this land for Portugal.

Finally, Cabral reached Calicut. His efforts to trade for spices went slowly. He ended up in a battle with Arab traders, and many people were killed. Still, Cabral set up a trading post in India and he returned to Portugal with a load of spices.

Vocabulary Strategy

Look at the phrase *Spice Islands* in the underlined sentence. Look in the context for clues to its meaning. Circle the words or phrases that help you learn its meaning.

The Portuguese Empire Expands

Soon Portugal was sending more ships to trade in Asia. They were also sending armed forces to gain control of many trading centers between the east coast of Africa and the west coast of India. Portugal managed to control trade in the region. ✓

Next, Portugal looked farther east. That's where the Moluccas were. These were the Spice Islands. They were in the northeastern part of what is now Indonesia. In 1511, Alfonso de Albuquerque (al FAHN soh du AL buh kur kee) seized the islands.

Portugal had a huge hold on the East. But its control was mainly limited to trade. Portugal held little territory.

✓ Reading Check

Between what two coasts did Portugal fight to control?

1. ______________________________

2. ______________________________

Challengers to Portugal

Portugal's empire brought it wealth, but the Dutch soon challenged Portugal's role in the East. During the 1500s, the Dutch were becoming an economic and military power in Europe.

In 1602, the Dutch East India Company was founded. The government gave the company a trade **monopoly** in Asia. That meant it had complete control of trade there.

The Dutch East India Company became a powerful force in Southeast Asia. From there, it set up many new trading posts and developed close ties with other Asian countries. It even had its own armies and used them to take over land and people.

England was also interested in Asian trade. In 1600, the East India Company was formed and led the British effort.

For a time, the East India Company and the Dutch East India Company competed in the East Indies. Soon, the English changed their focus to India. They drove out the Portuguese. Then they expanded their own trading operations. During the 1600s, England became the area's main trading power. ✓

At the same time, the Mughal Empire began to lose control of India. Groups began to fight for power. The French East India Company was one of the groups battling for control. In the mid-1700s, the British came out as the leading power in India. Over the next hundred years, Britain tightened its hold. In the mid-1800s, India became a **colony** of Great Britain.

Review Questions

1. What was the Dutch East India Company?

____

____

2. Why was England able to gain total control over India?

____

____

Key Terms

monopoly (muh NAHP uh lee) *n.* exclusive control of goods or services in a market
colony (KAHL uh nee) *n.* a territory ruled over by a distant state

Target Reading Skill

Summarize this section. Give the main point and two details.

____

____

____

✓ Reading Check

In what two areas of Asia did the English and Dutch focus their efforts?

1. ______________________________

2. ______________________________

Prepare to Read

Section 3
Europe Explores East Asia

Objectives

1. Learn about European efforts to expand trade in East Asia.
2. Understand European encounters with China and Japan, 1600–1700.

Target Reading Skill

Reread or Read Ahead Both rereading and reading ahead can help you understand words and ideas. If you do not understand a word or passage, use one or both of these techniques to explain the meaning of what you have read.

In some cases, you may wish to read ahead to see if the word or idea is explained later on. Sometimes a word is defined after its first use. The main idea of a sentence or paragraph may be discussed later in the section.

If you do not understand the main idea of a sentence or paragraph, try going back and rereading it. Look for details you may have missed earlier. Put together the facts you do understand. As you reread, concentrate on the parts that seem confusing.

Vocabulary Strategy

Use Context Clues Words work together to explain meaning. The meaning of a word may depend on its context. A word's context is the other words and sentences that surround it. The context gives you clues to a word's meaning.

Try this example. Say you do not know the meaning of the word *persecuted* in the following sentence:

> The missionaries and Japanese Christians were <u>persecuted</u> because of their religion, and many chose to leave Japan.

You could ask yourself, "What information does the sentence give me about the word?" Answer: "I know it is something that was done to people because of their religious beliefs. It must have been bad because many chose to leave. This tells me that persecuting someone must mean threatening or hurting that person because of his or her religion or other beliefs."

Section 3 Summary

In 1793, the British government sent a representative to ask for more British trading rights in China. The Chinese did not see any reason to grant them. They had no use for British products.

Other countries also wanted greater trade in East Asia from the 1500s through the 1700s. The Portuguese, the Dutch, and the Spanish all tried to tap the riches of the region.

Expanding European Trade

During the 1500s, European powers controlled trade and land in India and Southeast Asia. But there was an even more valuable prize nearby: China. It was famed for its porcelain, jade, and silk.

Portugal was beginning to explore trade in China. At first, the Chinese could see little reason to deal with them. Still, the Portuguese created a trading post at Macao (muh KOU) by 1557. But China strictly controlled this trade. And China did not officially grant Portuguese control of Macao. ✓

The Spanish also traded with China at this time. They worked out of their colony of the Philippines. Spain used gold mined in Mexico to pay for silks and other goods from China.

It was also during this time when Europeans first heard of Japan. A Portuguese ship had blown off course and landed there. More Europeans later returned to trade and spread Christianity.

✓ Reading Check

Who were the first Europeans to make contact with China in the early 1500s?

____

____

Vocabulary Strategy

What does the phrase *foreign devils* mean in the underlined sentence? What clues can you find in the surrounding words, phrases, or sentences? Circle the words in this paragraph that could help you learn what *foreign devils* means.

Target Reading Skill

Reread the bracketed paragraph to see why Europeans were not able to carry on wide trade with China.

✓ Reading Check

Which country dominated trade with Japan starting in the 1600s?

____

____

____

European Contacts with China and Japan

The Chinese saw themselves as the greatest empire in the world. They did not think much of "foreign devils," which is what they called Europeans. The Europeans also thought of themselves as superior. This attitude caused conflicts. When the Chinese did trade, they usually accepted only silver and gold. Europeans would have preferred to trade their goods.

Still, Europeans wanted to trade. The Dutch seized the island of Taiwan and used it as a base for trade with China and Japan. Years later, the Chinese drove them out and took control.

The British were also frustrated because the Chinese rulers kept tight control over trade. The Portuguese were the first to reach Japan. Soon Portuguese traders and **missionaries** returned, but by the late 1500s, Japanese rulers had begun to distrust the Portuguese. Religion was a major cause of this distrust. The missionaries and Japanese Christians were **persecuted**. The Portuguese soon left Japan. ✓

Next, the Dutch arrived in Japan. They were allowed to build a trading post. The Japanese kept close control over this trade. Until the 1800s, the Dutch were the only Europeans allowed to trade with Japan.

Review Questions

1. What were Chinese attitudes toward trade?

____

____

2. What was the effect of Portuguese efforts to spread Christianity in Japan?

____

____

Key Terms

missionary (MISH un her ee) *n.* one who is sent to do religious or charitable work in a foreign country

persecution (pur sih KYOO shun) *n.* the causing of injury or distress to others because of their religion, race, or political beliefs

Chapter 16 Assessment

1. Which of the following is linked to Prince Henry of Portugal?
   A. the Crusades
   B. the conquest of Cueta
   C. the East India Company
   D. the discovery of the Americas

2. Who led the first expedition that circumnavigated the globe?
   A. Vasco da Gama
   B. Christopher Columbus
   C. Vasco Núñez de Balboa
   D. Ferdinand Magellan

3. Who made the first Portuguese landing in Brazil and claimed the land for Portugal?
   A. Vasco da Gama
   B. Ferdinand Magellan
   C. Pedro Alvarez Cabral
   D. Alfonso de Albuquerque

4. Spanish trade with China was more active than other countries because the Spanish
   A. paid for Chinese goods with gold mined in Mexico.
   B. won armed conflicts with Chinese traders.
   C. secured a trading post at Macao.
   D. seized Taiwan as a trade base with China.

5. Which country was successful in trading with Japan?
   A. England
   B. Spain
   C. the Dutch
   D. France

Short Answer Question

Describe the sequence of events that led to Britain's control of India.

____

____

____

____

Prepare to Read

Section 1
Conquest in the Americas

Objectives

1. Learn what attitudes and events led to the Spanish exploration of the Americas.
2. Find out how the Spanish conquered Mexico.
3. Learn how the Spanish conquered Peru.

Target Reading Skill

Identify Main Ideas It's impossible to remember every detail you read. Good readers are able to find the main idea. The main idea is the most important point.

To help you find main ideas, look first at each heading. The headings will give you clues. Then, read the text. As you read, ask yourself what each paragraph is about. Sometimes the main idea of a paragraph is stated in the first sentence or two.

As you read, look for the main idea in each section.

Vocabulary Strategy

Recognize Signal Words Signal words give you clues. They help you understand what you read. They prepare you for what is coming next.

There are different kinds of signal words. Signal words may be used to show time, place, or direction. They may also show different kinds of relationships, such as contrast. Contrast shows the difference between things or ideas.

Here are some common signal words that show contrast:

but	*however*	*not*	*on the other hand*
even though	*yet*	*despite*	

Section 1 Summary

Spain's Exploration of the Americas

In 1492, the Spanish drove the Moors out of the Iberian Peninsula. Now they were ready to explore and claim new lands. Later that year, Queen Isabella and King Ferdinand sent Columbus to the Indies.

Centuries of war with the Moors had shaped Spanish culture. Spaniards admired the warriors who fought for glory and faith. The **conquistadors** would now seek glory in the Americas. At the same time, they would win great fortunes. ✓

Spain gained control of many islands in the Caribbean. They also conquered present-day Mexico, Central America, and parts of South America.

[The Spanish also conquered two great civilizations. Some native groups resisted for a while, but the conquistadors had better weapons. The Native Americans were no match for them. Also, thousands of Native Americans died from diseases brought by the Spanish. Some groups disappeared entirely.]

The Spanish Conquest of Mexico

In the 16th century, central Mexico was home to the Aztec (AZ tek) empire. Its capital was Tenochtitlán (teh nawch tee TLAN). That's where Moctezuma (mahk tih ZOO muh) ruled. The empire was huge and included many conquered peoples.

In 1519, the conquistador Hernán Cortés (hur NAHN kohr TEZ) arrived in Mexico. Rumors of the wealthy Aztec empire led him to Tenochtitlán. He took with him a force of several hundred soldiers.

Moctezuma welcomed the Spanish. According to legend, he thought Cortés was an Aztec god. According to Aztec beliefs, the pale-skinned god would one day come back to Mexico. ✓

The Aztecs soon realized Cortés wasn't the legendary god. Soldiers surrounded Cortés and his men.

Key Term

conquistador (kahn KEES tuh dawr) *n.* a Spanish conqueror of the Americas in the 16th century

✓ Reading Check

What effect did the long struggle with the Moors have on the Spanish people?

____

____

____

Vocabulary Strategy

Mark the Text

In the bracketed paragraph, a signal word is used to show contrast. Find the signal word and circle it. What is being contrasted here?

____

____

Target Reading Skill

What is the main idea of this section?

____

____

____

✓ Reading Check

Why did Moctezuma first welcome Cortés and his soldiers?

____

____

The Spaniards fought their way out of the city.

Cortés next put together a large army. In it were new troops from Spain. There were also thousands of Native Americans who hated Aztec rule. Cortés's army surrounded the city. There was a long **siege**. The battle ended in 1521. Tenochtitlán was in ruins. The Aztec Empire had ruled much of Mexico, but now it was completely defeated.

The Spanish Conquest of Peru

Cortés's success inspired other conquistadors, such as Francisco Pizarro (frahn SEES koh pea SAHR oh). He wanted to conquer the great Incan Empire, located in present-day Peru. The Inca had huge treasures of gold.

When Pizarro arrived in Peru, the Incan Empire had already been weakened by a **civil war**. Pizarro led 200 soldiers into the center of the empire. The Inca king, Atahualpa (ah tuh WAHL puh), watched the Spaniards closely, but he made the mistake of visiting their camp and Pizarro captured him. The Spanish forces, guns, and horses crushed Atahualpa's much larger army. The Incan soldiers had only spears and small weapons. Not a single Spaniard was killed in the fighting. ✓

Pizarro forced the Inca to pay a ransom for their king. A ransom is a large sum of money. He told the Inca to fill a room with gold if they wanted their king back alive. The Inca paid the ransom, but Pizarro had Atahualpa killed anyway. Without a leader, the Inca were not able to resist the Spanish army. Their empire was added to Spain's conquests in the Americas.

✓ Reading Check

Although the Incan army was much larger, why was Pizarro's army so successful?

____

____

____

Review Questions

1. Why was the year 1492 so important in Spanish history?

____

____

2. Who joined Cortés in his siege of Tenochtitlán?

____

____

Key Terms

siege (seej) *n.* the surrounding and blockading of a town

civil war (SIV ul wawr) *n.* a war between different regions of one country

Prepare to Read

Section 2
Colonies in Central and South Americas

Objectives

1. Learn how Spain and Portugal colonized the Americas.
2. Find out how the Spanish ruled their new colonies.
3. Understand the economic systems of the Spanish colonies.

Target Reading Skill

Identify Supporting Details The main idea of a paragraph or section is its most important point. The main idea is supported by details. Details give more information about the main idea. They tell you what, where, why, how much, or how many.

In this section, you will learn about colonies in the Americas. Look for details that provide more information about these colonies. How did Spain and Portugal rule? What were the colonies' economies like? Look for supporting details in each section.

Vocabulary Strategy

Recognize Signal Words Signal words give you clues. They help you understand what you read and prepare you for what's coming next.

There are different kinds of signal words. Some of the most common uses of signal words show time, place, or direction. They may also show how things are related, such as cause and effect.

Signal words that show cause	Signal words that show effect
because	as a result
if	consequently
on account of	so
since	then
	therefore

Some signal words that may show cause include *because, if, on account of,* and *since*. Signal words that show effect are *as a result, consequently, so, then*, and *therefore*.

Section 2 Summary

Europeans taught the Native Americans Christianity. The Native Americans blended Christian ideas with their traditions. Stones from Native American temples became part of new Christian churches. Native ceremonial sites became Christian holy places. The blend of Spanish Christianity and Native American religion became part of a new culture. ✓

Spain and Portugal Colonize Central and South America

The Spanish conquered a large portion of the Americas in the 1500s. Their lands stretched from southern South America north into the present-day United States. Some Native Americans fought against the invasion. Among them were the Maya in Mexico. But Spain won control of that region.

[In South America, Brazil did not come under Spanish control. Portugal claimed Brazil because Pedro Alvarez Cabral landed there. But, unlike Mexico and Peru, that area had no gold or other treasures. And it had no major cities. It was rich in valuable brazilwood. That is a dense and colorful wood. Therefore, many shiploads of the wood were sent to Portugal.]

Spanish Rule in the Colonies

To rule the Americas, Spain divided its lands into smaller units. They were called viceroyalties. Each viceroyalty was ruled by an official called a **viceroy**. Officials in Spain watched over the viceroys. ✓

The Catholic Church also helped rule the Spanish colonies. Its main reason for being in the Americas was to convert the Native Americans to Christianity. The clergy, or men ordained for religious service, acted as a local government. They enforced rules of behavior for both the Spanish and the Native Americans.

Key Term

viceroy (VYS roy) *n.* a governor of a country or colony who rules as the representative of a king or queen

---

✓ Reading Check

Name two ways Native Americans blended their traditional beliefs with Christianity.

____

____

____

____

Vocabulary Strategy

In the bracketed paragraph, a signal word is used to show cause and effect. Find the signal word and circle it. Then write the cause and effect below.

Cause: ______________________________

____

Effect: ______________________________

____

Target Reading Skill

What details in this section support the idea that the Catholic Church played a large role in governing the Spanish colonies?

____

____

____

✓ Reading Check

How did the Spanish govern the people in the Americas?

____

____

The clergy also stepped in when they thought the Spanish were abusing Native Americans. The clergy forced Native Americans to adopt Spanish ways as well as beliefs. But they also made it possible to blend Native American and Spanish cultures. They let the Native Americans keep some of their traditions and art. These then became part of a new culture.

The Economy of the Colonies

The new colonies made Spain rich. Shiploads of gold, silver, and other treasures were sent back across the ocean. **Plantations** grew valuable crops, like sugar cane.

The Spanish needed workers to mine gold and work the land. For this work, they used Africans. The Spanish brought these slaves to the Americas. The **encomienda** system gave the Spanish another source of labor. Spain gave encomiendas to conquistadors as rewards. Native Americans could be forced to work for Spanish **encomenderos**. The encomenderos were supposed to take care of the Native Americans they controlled. But conditions were often terrible. As the native peoples died from disease, the encomienda system weakened. Spain got grants of land, but still relied on Native American labor. ✓

✓ Reading Check

What's one reason why the encomienda system failed?

____

____

____

Review Questions

1. How was the Portuguese colony in the Americas similar to and different from the Spanish colonies?

____

____

2. How did the clergy affect the culture of the Native Americans?

____

____

Key Terms

plantation (plan TAY shun) *n.* a large estate or farm
encomienda (en koh mee EN dah) *n.* the right granted by the king to Spanish colonists to force Native Americans to work for them
encomenderos (en koh men DAY rohz) *n.* Portuguese colonists who were granted encomiendas

Prepare to Read

Section 3
Colonies in North America

Objectives

1. Identify the European countries that sought colonies in North America.
2. Understand the impact of European colonization on Native Americans.
3. Find out how the rivalry between France and England led to the French and Indian War.

Target Reading Skill

Identify Implied Main Ideas The main idea of a paragraph or section is its most important point. When you identify the main idea, you know what the paragraph or section is about. This will help you remember the most important points.

Sometimes the main idea is not stated exactly. Instead, all of the details add up to a main idea. In this case, the main idea is implied. It is up to you to put the details together to identify the main idea.

Carefully read the details of each section. Then state its main idea.

Vocabulary Strategy

Recognize Signal Words Signal words are words or phrases that give you clues. They help you understand what you read and prepare you for what's coming next.

There are different kinds of signal words. Often signal words show time, place, or direction. They may show different kinds of relationships, such as order, similarities, or cause and effect.

Signal words that may show time
then *when*
around (followed by a date)
in (followed by a date)
as early as (followed by a date)
in time *earlier*
later

Section 3 Summary

European Countries Seek Colonies in North America

In the 1600s, France, England, and the Netherlands also tried to start colonies in the Americas. ✓

The Dutch from the Netherlands started colonies in the Caribbean. They wanted to be part of the sugar cane trade. Sugar cane was highly valued in Europe. The Dutch started a colony on the North American continent. They called it New Netherland. But the English seized the colony in 1664. They renamed it New York.

Soon after Columbus discovered the new land, the French arrived in the Americas. In 1608, Samuel de Champlain (SAM yoo ul duh sham PLAYN) started the first French settlement, called Quebec. Catholic priests and monks soon followed. They converted Native Americans and traveled inland, away from the coast. Local Native Americans helped the French trade furs. The fur trade led to exploration. The French claimed the land from the Great Lakes down the Mississippi River to Louisiana.

The British were the most successful colonists. Their first settlement was in 1697, in Jamestown, Virginia. It did well when the Native Americans taught settlers how to grow tobacco.

In 1620, the English colony called Plymouth was settled by Pilgrims. The Pilgrims came looking for religious freedom, not for profit. Because of the success of that small settlement, more British **emigrated** to America. In time, the British had thirteen colonies in the new land.

Key Term

emigrate (EM ih grayt) *v.* to leave one country or region to settle in another

✓ Reading Check

Which five European countries established colonies in the Americas?

1. ______________________

2. ______________________

3. ______________________

4. ______________________

5. ______________________

Vocabulary Strategy

Mark the Text

As you read this section, look for the signal words that indicate when something happened. Circle the signal words when you find them.

Target Reading Skill

In one sentence, state the main idea of this section.

The Effect of European Colonization on Native Americans

When the Europeans arrived, Native American groups lived throughout North America. European diseases weakened or killed many native people. Those who survived lost their lands to European colonists. The English colonies along the East Coast were growing rapidly. For that reason, the Native Americans in this area faced the greatest problems.

Some Native Americans fought the colonists and won some battles, but usually lost the wars. They were pushed farther and farther inland as the British colonies grew.

The English and the French were already competing for trade in India and Europe. They were also competing as rivals in the new land. In 1754, they went to war in North America. This conflict is known as the French and Indian War. The French had several Native American groups as **allies** or friends. Native Americans acted as guides for French fur traders. But the English won that war and the French were driven out of most of North America. ✓

✓ Reading Check

Why did the Native Americans become allies of the French during the French and Indian War?

Native Americans helped the Pilgrims and the settlers of Jamestown survive. They did this by teaching them how to grow crops. Native American trails were the roads for the move west. Hundreds of Native American names are preserved across the continent.

Review Questions

1. How did the French and English colonies differ?

2. Name a place other than North America where England and France competed for power.

Key Term

ally (AL eye) *n* a country or group that is united with another for a common purpose

Prepare to Read

Section 4
Africa and the Atlantic Slave Trade

Objectives

1. Understand how slave trade began with exploration of Africa and colonization of South America and Central America. Learn how it spread to North America.
2. Discover what the triangular trade was and how it expanded.

Target Reading Skill

Identify Main Ideas To remember information, good readers identify main ideas as they read. The main idea is the most important point.

To help you find the main ideas, look first at each heading. The headings will give you clues. Then, read on to see what comes after each heading. As you read, ask yourself what each paragraph is about. Sometimes the main idea is stated in the first sentence or two.

As you read, look for the main idea in each section.

Vocabulary Strategy

Recognize Signal Words Signal words are words or phrases that give you clues. They help you understand what you read and prepare you for what's coming next.

There are different kinds of signal words. Signal words may be used to show time, place, or direction. They may also show relationships such as sequence. Sequence is the order in which things occur. It shows how events are related to each other.

Signal words that may show sequence	
first	*next*
then	*finally*
before	*earlier*
later	

Section 4 Summary

Vocabulary Strategy

Look at the underlined sentence. A signal word indicates sequence. Circle it. What is the order in which the actions take place? Write them below in the proper sequence.

Mark the Text

1. ______________________

2. ______________________

The trip of the African slave was terrible. One day he or she was a free person in an African village. The next, he or she was captured by slave traders. After being placed in chains, slaves were forced to walk for days to a slave trading fort. There, the Africans might sit for weeks or months. Eventually, they were loaded onto a ship. After a couple of months, the ship arrived in the Americas. Those who survived would begin a lifetime of slavery.

This story could have been told by millions of Africans. From the 1500s to the 1800s, the slave trade in Africa thrived. Slaves provided much of the work that built Europe's American colonies. It also changed the cultures of the Americas. Africans brought with them their traditions and values.

Slavery in the Americas

In the 1400s, Portugal had explored the western coast of Africa. During that time, it began capturing and trading **enslaved** human beings in Africa. To enslave means to make someone a slave. Slaves were considered the property of other people, and they had no rights. ✓

The Spanish used African slaves in their American colonies because so many Native Americans died from European diseases. The Portuguese also **imported** large numbers of African slaves to Brazil.

✓ Reading Check

Which European country began the European trade in African slaves?

____

____

____

Key Terms

enslaved (en SLAYVD) *v.* made into a slave and treated as property

import (im PAWRT) *v.* to bring in goods from a foreign country

The English colonies in North America were growing. They needed African slaves. This was especially true in the southern regions. There, the climate and soil were just right for crops like tobacco and sugar. To farm these crops, cheap workers were needed if profits were to be made.

European colonists preferred African slaves, who usually were not Christian. This may have made it easier for the colonist to excuse making other human beings work as slaves.

The Triangular Trade

The trade of enslaved Africans was part of a larger trade pattern. This pattern was called the triangular trade because it had three "sides." The first corner of the triangle was in Europe. There, ships were loaded with manufactured products. These items were shipped to Africa. This was the second point on the triangle. There, Europeans traded the products for African slaves. In the Americas, enslaved Africans were traded for resources such as tobacco and sugar cane. Those were then shipped back to Europe. There, they would be used for manufacturing, completing the triangle. ✓

The journey of enslaved Africans across the Atlantic Ocean was also called the Middle Passage. The ships were very crowded and many Africans died before reaching the Americas.

Slavery was important to the economies of several American colonies. In the 1600s and 1700s, it was an important part of trade between Europe and the American colonies.

Review Questions

1. In which century did Europeans begin trading in African slaves?

____

____

2. What was the Middle Passage?

____

____

Target Reading Skill

Mark the Text

Look at the first paragraph on this page. Which sentence represents the main idea of this paragraph? Circle it.

✓ Reading Check

Where was each point of the triangular trade located?

1. ____________________

2. ____________________

3. ____________________

Chapter 17 Assessment

1. The capital of the Aztec empire was at
   A. Yucatán.
   B. Atahualpa.
   C. Moctezuma.
   D. Tenochtitlán.

2. Portugal's colony in the Americas was located in
   A. Peru.
   B. the Caribbean.
   C. Brazil.
   D. Mexico.

3. To rule the Americas, Spain divided its lands into
   A. colonies.
   B. viceroyalties.
   C. provinces.
   D. encomiendas.

4. At the time of the French and Indian War, the English and French were already competing for power in
   A. India and Europe.
   B. India and China.
   C. Africa and China.
   D. Africa and Europe.

5. Which European country began the African slave trade?
   A. Spain
   B. Portugal
   C. France
   D. England

Short Answer Question

What were the three corners of the triangular trade?

____

____

____

____

____

CHAPTER 18

Prepare to Read

Section 1 Spain's Growing Power

Objectives

1. Understand why the Spanish Empire grew in the 1500s.
2. Learn about the reign of King Philip II.
3. Discover why Spain's power began to decline in the late 1500s.

Target Reading Skill

Previewing and Using Prior Knowledge Prior knowledge is what you already know about a topic. For example, viewing the preview to a movie gives you clues about the movie. Before reading a section, look at the headings. Think about what you already know about the section topic.

As you preview this section, write down what you know about Spain during the 1500s. As you read, connect what you are learning with what you already know.

Vocabulary Strategy

Recognize Roots Often, a few letters may be attached to the beginning or end of a word to make another word. For example, the letters *un-* may be attached at the beginning of a word. Or the letters *-ing* may be attached at the end of a word. After those extra letters are removed, what is left is called the root. A root is a word that is used to make other words. The word *well* is the root of the word *unwell*. The word *carry* is the root for *carrying*. Adding a few letters to the beginning or end of a word changes its meaning.

When you come across a new word, see if it contains any other words that you already know. You can use a new word's root to help you figure out what it means.

Section 1 Summary

The Spanish Empire Grows

In the late 1400s, Spain began a golden era of great power. Isabella and Ferdinand defeated the Moors, and Spanish explorers claimed land around the world. Spanish trips brought back tons of treasure from the Americas.

In 1517, Charles I became king of Spain. He also **inherited** another empire in Europe. It included the Netherlands and parts of Italy. He soon became emperor of the Holy Roman Empire. There, he was called Charles V. Spain also had lands in the Americas and the Philippines. ✓

Spain did well under Charles I. But his **reign** was full of challenges. As a Catholic, he fought Martin Luther and his followers in the Holy Roman Empire. But he was unable to stop them. He also helped lead the Catholic Reformation. Spain fought many wars with France while Charles was in power. He also faced military threats from the Ottomans. They had an empire based in what is now Turkey.

The Reign of Philip II

In the 1550s, Charles gave up his role as king of Spain and leader of the Holy Roman Empire. His brother, Ferdinand, took over the Holy Roman Empire and Charles's son, Philip II, became king of Spain. Under Philip II, Spain was perhaps the strongest and richest country on earth.

Philip was a firm believer in the Catholic Church. He also believed in absolute rule. He held all power over the government and the lives of the people. He did what he could to get rid of the people who were not Catholic.

Vocabulary Strategy

Each of the underlined words in these paragraphs contains another word that is its root. Circle the roots. The root of the first word, *golden*, is *gold*.

Mark the Text

✓ Reading Check

What two names were given to Spain's Charles?

1. ______________________

2. ______________________

Key Terms

inherit (in HAYR it) *v.* receive from a family member who has died
reign (RAYN) *n.* a period of rule

One way Philip did this was through the **Inquisition**. In some cases, people who refused to accept Catholic teachings were killed. Through the Inquisition, Philip managed to drive Protestants, Jews, and Muslims out of Spain.

There were new conflicts with the Ottomans. Philip put together a fleet that battled the Ottomans in the Mediterranean Sea. The Ottoman fleet was defeated. ✓

Philip later turned to another enemy. In the late 1500s, England was ruled by the Protestant queen Elizabeth I. At one time, Philip had tried to marry Elizabeth. In that way, he hoped to spread the Catholic faith to England. When that did not work, he looked to conquer England.

✓ Reading Check

Who threatened Philip II?

____

____

Spain's Power in Decline

Spain was a great naval power. To defeat England, Philip II put together a huge fleet of warships called the Spanish Armada. Spain believed the Armada was unbeatable. But English warships and bad weather nearly destroyed the Armada. ✓

This defeat weakened Spain. But there were other reasons for Spain's decline. Spain had suffered losses fighting Protestants in the Netherlands, and parts of the Netherlands declared independence.

Spain was also spending a lot of money to run its empire. The Jewish and Muslim people had played an important part in the Spanish economy. Now they were gone. This added to Spain's problems.

The Spanish leaders after Philip did not do as well. Soon, new countries would take over Spain's role as the major power in Europe.

✓ Reading Check

What two forces nearly destroyed the Spanish Armada?

1. ______________________________

2. ______________________________

Target Reading Skill

What do you know about the Reformation that helps you understand Philip's actions against people who were not Catholic?

____

____

____

Review Questions

1. How did Charles I help the Spanish Empire grow?

____

____

2. What part did religion play in the reign of Philip II?

____

____

Key Term

Inquisition (in kwuh ZIH shun) *n.* a Catholic organization that held trials for people accused of false beliefs

Prepare to Read

Section 2
France's Power Peaks

Objectives

1. Understand developments in the 1500s and 1600s that led to the rise of a strong French monarchy.
2. Learn about France under King Louis XIV.

Target Reading Skill

Preview and Set a Purpose Reading a textbook is different from reading a novel or the newspaper. To read effectively, you must set a reason for your reading.

Before you read this section, take a moment to look at it. Flip through the next two pages. Read each heading. They tell you what to expect to learn from each section. As you glance ahead, set your purpose for reading.

The title of this section is "France's Power Peaks." The objectives and headings are related to the title. In this section, you can expect to learn about the developments that led to a strong French kingdom. And you will learn about France under its strongest king, Louis XIV.

Vocabulary Strategy

Recognize Roots Often, a few letters may be attached to the beginning or end of a word to make another word. Usually, the letters attached to the root make one or more syllable. A syllable is a group of letters that are spoken as a single sound. Some syllables added at the beginning of words include *de-*, *non-*, and *un-*. Some syllables added at the end of words include *-ic*, *-ing*, and *-ly*. Think of some of the words you know that start or end with these syllables.

When you come across a new word, look at it closely. See if it contains any other words you already know. Use the new word's root to help you figure out what it means.

Section 2 Summary

A Strong French Monarchy

France had suffered a lot during the Reformation. Fighting was common between Catholics and Protestants. In France, Protestants were known as Huguenots (HYOO guh nahtz). The worst conflict was the St. Bartholomew's Day Massacre when Catholics murdered thousands of Huguenots.

Henry IV was a Huguenot who became king of France. In order to get the support of important groups in France he became a Catholic. But he also put in place important protections for Huguenots. Under Henry, France had a period of religious peace. His policies also helped the French economy do well.

When Henry IV died, he was followed by Louis XIII. At the time, Louis was only a young boy. One of the leaders of his **administration** was Cardinal Armand Richelieu (kahrd un ul ahr mund rish loo). Richelieu made many government policies. He wanted to build relations with Protestant governments, but he limited the power of the Huguenots in France. His work strengthened the power of the monarchy. ✓

France Under Louis XIV

When Louis XIV became king he was also a young boy. Because of this, he did not rule France directly for many years. During this time, there was a revolt in France. It was called the *Fronde* (frohnd). It created disorder and threatened the power of the king. Louis decided such a thing would never happen again. When he was 22, he finally took direct control of France. He intended to rule as an absolute monarch, or with complete power.

Key Term

administration (ad min is tray shun) *n.* a group of people who work with and for a leader

Vocabulary Strategy

Mark the Text

Each of the underlined words in these paragraphs contains another word that is its root. Circle the roots you find in these words. The root of the first word, *Protestants*, is *protest*.

Target Reading Skill

List two events that may have played an important role in Louis XIV's view of monarchy.

✓ Reading Check

Under which king did Cardinal Richelieu serve?

Louis XIV is famous for saying, "I am the state." This describes the idea that all power went through him. Under Louis XIV, local officials and nobles lost power. Louis XIV ruled on all matters of French life. He even chose the sun as his symbol because the sun is the center of the universe. Louis XIV is known as the Sun King.

Louis XIV believed in the **divine right of kings.** This meant that God decides who should be king. Therefore, rising up against the king was the same as rising up against God.

Huguenots suffered terribly under Louis XIV, who was Catholic. Many left France, including leading merchants and skilled workers. The loss of these people hurt the French economy. ✓

✓ Reading Check

What was Louis XIV's religion, and how did that affect France?

____

____

Louis XIV was willing to use France's military power. France was involved in several wars, which cost France a great deal. The worst was the War of the Spanish Succession. It grew out of a disagreement over whether Louis XIV's grandson should become king of Spain. It left France weak and in debt.

France was still a major power in Europe when Louis XIV died. But much of its power was gone. France would soon lose its colonies in North America. And England, the great sea power, was becoming Europe's leading power.

Review Questions

1. What was the St. Bartholomew's Day Massacre?

____

____

2. How did the *Fronde* help shape Louis XIV's attitudes about government?

____

____

Key Term

divine right of kings (du vyn ryt uv kinz) *n.* the idea that God decides who will be king

Prepare to Read

Section 3
Monarchies in Russia, Prussia, and Austria

Objectives

1. Learn about the rise of the Russian monarchy.
2. Discover why strong monarchs came to power in other parts of Europe.

Target Reading Skill

Preview and Predict Making predictions about what you will learn from your text helps you set a purpose for reading. It also helps you remember what you have read. Before you begin reading, look at the section's title, objectives, and headings. Then predict what the section will tell you. Based on your preview, you will probably predict that this section will tell you about how humans lived in Russia, Prussia and Austria.

List two facts you expect to learn about monarchies in Russia, Prussia, and Austria.

1. ______________________________

2. ______________________________

As you read, check your predictions. Were they accurate? If not, you may need to pay closer attention to previewing.

Vocabulary Strategy

Recognize Roots Often, syllables or groups of syllables are added to the beginning or end of a word to make a new word. The meaning of the new word is related to the original word. For example, we can add the syllable *un-* at the beginning of *well*. The new word, *unwell*, means the opposite of the original word, *well*. It is still related to the original word because it uses the original word as its root.

When you come across a new word, look at it closely. See if it contains any other words you already know. Use a new word's root to help you figure out what it means.

Section 3 Summary

Vocabulary Strategy

Each of the underlined words in these paragraphs contains another word that is its root. Circle the roots you find in these words. The root of the first word, *loved*, is *love*.

Mark the Text

Target Reading Skill

Is your prediction on target, according to what you've read so far? If not, revise or change it now.

____

____

____

✓ Reading Check

Which two monarchs helped lead Russia to join as leaders in Europe?

1. ______________________

2. ______________________

Peter I was the **czar** of Russia, but he loved the customs and manners of western Europe. He wanted the people of Russia to look and act like the people of western Europe. He ordered Russian men to shave off their beards. Those who did not would have to pay a beard tax!

You have read about strong monarchies in Spain and France. Peter I—or Peter the Great, as he was known—was a Russian example of a strong monarch. As you will see, many European nations were moving toward strong monarchies.

The Rise of the Russian Monarch

Peter the Great helped make Russia one of the leading powers of Europe. Peter I built a great army, which he used to wage war on Sweden. He wanted to give Russia land along the Baltic Sea. In this new territory, Peter built the city of St. Petersburg. It became the capital of his government. Peter the Great directed changes that affected many areas of Russian life.

The next great Russian ruler was Catherine the Great. She further expanded Russia's territory. She made major changes in the Russian economy. She wanted to modernize farming and industry. Her leadership helped place Russia more firmly among the great nations of Europe. ✓

Other Strong European Monarchs

Many European monarchs were using absolute rule in the 1600s and 1700s. This was true also in the countries of Prussia and Austria.

Prussia rose to power in the late 1600s. Its first ruler was Frederick William I. He began building a powerful army. It became the most important institution in Prussian life.

Key Term

czar (zahr) *n.* the title given to the Russian monarch

In 1740, Frederick II became king of Prussia. He also used the army to expand Prussia. He also made changes in education and the economy. He built a strong and united Prussia. For those reasons, he is remembered as Frederick the Great.

One of the countries Frederick the Great fought was Austria. It was ruled by Maria Theresa. Because she was a woman, she had not been raised to rule Austria. She came to the throne when her father, Charles VI, died without a male **heir**.

Maria Theresa ruled with great power. She built a strong army, which was effective in fighting Frederick the Great's army. She also set up a fair justice system and a strong government. She united Austria and made it one of Europe's leading powers. ✓

Strong Monarchies in Europe

Russia	Prussia	Austria
• Built a strong army • Used army to expand land • Reformed economy • Modernized farming and industry	• Built a strong army • Used army to expand land • Reformed education • Reformed economy • Strengthened and united Prussia	• Built a strong army • Used army to protect Austria • Created fair justice system • Created strong government • United Austria • Made Austria a leading power

Review Questions

1. What city did Peter the Great build?

____

____

2. Why was Maria Theresa not prepared to rule her country?

____

____

✓ Reading Check

What monarchs made Prussia and Austria strong and united?

Prussia: ____________________

Austria: ____________________

Key Term

heir (ehr) *n.* a person who inherits something from someone

Prepare to Read

Section 4
Limited Monarchy in England

Objectives

1. Learn about England's strong monarchs in the 1600s and their conflicts with Parliament.
2. Understand the events and outcome of the English Civil War.
3. Explore the significance of the Restoration and the Glorious Revolution.

Target Reading Skill

Previewing and Questioning Before you read this section, look at the title, headings, and objectives to see what the section is about. What do you think are the most important ideas in the section? How can you tell?

After you preview the section, write two questions that will help you understand or remember important points or facts in the section. For example, you might ask yourself:

- What was the English Civil War?
- What was the Glorious Revolution?

Find the answers to your questions as you read. Then keep asking questions about what you think will come next. Does the text answer your questions?

Vocabulary Strategy

Recognize Roots The meaning of a word that has a syllable added to either its beginning or end is related to the original word because it uses the original word as its root. In some cases, the spelling changes slightly. Often, a final *e* is dropped from the root when a new ending is added. For example, if *-y* is added to the end of the word *ease*, it is spelled *easy* (and **not** *easey*!). Sometimes, *-y* at the end of a word is often changed to *i* when a new ending is added. To build on the previous example, add the ending *-ly* to *easy*. First you have to change the final *y* to an *i*, and the result is the word *easily*.

Section 4 Summary

England's Monarchs in the Early 1600s

The Magna Carta gave the English people certain rights. It was a legal document that also said the monarchs had to obey the laws. These ideas became a strong tradition in English life. England's Parliament, or government, helped the monarch rule.

When Elizabeth I died without an heir, James I became king of England. He already had been king of Scotland for 36 years.

James I had different ideas about ruling England. He believed in the divine right of kings. He often acted as though he wanted to rule England by himself, without Parliament's help. This angered Parliament.

Charles I, James's son, became king and he was even more angry toward Parliament than his father had been. In fact, Charles I shut down Parliament. He did not allow it to meet for several years.

Relations between the king and Parliament got worse when Parliament was re-established. In time, the king's enemies in Parliament put together an army. This army battled against forces loyal to the king. **Civil war** broke out in England. ✓

English Civil War

The parliamentary force was called the Roundheads because they had short hair. Their first big battle with the king's forces was a tie. The Roundheads and their allies soon took control, however, and Charles I was taken prisoner.

The king's enemies were soon fighting among themselves. A group led by Oliver Cromwell (AHL uh vur KRAHM wel) won. They wanted to defend people's rights against the absolute power of the king. Parliament put Charles I on trial. He was found guilty of **treason** and was executed in 1649. ✓

Key Terms

civil war (siv ul wawr) *n.* a war among different parts of the same group or country

treason (tree zur) *n.* betrayal of one's country

Vocabulary Strategy

Each of the underlined words in this section contains a root that has had a spelling change before the ending was added. Write the full roots below.

✓ Reading Check

What did James I and Charles I think of Parliament?

✓ Reading Check

Of what crime was Charles I found guilty?

Target Reading Skill

Ask and answer a question about Cromwell and the English Civil War.

Question: ______________________

____

Answer: ______________________

____

England was now led by Oliver Cromwell and Parliament. But Cromwell found Parliament hard to work with. After a few years, he closed Parliament and became the absolute ruler of England. Because he was not a king, he ruled as lord protector.

The Restoration and Glorious Revolution

During Cromwell's time, many people wanted the monarchy back. They even asked Cromwell to become king, but he refused. When he died, his son Richard took power.

Soon, Charles I's son arrived in England and brought a small army with him. He had escaped to France when his father was killed. Charles II gained the support of the English people and forced Richard Cromwell from power. Charles II became king of England. But arguments with Parliament continued. Charles asked for money and troops from King Louis XIV of France.

Charles's brother, James II, took power next. The clash with Parliament got worse. Parliament asked William of Orange, the ruler of Holland, to take power. That's when James left England. A year later, William III and Mary II became England's king and queen. This change of power is called the **Glorious Revolution**. It took place peacefully. The new monarchs agreed to a document called the Bill of Rights. It made Parliament more powerful than the monarchy. It also protected English citizens. ✓

✓ Reading Check

Who followed James II as rulers of England?

____

____

____

Review Questions

1. Who was king when the English Civil War started?

____

____

2. What was the English Bill of Rights?

____

____

Chapter 18 Assessment

1. What was the Inquisition?
   - A. a Catholic organization that held trials for people accused of false beliefs
   - B. a council that helped Charles V rule the Holy Roman Empire
   - C. the Spanish council that helped Philip II rule Spain
   - D. a war between the Spanish and the Ottomans

2. Which of the following best explains the importance of the Spanish Armada?
   - A. It was a great victory that gave France even more power in Europe.
   - B. The defeat of the Armada led to the decline of Spanish power.
   - C. The Armada improved Russian access to the Baltic Sea.
   - D. The Armada defeated the Ottoman fleet.

3. Cardinal Richelieu was a key figure in the administration of which ruler?
   - A. Henry IV of France
   - B. Louis XIII of France
   - C. Louis XIV of France
   - D. Maria Theresa of Austria

4. Which Russian ruler moved the capital to St. Petersburg?
   - A. Catherine the Great
   - B. Maria Theresa
   - C. Frederick the Great
   - D. Peter the Great

5. Which of the following figures is connected with the English Civil War?
   - A. William III and Mary II
   - B. James I
   - C. Oliver Cromwell
   - D. Cardinal Armand Richelieu

Short Answer Question

What is absolute rule?

____

____

____

____

CHAPTER 19

Prepare to Read

Section 1 The Enlightenment

Objectives

1. Learn about the approaches to science that began in the 1500s.
2. Identify discoveries of the Scientific Revolution.
3. Understand the ideas of the Enlightenment.
4. Find out how the Enlightenment affected governments.

Target Reading Skill

Using Context Clues As you read, you may find a word that is unfamiliar to you. Or you may find a word that is used in an unfamiliar way. Look for clues in the context to help you understand the word's meaning. The context is the surrounding words, phrases, and sentences.

For example, you can use a context clue to figure out the meaning of *royalty*:

People believed kings and other *royalty* could collect taxes.

The phrase *kings and other royalty* is a clue that royalty are people who are like kings.

Vocabulary Strategy

Use Roots and Suffixes A suffix is one or more syllables attached to the end of a word to make a new word. The word the suffix is attached to is known as the root. The new word is a combination of the two meanings.

Some common suffixes are listed below, along with their meanings. Notice some of them have more than one form or meaning. Learning to identify suffixes will help you understand what you read.

Suffix	Meaning	Example
-al	of or like	coastal
-ation	act of; condition of being; result of	alteration; starvation
-ism	act or practice of; doctrine of	terrorism; socialism
-ment	act or result of; condition of being	improvement; disappointment

Section 1 Summary

Scientific Discoveries Encourage New Attitudes

New ideas inspired by humanism and the Reformation spread across Europe in the 1500s and 1600s. Scientists began to understand the world in a new way. They began to rely more on reason and logic such as the **scientific method**. Experiments using the scientific method can be repeated by others. Discoveries made by scientists of this period changed the way people lived.

Sometimes the results of these experiments did not agree with the teachings of the Roman Catholic Church. Galileo Gallilei (gal uh LEE oh gal uh LAY) proved that the planets revolved around the sun. The Church taught that the sun and planets revolved around Earth. Galileo was put on trial by the Catholic Church and sentenced to life in jail. Other scientists and writers were also jailed for going against the church. Their writings were banned. ✓

New ideas spread throughout Europe and changed the way people thought about religion, politics, human nature, and society.

The Scientific Revolution

Galileo lived and worked during a period now called the Scientific Revolution. It began in about the mid-1500s and lasted for 200 years. The first book showing the structure of the human body was created in 1543. William Harvey, an English doctor, discovered how the heart circulates blood in the body. ✓

In the mid-1700s, the British scientist Sir Isaac Newton studied the motion of the planets and objects on Earth. His theories about **natural laws** included laws of motion and gravity.

Key Terms

scientific method (sy un TIF ik METH ud) *n.* a way of performing experiments
natural laws (NACH ur ul lawz) *n.* the patterns that control the behavior of the universe

Vocabulary Strategy

Mark the Text

The words below appear in this section and each contains a suffix. Underline the suffix in each word. As you do so, think about what each suffix means.

humanism
teaching
natural
organization
royalty
government

✓ Reading Check

How did the Catholic Church react when scientific theories differed from church teachings?

____

____

✓ Reading Check

How did William Harvey advance scientific knowledge?

____

____

✓ Reading Check

What five areas were affected by the Enlightenment?

1. ____________________

2. ____________________

3. ____________________

4. ____________________

5. ____________________

Target Reading Skill

What context clues help you understand what *Enlightenment* means?

____

____

✓ Reading Check

Which European rulers were affected by Enlightenment thinking?

____

____

____

New Ways of Thinking

Scientists and thinkers used Newton's approach to look for other natural laws. They looked for natural laws in human behavior as well. Scientific organizations were formed to share new knowledge.

This movement became known as the **Enlightenment**. It is sometimes called the Age of Reason because people thought the world could be understood through intelligence. It affected politics, art, literature, science, and religion. ✓

The Enlightenment Affects Government

For many years, European monarchs claimed to have **divine right**. An English writer, Thomas Hobbes, even published a book that supported the power of royalty. He thought people needed a king to keep order.

Others, such as English writer John Locke disagreed. He wrote that a government should rule only if it protected people's **natural rights**. Otherwise, people should overthrow the government.

Frederick the Great of Prussia made changes inspired by Enlightenment ideas. He kept absolute power, but he believed he should work for the good of all. He made laws more fair to all people.

Joseph II of Austria allowed religious freedom and limited the power of the Catholic Church. He reformed laws, freed the serfs, and allowed opposing ideas to be published. ✓

Review Questions

1. How did the Scientific Revolution affect thinkers across Europe?

____

____

2. Explain how Enlightenment ideas helped some peasants and serfs in Europe.

____

Key Terms

Enlightenment (en LYT un munt) *n.* science and natural laws bringing people to a more enlightened state

divine rights (duh VYN rytz) *n.* the theory that monarchs were chosen by God to rule others and answered only to God

natural rights (NACH ur ul rytz) *n.* the rights to life, liberty, and property

CHAPTER 19

Prepare to Read

Section 2 Political Revolutions

Objectives

1. Learn why Great Britain established colonies in North America.
2. Understand the American Revolution.
3. Identify reasons for the French Revolution.
4. Explore the effects of the French Revolution.

Target Reading Skill

Recognizing Nonliteral Meanings Sometimes figurative, or descriptive, language is used to explain a meaning. Figurative language is poetic. It does not mean what the words seem to mean. It uses figures of speech, such as metaphors, to create an image. Literal language means exactly what it says.

As you read, look for words that have figurative meanings and substitute a word that gives a more literal meaning.

For example, look at the word *spark* in the following sentence:

These new beliefs would *spark* a revolution in North America.

What is a word that could replace *spark*?

Vocabulary Strategy

Use Roots and Suffixes A suffix is one or more syllables attached to the end of a word to make a new word. The word the suffix is attached to is known as the root. The meaning of the suffix can change the meaning of the new word. The new word is a combination of the two meanings.

Some suffixes are listed below, along with their meanings. Notice some of them have more than one form or meaning. Learning to identify suffixes will help you understand what you read.

Suffix	Meaning	Example
-ative	of or relating to, serving to, tending to	informative
-dom	position or domain of; condition of being	kingdom; wisdom
-ion	the act or condition of; the result of	reaction; production

Section 2 Summary

Britain Establishes Colonies in North America

Great Britain used its North American **colonies** to make money. Private companies had established some settlements hoping to make profits. ✓

By the mid-1700s, most of the colonies were ruled by royal governors. Laws said that all goods shipped from the colonies had to be sent on British ships. The British government also provided protection.

The American Revolution

The British wanted the colonies to help pay for their defense, but the colonists did not have elected representatives in Parliament (PAHR luh munt). Some leaders in the colonies argued that the British were not respecting their natural rights.

The colonists tried to get the British to change their policies. When this did not work, colony representatives signed the Declaration of Independence in Philadelphia in July 1776. Led by George Washington, the colonists won a war for independence in 1781.

Leaders of the newly independent colonies agreed to be governed as one country under the Articles of Confederation (AHR tih kulz uv kun fed ur AY shun). But the national government was weak and there were conflicts between colonies. In 1787, representatives met to write a **constitution**. A Bill of Rights was added. These amendments guaranteed specific rights to the people. ✓

Revolution in France

The American Revolution was one of the first in which ordinary citizens overthrew a royal power. Its success sparked an interest in **democracy** in France.

Key Terms

colony (KAHL uh nee) *n.* a territory that is ruled by another country and is usually very far from the ruling country

constitution (kahn stuh TOO shun) *n.* a set of rules explaining the structure and powers of the government

democracy (dih MAHK ruh see) *n.* a political system in which people freely elect government leaders

✓ Reading Check

Why did private companies help establish colonies in North America?

____

____

____

Vocabulary Strategy

Mark the Text

The words below appear in this section and each contains a suffix. Underline the suffix in each word and think about what each suffix means.

settlement

protection

representative

amendment

✓ Reading Check

How were the Articles of Confederation and the Constitution different?

____

____

Target Reading Skill

Look at the word *sparked* in this paragraph. What is a word that you can use to replace *sparked*?

____

____

In 1789, France was almost out of money. There were food shortages. The common people wanted a more representative government and called a National Assembly to write a new constitution. King Louis XVI sent troops to break up their meeting.

On July 14, French citizens stormed the Bastille (bas TEEL). It was a Paris prison where they hoped to find weapons. The fighting spread across the country.

During the next two years, the National Assembly changed the French government. It passed the Declaration of the Rights of Man and of the Citizen. It set up a representative government and expanded voting rights.

The king, nobles, and clergy opposed many of these changes. Many nobles left the country and convinced the rulers of Prussia and Austria to invade France. As these armies got close to Paris, the king and his family were arrested. ✓

✓ Reading Check

Why did Prussia and Austria invade France?

____

____

Effects of the French Revolution

A period of violence known as the Reign of Terror (rayn uf TEHR ur) began. Hundreds of thousands of people were arrested. About 17,000 were executed. The Jacobins (JAK uh binz) were a radical group that ruled as dictators.

The Jacobins passed some reforms. They included free schooling for all children and a tax system based on income. An army was raised to fight against European powers that opposed the changes in France. ✓

✓ Reading Check

What was a reform passed by the Jacobins?

____

____

____

After the Reign of Terror, a new government was formed. It was called the Directory. It did away with many of the reforms the Jacobins had passed.

Review Questions

1. How did Americans change their form of government after they won the Revolutionary War?

____

____

2. What political group ruled France during the Reign of Terror?

____

____

CHAPTER 19

Prepare to Read

Section 3 The Age of Napoleon

Objectives

1. Learn how Napoleon rose to power in France and began a large empire.
2. Understand some reforms Napoleon made and why he lost power.

Target Reading Skill

Using Context Clues When you come across an unfamiliar word, you can often figure out its meaning from its context. Context refers to the surrounding words, phrases, and sentences. Sometimes the context will include a definition. Sometimes the context gives a description of a word. The following sentence gives a description of the word *alliance*.

> At one time, France and Spain formed an *alliance* to fight together against the British.

What does the word *alliance* mean?

Vocabulary Strategy

Use Roots and Suffixes A suffix is one or more syllables attached to the end of a word to make a new word. The meaning of the suffix can change the meaning of the new word. The new word is a combination of the two meanings.

Some common suffixes are listed below, along with their meanings and examples. Notice that some of them have more than one form. Also, some have more than one meaning. Learning to identify suffixes, and knowing what they mean, will help you understand what you read.

Suffix	Meaning	Example
-ance	act or process; quality or state of	continuance; importance
-ant, -ent	that has, shows, or does	defiant; insistent
-est	most (added to an adjective or adverb)	greatest
-ic	like or having to do with	angelic
-or, -er	a person or thing that does something	actor; worker
-ship	the quality or condition of; skill as	friendship; leadership

Section 3 Summary

Napoleon Takes Power and Builds an Empire

French armies made gains against other European empires in the late 1700s. At the same time, the power of the Directory was weakened. A young military officer, Napoleon Bonaparte, had gained fame from fighting against the Austrian Empire.

In 1799, Napoleon learned Austria, Great Britain, Turkey, and Russia had joined together to defeat France. He took away power from the Directory. After ten years of war, the French people wanted a strong leader. In 1802, they made Napoleon leader for life. Two years later, he made himself emperor. ✓

Napoleon continued his wars against other European kingdoms. He wanted to build the greatest empire in history. By 1812, he controlled most of Europe. He made alliances with other countries to extend his control. Often, he put friends and relatives in power in the countries he had conquered. That way, he guaranteed their friendship and support. Only Great Britain was strong enough to resist him.

The Napoleonic Era

Napoleon ruled as a dictator. A dictator is a person who has absolute power. Even so, he carried out many reforms that had first been thought of during the French Revolution. They made him very popular with the French people.

One important reform was the **Napoleonic Code**. It was a simplified version of the French legal system. It protected property rights and expanded the power of employers over employees.

✓ Reading Check

How did Napoleon first become popular with the French people?

____

____

____

Vocabulary Strategy

Mark the Text

The words below appear in this section and each contains a suffix. Underline the suffix in each word. As you do so, think about what each suffix means.

kingdom
greatest
alliance
friendship
dictator
Napoleonic

Key Term

Napoleonic Code (huh poh lee AHN ik kohd) *n.* a set of laws that protects individual liberty, the right to work, and the right to one's own opinions

During the Revolution, the Catholic Church had come under government control, and Napoleon gave Catholics the right to worship as they wanted. He also started schools and built roads and canals. He set up a central bank, controlled prices on food and other needs, and supported new business and industry.

But Napoleon did not allow anyone to question his decisions. His wars cost France a lot, destroyed some of the great cities of Europe, and killed many thousands of people.

Napoleon was unable to defeat Great Britain. For years, he tried to weaken Britain's economy. He set up a **blockade** of Britain. ✓

✓ Reading Check

Why did Napoleon set up a blockade of Great Britain?

____

____

____

Next, Napoleon invaded Russia. He met with defeat. Four European countries joined forces against France. After a string of losses, the French refused to fight. Napoleon was **exiled** from France in 1814. A new king, Louis XVIII, was put on the throne.

A year later, Napoleon escaped from exile and returned to France. Louis XVIII fled the country. That same year Napoleon was defeated at the Battle of Waterloo in Belgium. He was again exiled. This time, exile lasted until his death in 1821.

Target Reading Skill

What context clues help to define the term *exile*?

____

____

Napoleon's rule had a great effect on France. Many of his reforms are the basis for today's French government and society. Many of the laws and systems in France are still based on Napoleonic Code. Although the lands Napoleon conquered were run fairly, the people wanted to rule themselves. They wanted to create nations of their own.

Review Questions

1. How was France threatened when Napoleon took control?

____

____

2. Which country was France's strongest enemy?

____

____

Key Terms

blockade (blah KAYD) *n.* the banning of trade
exile (EK syl) *v.* to send away

CHAPTER 19

Prepare to Read

Section 4 The Industrial Revolution in Europe and the United States

Objectives

1. Learn how farming methods improved and why the population in Europe grew quickly.
2. Understand reasons that Great Britain led the Industrial Revolution.
3. Find out how the United States expanded and improved industrial techniques.
4. Consider how the Industrial Revolution changed people's lives.

Target Reading Skill

Recognizing Nonliteral Meanings Sometimes figurative, or descriptive, language is used to convey meaning. Figurative language is poetic and may not mean what the words would seem to mean. Instead, it uses figures of speech, such as metaphors, to create an image. Literal language means exactly what it says.

As you read, look for words that have figurative meanings and substitute a word that gives a more literal meaning.

In the sentence below, what does *soared* mean?

Food was hard to find, so food prices *soared*.

Vocabulary Strategy

Use Roots and Suffixes A suffix is one or more syllables attached to the end of a word to make a new word. The word the suffix is attached to is known as the root. The suffix can change the meaning of a word.

A few suffixes are listed below. Learning to identify suffixes, and knowing what they mean, will help you understand what you read.

Suffix	Meaning	Example
-able, -ible	capable of being; likely to	breakable; combustible
-ful	full of, characterized by, having	joyful; beautiful; artful
-less	without	treeless

Section 4 Summary

Changes in the Rural Population

Before the 1700s, most people in Great Britain and Europe lived as they had lived for hundreds of years. After 1700, the British began to study farming as a science, making farming more profitable. Changes in farming made it easier to produce more food. The population grew quickly. This increased the demand for goods such as **textiles**.

In the 1760s, new machines were invented that could make textiles more cheaply and quickly than before. Merchants built successful **factories**. More and more factories shot up all over Great Britain. By the 1780s, there were over 120 textile mills in Britain. ✓

Merchants who made other products began to build factories to increase their profits. These developments were the beginning of the **Industrial Revolution**.

Great Britain Leads the Industrial Revolution

The Industrial Revolution began in the 1760s. Britain had large deposits of coal and iron. Coal was used as fuel for the industrial machines. Iron was used to build the machines and support large buildings. Later, it was used to build railroads. ✓

Great Britain also had a stable government and powerful empire. Its colonies provided natural resources and a market for finished products.

An English inventor created the steam engine and Scottish inventor James Watt made it practical for use. In 1825, the world's first steam railroad went into service in England. This made it possible to travel much farther in less time.

Key Terms

textiles (TEXT tylz) *n.* woven cloths used to make goods
factories (FAK tuh reez) *n.* buildings in which people work
Industrial Revolution (in DUS tree ul rev uh LOO shun) *n.* the development of new machines and the creation of factories

Vocabulary Strategy

Mark the Text

The words below appear in this section and each contains a suffix. Underline the suffix in each word. As you do so, think about what each suffix means.

farming
profitable
cheaply
development
industrial

Target Reading Skill

The phrase *shot up* is used figuratively in the second paragraph. What is another phrase you could substitute for *shot up*?

____
____

✓ Reading Check

How were coal and iron used during the Industrial Revolution?

Coal: ______________________________
____

Iron: ______________________________
____

Industrial Expansion in the United States

The United States had many of the same industrial advantages as Great Britain. It had large supplies of natural resources and a stable government and economy.

Eli Whitney, a gun manufacturer, developed a new technique using **interchangeability** of parts. Before this, guns had been made one at a time. By making parts interchangeable, companies could begin to make products in much greater numbers. This led to a rapid growth in production in the United States because it could be used for many products. ✓

✓ Reading Check

Who created the idea of interchangeable parts?

____

____

____

Industrialization quickly spread. By 1860, more than half the miles of the world's railroad tracks were in the United States. The invention of the telegraph made it possible to communicate quickly over many miles. Americans also discovered new ways to grind grain and to make gasoline and other products from oil.

Effects of Industrialization

The Industrial Revolution changed working conditions and life in cities. It increased wealth. New factories drew workers to fill jobs. Cities grew rapidly. ✓

✓ Reading Check

Why did new cities grow so quickly during the Industrial Revolution?

____

____

Factory workers often worked long hours and conditions were dangerous. Women and children did some of the worst jobs. Many of the machines were not safe. The air was often hard to breathe because of dust. But the quality of life improved for the working class.

Review Questions

1. Why did Great Britain lead the Industrial Revolution?

____

____

2. What features did the U.S. share with Great Britain that allowed industrialization to develop rapidly?

____

____

Key Term

interchangeability (in tur chaynj uh BIL uh tee) *n.* making the same parts of a product identical

Chapter 19 Assessment

1. Which scientist wrote about natural laws of motion and gravity?
   - A. Galileo Galilee
   - B. William Harvey
   - C. Sir Isaac Newton
   - D. James Watts

2. According to Locke, what should people do if a government does not grant them their natural rights?
   - A. They should overthrow the government.
   - B. They should rely on the church.
   - C. They should move to another country.
   - D. They should elect a new president.

3. The original government of the newly independent United States was established under the
   - A. Directory.
   - B. Parliament.
   - C. National Assembly.
   - D. Articles of Confederation.

4. Which of the following was a provision of the Napoleonic Code?
   - A. It protected property rights.
   - B. It protected individual liberty.
   - C. It protected the right to one's opinion.
   - D. All of the above

5. What is one result of the Industrial Revolution in the nineteenth century?
   - A. Peasants supported the rule of Napoleon.
   - B. Competition for colonies in North America decreased.
   - C. Cities in Europe and the United States grew.
   - D. The pace of scientific discoveries slowed.

Short Answer Question

Why is the Enlightenment sometimes called the Age of Reason?

Prepare to Read

Section 1
Nationalism and Expansion in Europe

Objectives

1. Learn how Enlightenment ideas and changes in Europe in the early 1800s led to a rise in nationalism.
2. Understand changes in France after the fall of Napoleon.
3. Identify causes and results of revolutions in Europe in 1848.
4. Find out how European countries expanded their control.

Target Reading Skill

Identifying the Main Idea The main idea of a paragraph or section is its most important point. The main idea is supported by details that give additional facts. Details tell you what, where, why, how much, or how many.

The main idea of the section titled "The Rise of Nationalism" is the rise of nationalism throughout Europe.

As you read, notice how the facts tell you more about the rise of nationalism in Europe. These are the details that support the main idea.

Vocabulary Strategy

Word Origins Many words in English were borrowed from other languages. Usually, the spelling will change.

In this chapter, you will read the words *revolt* and *revolution*. They both come from the same Latin word, *revolvere*, which means "to revolve."

The word *revolt* can be either a verb or a noun. That is, it can show action, or it can name something. We can say, "The people revolted against their oppressors." In that case, revolt is a verb. Or we can say, "There was a peasant's revolt in Italy." In that case, it is a noun.

The word *revolution* can only be a noun. But *revolutionary* and *revolutionize* have been formed by adding suffixes to it. The suffix *-ary* turns the word into an adjective, or a word that describes something. The suffix -*ize* turns it into a verb, a word that shows action.

Section 1 Summary

After Napoleon's defeat, governments from all over Europe met in Vienna, Austria, to discuss how his empire should be divided.

In the end, kings and queens were put back into power. The Congress of Vienna helped prevent a large war in Europe for 100 years. But many of the countries they created would not last.

The Rise of Nationalism

Napoleon encouraged national songs, holidays, flags, and other symbols to promote patriotic feelings for France. His conquests helped spread ideas about national pride throughout Europe.

The Congress of Vienna tried to put royal families back into power, but the move toward **nationalism** was too strong. During the next 35 years, people across Europe revolted against royal families. They wanted to create and govern their own countries. ✓

France After the Fall of Napoleon

After Napoleon's defeat, King Louis XVIII was put into power. He let voters elect representatives to parliament, but he kept the most important powers for himself.

After Louis's death, his younger brother, Charles X, became king. Charles believed that kings ruled by divine right. He tried to reject the French constitution, but the people revolted. They named a new king, Louis-Philippe, and wrote a new constitution.

Louis-Philippe was known as the "citizen king" because he ruled by consent of the people. ✓

Revolutions Across Europe

These changes in France inspired nationalists in other countries. Revolts in Italy and Switzerland had some success. But the only revolt that created an independent country was in Belgium.

Key Term

nationalism (NASH uh nul iz um) *n.* a feeling of strong loyalty or attachment to a culture, language, and/or territory

Vocabulary Strategy

The word *patriotic* is related to the Latin word *patria*, "fatherland." What are patriotic feelings?

____

____

✓ Reading Check

Why was nationalism especially strong in France?

____

____

✓ Reading Check

Why was Louis-Philippe known as the citizen king?

____

____

The Vienna Congress had joined Belgium, Holland, and Luxembourg to form the Kingdom of the Netherlands. People in these areas spoke different languages and had different religions. They did not want to be one kingdom. ✓

Revolutions of 1848

Louis-Philippe began to act like a royal king from the past. He was overthrown in 1848 and there was an election in which all citizens were allowed to vote. Napoleon III was elected president. A few years later, he declared himself emperor and ruled as a **dictator**.

The Austrian Empire included people of many nationalities. The 1848 revolution in France inspired a revolt in Vienna against the Austrian empire. Other revolutions broke out among the Hungarians, the Czechs, and the Italians. But Austrian troops put down these nationalist movements. ✓

Germans in Berlin also rebelled in 1848, demanding a new constitution. Germans met to write a constitution that would unify the 39 independent German states, but they failed to agree. Prussia regained control.

Italy became independent in 1861. Germany became independent in 1871.

European Expansion and Imperialism

Europeans began to expand their power in Asia, Africa, and the Middle East. The French and the British were the leaders in this move. A new era of **imperialism** began as European countries took over new lands. ✓

Review Questions

1. How did Napoleon instill French pride?

2. How did the overthrow of Charles X change the rights of French citizens?

Key Terms

dictator (DIK tay tur) *n.* a ruler who has complete power

imperialism (im PIHR ee ul iz um) *n.* the policy of forming and maintaining an empire, usually by taking over foreign colonies

✓ Reading Check

What new country was formed by a nationalist revolution in Europe?

✓ Reading Check

Where did the Austrian nationalist movement begin? What other nationalist groups joined the revolt?

Target Reading Skill

What details explain how the revolts in Austria were similar to other revolts in 1848?

✓ Reading Check

In which areas of the world did the Europeans look to expand their control?

Prepare to Read

Section 2
Imperialism in Africa and the Middle East

Objectives

1. Identify the reasons for European colonization in Africa.
2. Examine how European powers made claims on the right to rule Africa.
3. Learn how Africans resisted European colonization.
4. Understand the causes of the Boer War.
5. Understand how Britain gained control of colonies in the Middle East.

Target Reading Skill

Identifying the Main Idea The main idea of a paragraph or section is its most important point. When you identify the main idea, you know what the paragraph or section is about. This will help you remember the most important points.

In some sections, the main idea is not stated directly. All the details in a paragraph or section add up to a main idea. In this case, the main idea is implied. It is up to you to put the details together. You will then be able to see the main idea.

When the main idea is implied, you must determine the main idea from key facts or ideas contained in the section. As you read, consider what the sentences describe and then connect the details to find the main idea.

Vocabulary Strategy

Word Origins Many words in English were borrowed from other languages, but the spelling usually changes.

In this section, you will read the word *campaign*. It comes from the French word *campagne*, which means "open country"—specifically, open country that is suitable for military maneuvers. It has come to mean "military expedition."

Section 2 Summary

European Interest in Africa Grows

In the early 1800s, European nations traded with kingdoms on the northern coast of Africa. Along the West African coast, they mainly engaged in the slave trade. Africans and Arabs controlled interior trade routes. ✓

But European governments, companies, and churches began sending people to explore Africa's interior. By the 1870s, Great Britain and France were competing for trade routes in western Africa. The Germans and Belgians were competing for African lands.

The Scramble for Africa

To avoid wars, European leaders gathered in Berlin in 1884 to make rules for claiming land in Africa. They wanted to set up trading **monopolies**. No African leaders were at the conference.

The Berlin conference set up **partitions** of African lands. Seven countries established areas of control over the next twenty years. They were Spain, Belgium, Portugal, France, Great Britain, Italy, and Germany. ✓

European countries wanted Africa's rich natural resources. After making claims, they set up colonial governments. They built roads and railways to ship goods to ports. Christian **missionaries** ran schools and hospitals throughout the continent.

African Resistance to Colonization

Europeans took over nearly all of Africa by 1914. In many places, they had to fight native groups for control. But the Africans' spears and musket guns were no match for European machine guns. As the scramble for Africa went on, battles became bloodier. In separate **campaigns**, France took control of Madagascar (mad uh GAS kur) and Morocco.

Key Terms

monopoly (muh NAHP uh lee) *n.* the areas in which only one government or company has the right to trade
partition (pahr TISH un) *n.* a division
missionary (MISH un her ee) *n.* people who traveled to other places to convert others to Christian beliefs
campaigns (kam PAYNZ) *n.* a series of military operations in a war

✓ Reading Check

Where in Africa did the Europeans trade in the early 1800s?

____

____

✓ Reading Check

Which European countries set up colonies in Africa?

1. ______________________
2. ______________________
3. ______________________
4. ______________________
5. ______________________
6. ______________________
7. ______________________

Vocabulary Strategy

The word *musket* comes from the French word *mousquet*. What do you think a musketeer is?

____

____

✓ Reading Check

What two African countries successfully resisted the European colonizers in Africa?

The Italians tried to take control of Ethiopia, but the Ethiopians defeated them. The Ethiopians went on to conquer lands to the south and southwest.

Liberia, on Africa's west coast, also kept its independence. It had been settled by freed slaves from the United States. ✓

The missionary schools spread new ideas about how Africans could control their own lives. Growing unrest led to independence movements in the 20th century by African nationalists.

✓ Reading Check

How did the discovery of diamonds and gold in the Boer republics contribute to the Boer War?

The Boer War

In southern Africa, tensions between the British colonial government and Dutch settlers led to war. When Britain seized the Cape Colony, many Dutch settlers, called Boers (bohrz), moved north. They founded two new republics. The British also started a second colony to the east.

Diamonds and gold were discovered in the Boer republics. The British claimed these lands at the Berlin Conference. After a two-year war, the British army defeated the Boers and Britain took over all of South Africa. ✓

✓ Reading Check

What two seas did the Suez Canal connect?

1.

2.

Target Reading Skill

What details in the section about the Boer War help show the main idea?

Britain Seeks Control in the Middle East

The Ottoman Empire once ruled a large part of the Middle East. Napoleon's armies invaded Egypt, but with British help, the French were driven out.

A series of weak rulers then controlled Egypt with British support. A French company was given the right to build a canal at Suez (SOO ez). It would link the Mediterranean and Red seas. In the early 1880s, a series of political revolts broke out, but the British maintained control of Egypt. ✓

Review Questions

1. List the nations involved in the scramble for Africa.

2. Why did most armed resistance by Africans fail?

Prepare to Read

Section 3
Imperialism in Asia and Latin America

Objectives

1. Understand how Britain gained control of China.
2. Explore how Britain ruled India through the East India Company.
3. Find out why Japan successfully resisted Western colonial powers.
4. Learn the effects of revolutions that brought independence to Latin American countries.

Target Reading Skill

Identifying the Implied Main Idea Sometimes the main idea of a paragraph or section is implied rather than directly stated. All the details in a paragraph or section add up to a main idea. In this case, the main idea is implied. It is up to you to put the details together to form the main idea.

For example, the implied main idea of the second paragraph on the next page could be stated this way:

> Instability in China allowed foreign nations to get concessions from the Chinese government.

As you read, note the main ideas that paragraphs and headings imply.

Vocabulary Strategy

Word Origins Many words in English were borrowed from other languages. Sometimes English words just have foreign roots. For example, many words have been made by combining Latin roots. In this chapter, you will read the word *rebellion*. It is formed by adding the prefix *re-* to the Latin root *bellare*:

> *re-* ("again") + *bellare* ("to wage war")

A prefix is a syllable that is added at the beginning of a word or root that changes the word's meaning.

The words *rebel* and *rebellious* are related to *rebellion*. *Rebellion* is a noun, or a word that names something. *Rebel* can be a verb, or a word that shows action, or it can be a noun. (A rebel is a person who rebels.) *Rebellious* is an adjective, which describes something.

Section 3 Summary

Target Reading Skill

What is the implied main idea of the last paragraph?

Expanding Empires in Asia

In the early 1800s, China sold many products to other countries but bought very few. The British forced the Chinese to sign a treaty allowing more trade. It also let Christian missionaries come to China.

The Qing (ching) dynasty could not manage China's problems. There was a 14-year rebellion, or battle against the government. Foreign nations pushed China to give more freedom to foreigners.

Some people wanted to improve Chinese society using Western ideas. Others wanted to limit foreign power. In 1900, a group of nationalists attacked foreigners in many Chinese cities. Troops from Japan and Europe defeated them and forced China to allow even more foreign influence.

In 1600, Britain granted the East India Company a monopoly on trade with India. By the mid-1700s, the Moghul (MOH gul) Empire was weak and the East India Company took over much of the region. Rebellions resulted in British control of the company. The British used **direct rule** and **indirect rule** to govern the colony.

The British improved education, transportation, and communications in India, but limited Indians' chances to become high government officials. Nationalism in India grew. The Indian National Congress made changes to British rule.

In the early 1800s, Japan only traded with Russia and China. Matthew Perry, of the United States, led a small fleet of ships to Japan to open Japanese ports to trade. Perry's request was refused. Eventually, five ports were opened. The Japanese government also gave **extra-territorial rights** to Americans. It made similar agreements with other countries. ✓

✓ Reading Check

Why did Matthew Perry visit Japan?

Key Terms

direct rule (duh REKT rool) *n.* a country's authority over a colony
indirect rule (in duh REKT rool) *n.* the governing of local populations by enforcing colonial law
extra-territorial rights (eks truh tehr uh TAWR ee ul rytz) *n.* the rights of foreigners to be protected by their nation's laws

In 1868, a group called the Meiji Restoration seized power and ruled until 1912. During that time, Japan's government invested in industries, railways, and communications. The education system was reformed and the military modernized.

Japan was now one of Asia's strongest countries. It began an age of imperialism and took control of Taiwan and the Korean peninsula.

Independent Nations in Latin America

Spain controlled Central America and western South America. The spread of Enlightenment ideals and Napoleon's invasion of Spain and Portugal gave colonies a desire for independence. Revolts ended Spanish rule in Latin America. ✓

When Napoleon invaded Portugal, the Portuguese royal family fled to Brazil. They returned to Portugal years later, but left their son, Dom Pedro, to rule Brazil. Pedro declared independence and his son, Pedro II, did much to modernize Brazil.

Most of the new states in Central and South America wrote constitutions similar to that of the United States. But many rulers ignored them and ruled as dictators. Future generations of European settlers did not share power with **indigenous** peoples.

Development required British and U.S. loans. In return, these countries wanted a bigger role in Latin America. This is called **economic imperialism**. The United States protected Latin American countries from European powers. Nationalists felt foreign influence was too strong.

Review Questions

1. Define direct rule and indirect rule.

____

2. How were the policies of the governments of Japan and China similar in the early 1800s?

____

____

Key Terms

indigenous (in DIJ uh nus) *adj.* the original inhabitants of a region

economic imperialism (ek uh NAHM ik im PIHR ee ul iz um) *n.* one country's control over another country through economic policies

Vocabulary Strategy

The word *indigenous* comes from the Latin word *indigena*, or "native." What are indigenous peoples?

____

____

✓ Reading Check

List two reasons why Spain's colonies revolted.

1. ______________________________

2. ______________________________

Chapter 20 Assessment

1. Louis-Philippe of France was called the
- **A.** sun king.
- **B.** people's king.
- **C.** citizen king.
- **D.** constitutional king.

2. What European nation became independent as a result of a nationalist revolt?
- **A.** Italy
- **B.** Belgium
- **C.** Hungary
- **D.** the Czech Republic

3. Which of the following countries took part in the scramble for Africa?
- **A.** France
- **B.** Portugal
- **D.** Germany
- **D.** All of the above

4. What was one result of the Meiji Restoration in Japan?
- **A.** Japan's military power grew.
- **B.** Japan became a colony of Great Britain.
- **C.** Japan's influence in Korea declined.
- **D.** Japanese ships were barred from Chinese ports.

5. What is one of result of Napoleon's invasion of Spain and Portugal?
- **A.** Napoleon became emperor of Brazil.
- **B.** Control of Brazil shifted from Portugal to Spain.
- **C.** French became the official language in the Latin American colonies.
- **D.** Colonies in Latin America began a series of rebellions against Spanish colonial rule.

Short Answer Question

How did Britain and the United States gain influence in Latin America?

____

____

____

Prepare to Read

Section 1 World War I

Objectives

1. Identify the causes of World War I.
2. Learn why the war resulted in battlefield stalemates.
3. Find out how U.S. intervention led the Allies to victory.
4. Learn about peace terms and their effect on postwar Europe.

Target Reading Skill

Identify Causes and Effects When you're reading, it's important to see the causes and effects. A cause makes something happen and an effect is what happens. As you read, ask yourself what happened. The answer to that question is the effect. Then ask yourself why it happened. The answer to that question is the cause.

Recognizing causes and effects helps you understand how events are connected to each other. As you read this section, note both the long-term and short-term causes of World War I.

Vocabulary Strategy

Use Word Parts A prefix is one or more syllables attached to the beginning of a word to make a new word. The word the prefix is attached to is known as the root. When a prefix is added to a root, the new word has a different meaning. The new word is a combination of the two meanings.

In this chapter, you will read the word *archduke*. It contains the prefix *arch-*, which means "highest" or "chief." Other words that use the prefix include *archbishop* and *archangel*.

Section 1 Summary

On June 28, 1914, Austrian Archduke Francis Ferdinand and his wife Sophie were killed in Sarajevo (sa ruh YAY voh). This was the spark that ignited World War I.

The Causes of World War I

Historians disagree about the cause of World War I. The direct cause was the archduke's murder, but there were other causes such as nationalism, imperialism, and **alliances**.

Nationalism is a feeling of loyalty to a culture, language, or territory. Before World War I, such feelings had been strong in the Balkans (BAWL kunz). Nationalism was also strong in other parts of Europe.

Imperialism is building an empire, usually by taking over foreign colonies. Imperialist rivalries also led to the war. European nations fought for control in Africa and the Middle East.

The major powers made alliances with other countries to keep peace. There were two major alliances in 1914: France, Russia, and Britain made up the Triple Entente (TRIP ul ahn tahnt) or allies; Germany, Austria-Hungary, and Italy formed the Triple Alliance.

When Ferdinand was murdered, the leaders of Austria-Hungary declared war on Serbia (SUR bee uh). To protect its ally, Germany declared war on Russia. Germany then declared war on Russia's ally, France, and invaded Belgium in order to attack France. Belgium was a **neutral** country. The British then declared war on Germany. In a few weeks, all of Europe was at war.

Battlefield Stalemate, 1914–1917

By the winter of 1915, the Allies were stalled on all fronts. Armies began three years of trench warfare.

Key Terms

alliance (uh LY uns) *n.* a close association between nations
neutral (NOO trul) *adj.* not taking any side

Vocabulary Strategy

The word *archduke* contains the prefix *arch-*, which means "highest" or "chief." What is an archduke?

____

____

Target Reading Skill

What was the effect of the system of alliances?

____

____

✓ Reading Check

List three causes of World War I.

1. ______________________________
2. ______________________________
3. ______________________________

Most of the burden fell on foot soldiers who were protected by a network of trenches. The soldiers formed charges against enemy lines but were often cut down by artillery or poison gas. By 1917, millions were dead. ✓

U.S. Involvement and Allied Victory

The United States had stayed neutral, but German submarines sank several American merchant ships. The U.S. response to declare war on Germany helped the Allies.

In 1917, the Bolshevik Revolution took place in Russia, and the government had to pull out of the war in Europe. The Germans could now add more troops to the Western Front. ✓

When American soldiers arrived in Europe, it was too much for the Germans. They signed an armistice, or cease-fire agreement, on November 11, 1918.

A Hard and Bitter Peace

The Treaty of Versailles (TREE tee uv vur SY) was signed in 1919 in the French town of Versailles.

The treaty forced Germany to take blame for the war and to turn over land to the Allies. Germany also had to pay **reparations** to the Allies. Many historians believe the Germans resented the harsh terms of the treaty, and that resentment led to World War II.

The treaty also set up the League of Nations. U.S. President Woodrow Wilson hoped it would promote democracy and prevent wars. ✓

Review Questions

1. What was the most important effect of the U.S. entry into World War I?

____

____

2. What effects did the Treaty of Versailles have on Germany?

____

____

Key Term

reparations (rep uh RAY shunz) *n. pl.* payments for harm done to other countries

✓ Reading Check

Which part of the military bore the brunt of most battles in World War I?

____

____

____

✓ Reading Check

Which event allowed the Germans to add more troops to the Western front?

____

____

____

✓ Reading Check

What steps were taken to promote democracy and prevent future wars?

____

____

____

Prepare to Read

Section 2
The Russian Revolution

Objectives

1. Understand why the Russian people revolted against the czar.
2. Learn about the revolutions in 1917.
3. Identify the main features of the new revolutionary government.
4. Understand why the Russian Revolution led to civil war and dictatorship.

Target Reading Skill

Recognize Multiple Causes A cause makes something happen and an effect is what happens. Often, an effect can have more than one cause. For example, the Russian Revolution had many causes. As you read this section, identify at least three causes of the Russian Revolution. Make a chart like the one below to record the information.

Vocabulary Strategy

Use Word Parts When you come across a new word, you may be able to figure out its meaning if you break it into parts. For example, if you did not know what *snowball* means, you could break it into *snow* and *ball*. A snowball is a ball of snow. Many words in English are made by combining two or more words. Such words are referred to as *compound words*. As you read, use what you know about compound words to help you understand word meanings.

Here are some common compound words:

anybody	*baseball*	*businessperson*	*countryside*
downtown	*farmland*	*homeland*	*landform*
mainland	*mountaintop*	*northeast*	*seashore*
skyscraper	*southwest*	*waterway*	*worldwide*

Section 2 Summary

The Revolt against the Czar

Russia was ruled by a czar (zahr), who had the power of a king. Czars ruled with the support of wealthy nobles and landowners.

In 1900, most of the Russian people were peasants who worked for nobles. They were very poor and had few rights. Russia still relied mostly on farming long after the Industrial Revolution had taken hold elsewhere. ✓

By 1905, Russia began to develop. There was a small group of **capitalists** that started factories and railroads. A class of industrial workers grew up.

Manufacturers wanted more economic freedom and political power. Workers were drawn to Marxist (MAHRKS ist) **socialism**. The Marxists split into two groups, the Mensheviks (MEN shuh viks) and the Bolsheviks (BOHL shuh viks). Vladimir Lenin (vlad uh MIHR LEN in) was the leader of the Bolsheviks.

On January 22, 1905, there was a large demonstration for reform in St. Petersburg. The czar's police fired guns into the crowd, which began a series of strikes and riots throughout Russia. Czar Nicholas II used force to stop the protests, but he also made some reforms. Russia got its first elected legislative body, the Duma (DOO mah).

The Year of Revolution

Russia entered World War I, but it turned out to be a military, economic, and political disaster. It set the stage for **revolution**.

Russia's horrible wartime conditions led to huge strikes and demonstrations. Czar Nicholas II was forced to give up power. Later, he and his family were executed. The Duma was left in control.

Key Terms

capitalist (KAP ut ul ist) *n.* someone who provides ideas and money for investing in businesses
socialism (SOH shul iz um) *n.* a social system that seeks to abolish all forms of social classes and create a society of complete equality
revolution (rev uh LOO shun) *n.* a change or overthrow of a government or social system

✓ Reading Check

What was the largest social class in Russia in 1900?

____

____

Vocabulary Strategy

Mark the Text

The words below appear on this page. Each is a compound word. Draw a vertical line to separate the two words that form the compound. Circle the words in the text as you read them.

landowners

railroads

wartime

Workers formed their own elected body called a **soviet**. There were many soviets set up by laborers that fought the Duma for control.

Lenin and other Bolshevik leaders had been banned from Russia since 1907. In 1917, Germany let them return, hoping to weaken the Russian war effort.

The Bolsheviks tried to take over the government and gained majorities in several key soviets. In 1917, Bolshevik workers arrested cabinet members and took control of Moscow (MAHS kow). They had led the world's first socialist revolution. ✓

A New Government

After the revolution, workers seized factories and peasants seized land from the nobles. There were many reforms, including equal rights for women. ✓

Post-Revolutionary Russia

In March 1918, the new government dropped out of World War I, but Russia had to give Germany large amounts of land.

This and other Bolshevik policies angered many Russians. In 1918, they revolted against the government and two years of civil war followed. The Bolsheviks won, but many reforms were cancelled.

The Bolsheviks became known as the Communist Party. After Lenin died, Communist Party leader Joseph Stalin (HOH zuf STAH lin) took control. He became Russia's new dictator. ✓

Review Questions

1. Which two new social classes sprang up in Russia as it began to build factories?

2. Why did the Germans decide to let Lenin back into Russia in 1917?

Key Term

soviet (SOH vee ut) *n.* an elected worker's council or committee

✓ Reading Check

Who took over the Russian government in 1917?

✓ Reading Check

Name one feature of the new Russian government.

✓ Reading Check

Who took power after Lenin died?

Target Reading Skill

What multiple causes led to the revolt against the Bolshevik government?

CHAPTER 21

Prepare to Read

Section 3 Crises Around the World

Objectives

1. Discover why U.S. citizens were hopeful at the start of the 1920s.
2. Understand the causes of the Great Depression.
3. Explore the two major responses to the Great Depression.
4. Learn about the growth of Japan as a major power.

Target Reading Skill

Understanding Effects Remember, a cause makes something happen. The effect is what happens as a result. Sometimes one cause may produce several effects. For example, the Great Depression had many different effects on countries around the world. As you read, note three effects of the Great Depression and write them in a chart like the one below.

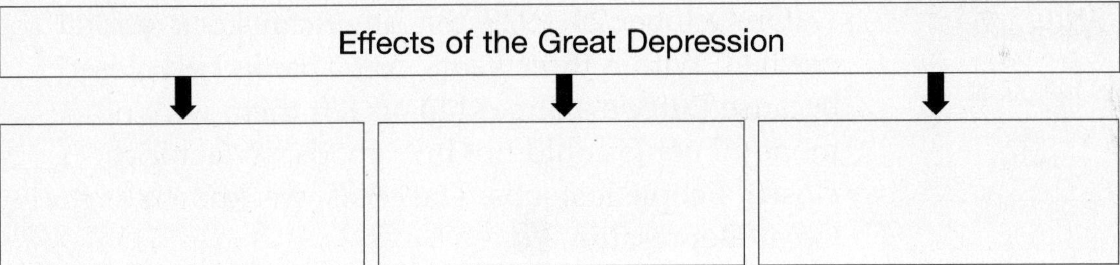

Vocabulary Strategy

Use Word Parts A suffix is one or more syllables attached to the end of a word to make a new word. The word it is attached to is known as the root. When a suffix is added to a root, the new word has a new meaning.

In this chapter you have read many words that end in the suffix *–ism*, which means "doctrine" or "system." You have read *imperialism, nationalism, communism, socialism*, and *capitalism*. In this section, you will read another, *fascism*. These doctrines are often referred to as "isms."

The suffix *-ist* is used to indicate a person who follows one of these doctrines or systems. So, a follower of imperialism is an imperialist.

Section 3 Summary

✓ Reading Check

What problem briefly hurt the German economy?

____

____

Vocabulary Strategy

Fascism is one of the "isms." What is a person who follows fascism called?

____

____

✓ Reading Check

Why did the banks run out of money?

____

____

Target Reading Skill

What were some of the effects of the New Deal?

____

____

A Time of Hope

There was major economic recovery after World War I. The automobile and technologies such as radio and movies created new industries. In 1929, European trade reached a level it would not equal again until 1954. The German economy was hit by **inflation**, but it quickly recovered. ✓

Worldwide Economic Depression

By the late 1920s, the economies of the United States and Europe slowed. Wages had not risen along with profits, and production grew faster than sales.

The biggest cause was Europe's huge debt to the United States. Britain and France planned to pay their debts with money from German reparations, but Germany could only pay if it borrowed from the United States. When the Europeans could not pay their loans, U.S. banks had problems.

On October 24, 1929, the American stock market crashed. Within three years, 5,000 banks had closed because Europe's unpaid loans left them with no money. People could not buy goods, so factories closed. People lost jobs. The crisis was known as the Great **Depression**. ✓

Responses to the Great Depression

The United States, France, and Britain made reforms democratically. Italy and Germany turned to **fascism**.

In the United States, the New Deal created new jobs by funding public works projects. The New Deal also funded unemployment insurance and social security. It expanded rights of labor unions, reformed the banking system, and began price supports for farmers.

Key Terms

inflation (in FLAY shun) *n.* an increase in prices and the amount of money in circulation
depression (dee PRESH un) *n.* a downturn in the economy
fascism (FASH ism) *n.* a type of authoritarian government

Italy was on the winning side in World War I. But after the war, it was left with a poor economy and unemployment. Socialists and Communists won in the 1921 elections. Army and business leaders were afraid of a communist takeover, so they turned to fascism. A year later, the Fascist party took over.

After the war, Germany seemed headed for democracy, but then Adolf Hitler (AD awlf HIT lur) began to gain power. He was the leader of the National Socialist German Worker's Party, or "Nazis" (NAHT seez). The Nazis wanted to unite German-speaking peoples against communists and Jews. The Jews became the **scapegoat** for Germany's defeat. ✓

In 1933, Hitler became chancellor, or leader, of Germany. He outlawed other political parties and broke up unions. Jews were robbed of their property and rights. The Nazis sent Jews, Gypsies, Slavs, other minorities, and communists to concentration camps. More than 6 million Jews were murdered there.

Hitler set Germany on the road to another war.

Japan: Growing Power in the Far East

Since the late 1800s, Japan had been building up its military, schools, agriculture, and industry. It gained land by winning wars against China and Russia. In the 1930s, Japan invaded China again. The United States supported China against Japan. Japan joined Nazi Germany and fascist Italy in a military alliance. ✓

Review Questions

1. What helped to create new industries after World War I?

____

____

2. How did the New Deal put people back to work?

____

____

Key Term

scapegoat (SKAYP goht) *n.* a person who bears the blame for others' mistakes

✓ Reading Check

What were members of the National Socialist German Worker's Party called?

____

____

____

✓ Reading Check

Why did the United States support China against Japan?

____

____

____

Prepare to Read

Section 4 World War II

Objectives

1. Explore the causes of World War II.
2. Learn about Germany's early successes.
3. Discover how 1941 was a turning point in the war.
4. Understand why the Allies achieved success.

Target Reading Skill

Recognizing Cause-and-Effect Signal Words As you read, watch for clues that show cause and effect. Often, a word will give you a signal that what is being described is either a cause or an effect.

This section contains information about many of the important events of World War II. To help keep the order of events clear, look for words such as *before*, *after*, *meanwhile*, *then*, and *next*. They signal the order in which events took place.

Vocabulary Strategy

Using Word Parts Sometimes when you come across a new word, you can figure out what it means if you break it into parts. If a word contains a prefix or suffix, look for the root. The root is the word that the prefix or suffix is attached to. Add the meanings of the root and prefix or suffix and you will have found the meaning of the new word.

Sometimes when a prefix or a suffix is added to a root, the root's spelling is changed.

- A final vowel, such as *a* or *e*, may be dropped: *Buddha* + *-ism* = *Buddhism*
- A final *y* may change to *i*: *happy* + *-ly* = *happily*
- A final consonant may be doubled: *war* + *-ing* = *warring*
- The *e* before a final *r* may be dropped: *disaster* + *-ous* = *disastrous*

Section 4 Summary

Many people think the **Holocaust** is the most evil event in the modern era. It was the Nazis' murder of millions of Jews and other minorities during World War II.

Causes of World War II

In many ways, World War II was the result of unfinished business of World War I. Nationalism didn't disappear.

Many Germans felt humiliated by the terms of the Treaty of Versailles. Hitler wanted to get over this. Germany stopped paying reparations and built up its army. In October 1936, Germany and Italy signed a treaty creating the Rome-Berlin Axis.

In 1938, Hitler united Austria with Germany and then took over part of Czechoslovakia (chek uh sloh VAH kee uh). France and Britain followed a policy of **appeasement**. They signed the Munich Pact (MYOO nik pakt), agreeing to the takeover. ✓

In 1939, Hitler took over the rest of Czechoslovakia. Britain and France prepared their militaries and formed alliances with Turkey, Greece, Romania, and Poland.

Hitler invaded Poland on September 1, 1939. Two days later, Britain and France declared war on Germany and World War II began.

Early German Successes and the Battle of Britain

On May 13, 1940, German forces reached the Maginot Line (MAZH uh noh lyn). It was a fortified line the French had built to stop a German attack, but it didn't work. By late June, Germany had taken over France. ✓

Key Terms

Holocaust (HAHL uh kawst) *n.* the term used to refer to the Nazis' murder of millions of Jews and minorities during World War II

appeasement (uh PEEZ munt) *n.* the giving in to the demands of an aggressor in order to keep the peace

Vocabulary Strategy

Mark the Text

The words below appear in this section. Each of these words contains a prefix or a suffix. Underline the prefix or suffix in each word. Think about how each prefix or suffix changes the meaning of the root. Circle the words as they appear in the text.

nationalism

disappear

appeasement

alliances

✓ Reading Check

How was the Munich Pact an example of appeasement?

____

____

✓ Reading Check

What was the Maginot Line?

____

____

____

Identify signal words in the bracketed paragraph.

Germany now controlled all of Western Europe except Britain and neutral countries Switzerland and Sweden. British pilots were able to hold off the Nazi air force in the Battle of Britain.

1941: Turning Points in the War

[In June of 1941, Hitler attacked the Soviet Union and German troops advanced toward Moscow. But then the harsh winter set in and the Germans were unprepared.]

The United States stayed neutral, but it helped Britain and the other Allies through the Lend-Lease program, which provided aid. In the meantime, Japan was expanding in Asia. On December 7, 1941, Japanese planes attacked the U.S. naval base at Pearl Harbor, Hawaii. As a result, the United States entered the war.

The Allies' Success

One of Germany's failures came at Stalingrad (stah lin GRAHT), in the Soviet Union. German troops surrendered in January, 1943. This was Germany's first major defeat. Soviet forces pushed westward. ✓

✓ Reading Check

What events signaled a turning point in the war?

On June 6, 1944, the Allies landed at Normandy (NAWR mun dee), on the northern coast of France. This event is known as D-Day. Within six months, the Allies had reached Germany. On May 8, 1945, the Allies declared victory in Europe.

In 1945, a U.S. air campaign ended with the dropping of the **atomic bomb** on the Japanese cities of Hiroshima (HIHR uh SHEE muh) and Nagasaki (nah guh SAH kee). Both cities were destroyed. Five days later, Japan surrendered and World War II was over.

Review Questions

1. How did things go for Germany during the first year of the war?

2. How did the atomic bomb affect World War II?

Key Term

atomic bomb (uh TAHM ik BAHM) *n.* an extremely destructive bomb whose power results from the chain reaction of nuclear fission

Chapter 21 Assessment

1. A person from which country would be more likely to feel the Treaty of Versailles was unfair?
   A. France
   B. Germany
   C. Great Britain
   D. Italy

2. Who would be most likely to support socialism?
   A. a noble
   B. a worker
   C. a dictator
   D. a capitalist

3. Who controlled Germany in the 1930s and 1940s?
   A. Czar Nicholas II
   B. Lenin
   C. Stalin
   D. Hitler

4. What happened as a result of the American stock market crash of 1929?
   A. World War I began.
   B. World War II began.
   C. The Russian Revolution began.
   D. The Great Depression began.

5. What was the direct cause of World War II?
   A. the invasion of Poland by Germany
   B. Germany's takeover of Czechoslovakia
   C. the bombing of Pearl Harbor by the Japanese
   D. the murder of the Archduke Francis Ferdinand

Short Answer Question

Which social problem was most responsible for promoting the growth of fascism in Europe in the 1920s?

Prepare to Read

Section 1
Europe and North America

Objectives

1. Find out about the Cold War.
2. Learn about two hot wars: Korea and Vietnam.
3. Examine the fall of the Soviet Union and the effect on European nations.
4. Recognize the strong nations and economies in North America.

Target Reading Skill

Paraphrasing When you paraphrase, you are putting something into your own words, which can help you understand what you read. As you read, "say back" the sentences or paragraphs. That way, you will make sure you understand what you have read.

For example, look at this sentence: "During World War II, the Soviet Union and the nations of the West worked together to defeat Nazi Germany." You could paraphrase it this way: "The Soviet Union cooperated with the West to defeat Germany in the Second World War."

As you read this section, paraphrase the information following each heading.

Vocabulary Strategy

Word Origins English has "borrowed" more words than any other language. These words have made the English language rich and colorful. They have also made the language very precise. For example, when we talk about the Russian space program, we often use Russian terms. Russian space explorers are called *cosmonauts*, not *astronauts*. When we hear the word *cosmonaut*, we know that it refers to a Russian space explorer, not an American.

In this section, you will read two other Russian terms that have become part of the English language. They are *glasnost* and *perestroika*. They were first used during the final years of the Soviet Union. In Russian, *glasnost* means "opportunity to be heard." *Perestroika* means "reconstruction" or "restructuring."

Section 1 Summary

The Cold War

During World War II, the Soviet Union and the nations of the West worked together. Afterward, they divided control of the defeated Axis countries. Eastern Europe was controlled by the USSR. Communist governments were put in power. Democratic governments were set up in Western Europe. Distrust grew between the USSR and the West. This was known as the **Cold War**.

Democracies and communist countries competed for power and influence, but they never used their armies against each other. The U.S. and USSR build up of military and weapons was called the **Arms Race**.

During the Cold War, the USSR and its allies supported communist groups with money, supplies, advisors, and soldiers. U.S. and Western democracies fought the spread of communism. ✓

Two Hot Wars: Korea and Vietnam

After World War II, Korea was divided: North Korea became a communist country; South Korea was not communist. It was supported by the United States.

In 1950, North Korea tried to unite all of Korea under its control. The United States sent soldiers to push the invaders out. In 1953, an armistice was signed and the two sides agreed to stop fighting. The country is still divided.

Vietnam was divided. The communist rebels in the north wanted to unite the country under communist rule. U.S. aid, including troops, was sent to South Vietnam. ✓

Even with U.S. help, South Vietnam could not defeat the North. After many years of fighting, U.S. troops were pulled out and Vietnam became a single country under communist rule.

Key Terms

Cold War (kohld wawr) *n.* the period between 1945 and 1989, when the United States and USSR competed for influence

Arms Race (ahrmz rays) *n.* the buildup of military forces

Target Reading Skill

Paraphrase or restate the information in the section titled "The Cold War."

✓ Reading Check

What was the Cold War?

✓ Reading Check

Why did the United States enter the wars in Korea and Vietnam?

The Soviet Union Falls and Europe Unites

In 1985, Mikhail Gorbachev (mee kah EEL GAWR buh chawf) came to power in the Soviet Union. He hoped to make reforms. He called for **glasnost**, or openness, and **perestroika**, or change in the government.

Vocabulary Strategy

In Russian, the word *glasnost* means "opportunity to be heard." How does that definition compare with the way the word is used here?

____

____

____

The changes did not work at first. Some people wanted to return to old-style communism. In 1991, Gorbachev resigned and the Soviet Union came to an end. Its republics became independent countries, of which the Republic of Russia is the largest. Some republics joined a new Russian Federation.

Economic cooperation helped Western Europe recover from World War II. Six nations signed a treaty to form the Common Market, which expanded free trade. It also set up the European Parliament.

In the 1980s and 1990s, the Common Market expanded and took the name European Union (EU). It pushed for economic and political unity. ✓

✓ Reading Check

Name two ways Europeans benefited from the Common Market and European Union.

1. ____________________

2. ____________________

Strong Nations and Economies in North America

After the fall of communist USSR, the United States was the only superpower. Its military is the strongest in the world, and it remains a rich nation. ✓

✓ Reading Check

What makes the United States the world's only superpower?

____

____

____

Canada is shaped by immigrants. It is a major democratic and industrial power.

Review Questions

1. Identify the two main kinds of government in Eastern and Western Europe after World War II.

____

____

2. How are the Cold War and the Arms Race connected?

____

____

Key Terms

glasnost (GLAHS nawst) *n.* openness
perestroika (pehr uh STROI kuh) *v.* change in Soviet government

Prepare to Read

Section 2 Latin America

Objectives

1. Understand why Mexico has experienced reform, but little economic growth.
2. Learn about Central American revolutions.
3. Find out about unstable governments and economies in South America.
4. Learn about the Cuban revolution.

Target Reading Skill

Rereading or Reading Ahead Both rereading and reading ahead can help you understand words and ideas. In some cases, you may wish to read ahead to see if the word or idea is explained later on. Sometimes a word is defined after its first use in a text. The main idea may be discussed later in the section.

If you do not understand the main idea of a sentence or paragraph, try rereading it. Look for details you may have missed. As you reread, concentrate on the parts that seem confusing.

Vocabulary Strategy

Word Origins Many people in Latin America speak Spanish. As you read about Latin America, you will come across Spanish words. You may recall words like *conquistador* and *encomienda*. They are both Spanish. In this section, you will read *guerrilla* and *contra*. *Guerrilla* comes from the Spanish word *guerra*, which means "war." The literal meaning of *guerrilla* is "little war." *Contra* is a shortened form of *contrarrevolucionario*, which means "counterrevolutionary." A counterrevolutionary is a person who is opposed to a revolution.

Section 2 Summary

Mexico: Reform but Little Growth

Since World War II, Mexico has tried to improve its economy, but with mixed results. It has tried hard to pay a big foreign debt. This debt has kept the economy from growing. Many people live in poverty.

In 1994, Mexico joined Canada and the United States in the **North American Free Trade Agreement (NAFTA)**. It lowered investment barriers among the three countries. NAFTA has brought some new business to Mexico, but it also hurt Mexican manufacturers. They could not compete with the amount of goods brought in from the United States. ✓

The Mexican people have also tried to reform their government. One political party had been in power since 1929, but it lost control in the 2000 presidential elections.

Revolutions and Wars in Central America

During the early 1900s, dictators and military strongmen ruled Guatemala, most of them supported by the United States. In 1944, liberal leaders began reforms, but these leaders were overthrown in 1954. Harsh military rule plunged the country into civil war. Finally in 1996, a democratic government took control.

[Civil war also broke out in El Salvador. The government fought against **guerrillas**. The United States pressed the government to make reforms. It also gave military and financial aid.]

The Somoza (soh MOH zah) family ruled Nicaragua for years. In 1979, they were driven from power by the **Sandinistas**.

✓ Reading Check

What three countries belong to NAFTA?

1. ______________________________

2. ______________________________

3. ______________________________

Target Reading Skill

Reread the section in brackets on El Salvador to help you better understand the meaning of *guerrilla*. Who were the Salvadoran guerrillas fighting against?

____

____

Key Terms

NAFTA (North American Free Trade Agreement) (NAF tuh) *n.* a trade agreement that lowered trade barriers among the United States, Canada, and Mexico

guerrilla (guh RIL uh) *n.* a member of a small defensive force of soldiers that makes surprise raids

Sandinista (san duh NEES tuh) *n.* a member of a political movement that overthrew the Somoza regime in Nicaragua

The United States supported the **contras**. They were guerrillas who fought against the Sandinistas. A peace treaty was signed in 1987, and there have been moderate governments since then. ✓

Unstable Governments and Economies in South America

In 1964, a military dictatorship took over Brazil, and it lasted nearly 20 years. The economy boomed, but people wanted democracy. In 1989, Brazil returned to democracy, but poverty and inequality led to the election of a socialist president.

After World War II, Argentina was led by a former army colonel named Juan Perón (hwahn pay RAWN). He was overthrown in 1955 by the military. In 1973, Perón was reelected. He died a year later and his wife took over. Two years later, she was overthrown.

During the 1980s, the military waged a "dirty war" against those who opposed the government. In 1983, civilian rule was restored. ✓

The Cuban Revolution

In 1959, workers and peasants, led by Fidel Castro, overthrew Cuba's dictator. Castro turned to the Soviet Union for support. In 1961, a U.S.-backed invasion failed to remove Castro from power. The next year, the United States discovered Soviet missiles in Cuba. The world came to the edge of nuclear war, but the Soviets agreed to remove their missiles. Castro is still in power, with a strict communist rule. He has one of the worst human-rights records in the region. ✓

Review Questions

1. How has the government of Guatemala changed?

____

____

2. What led to a socialist president in Brazil?

____

____

> **Key Term**
>
> **contra** (CON truh) *n.* guerrilla supported by the United States, who fought the Sandinistas

Vocabulary Strategy

To whom were the contras opposed?

____

____

✓ Reading Check

List three Central American countries that experienced revolutions or civil wars after World War II.

1. ___________________________
2. ___________________________
3. ___________________________

✓ Reading Check

Who was the target of the "dirty war"?

____

____

____

✓ Reading Check

In what year did Castro become Cuba's leader? In what year did a failed invasion try to overthrow Castro? In what year did the Soviets put missiles in Cuba?

____

____

____

Prepare to Read

Section 3 Asia

Objectives

1. Learn about Japan's postwar economy.
2. Understand the tensions between India and Pakistan.
3. Find out about China's move toward a more open economy.

Target Reading Skill

Paraphrasing When you paraphrase, you are putting something into your own words, which can help you understand what you read. Paraphrasing will also help you remember what you have read.

For example, read this sentence: "After the communist takeover of China in 1949, the country became a one-party dictatorship on the model of the Soviet Union, with complete government control of the economy." You could paraphrase it this way: "In 1949, the communists set up a Soviet-style dictatorship in China."

As you read, paraphrase the information following each heading.

Vocabulary Strategy

Word Origins Many English words come from names of people or places. For example, fine ceramic called porcelain was first made in China. Now dinnerware made from porcelain is referred to as *china*.

The word *India* comes from the Persian word for "Hindu." The word was often used to refer to places in East Asia. The islands referred to as the East Indies are not actually part of India, but they *are* in East Asia. And the West Indies aren't close to India at all. In fact, they aren't in Asia. They are in the Americas.

Cashmere is a kind of very fine goat wool, and is named for the region from which it comes. *Cashmere* is an old way of spelling *Kashmir*.

Section 3 Summary

The war left cities crumbling throughout Japan. Farm output had also suffered from bad weather. Rice harvests were at only two thirds of the level before the war.

With the end of the war, Japan had to accept foreign occupation. It was the first time in their history. They borrowed Western ideas and technology and put them to use. In time, Japan became an economic superpower.

Japan's Recovery and Strong Economy

After World War II, the Japanese economy struggled. Inflation was high. The United States helped Japan recover and its economy grew quickly.

Real growth and changes began in 1949. Japan became a manufacturing, trade, and transportation power. By the 1970s, Japan was a leader in electronics. Its brands led the market for TVs and stereos. Later, Japan improved the technology by introducing VCRs, DVD players, and computer components. Japan's auto industry produced such good cars that its industry began to overtake U.S. automakers. Today, some of the best-selling car brands in the world are Japanese. ✓

Since 1990, the Japanese economy has slowed quite a bit. Prices keep falling, and major public-works projects have not brought Japan out of its slump.

India and Pakistan: Still Enemies

When India won its independence, it was divided into two nations: India was mainly Hindu. Pakistan was mainly Muslim. India adopted a democratic form of government. Pakistan has gone through periods of democracy and of military dictatorship.

✓ Reading Check

What items does Japan manufacture?

____

____

____

Vocabulary Strategy

How is *Cashmere* spelled now?

____

____

Relations have always been tense between the two countries. They have fought three major wars. The first was in 1947. All of the wars have been fought over **Kashmir**. In 1949, the United Nations sponsored a peace agreement that divided Kashmir. Later, free elections were scheduled, but the plan didn't work. Fighting broke out again in 1965 and 1971.

Target Reading Skill

Paraphrase the problem between India and Pakistan.

____

____

____

War became likely again in 1998, when both countries tested nuclear bombs. Fighting over Kashmir continues to flare up. ✓

China's Move Toward an Open Economy

In 1949, the government communists took over China and it became a one-party dictatorship. The government had full control over the economy and built up heavy industry and military power. But there were few choices of goods, and they were of poor quality.

✓ Reading Check

Which territory has remained a source of conflict between India and Pakistan?

____

____

By the 1970s, China's economy had stalled. The government decided to make contact with the United States. In 1979, the two countries set up diplomatic relations, and China began to open its economy to investment from private corporations. Since then, it has developed one of the fastest-growing economies in the world. ✓

✓ Reading Check

When did China and the United States establish full diplomatic relations?

____

____

Review Questions

1. What is the main religion in India?

____

____

2. What is a major cause of growth of the Chinese economy in recent years?

____

____

Key Term

Kashmir (KASH mihr) *n.* a mostly Muslim area in the northern part of the Indian subcontinent that is claimed by both India and Pakistan.

Prepare to Read

Section 4
Africa and the Middle East

Objectives

1. Learn about the new countries in Africa and some of the challenges they face.
2. Learn about the Arab-Israeli conflict.
3. Understand the importance of oil in the Middle East and Persian Gulf.

Target Reading Skill

Summarizing You will learn more from your text if you summarize it. When you summarize, you use your own words to restate the key points. A summary includes important events and details in the order the events occurred. It also makes connections between the events.

Summarize by using the following steps:

1. Identify main ideas.
2. State them in the order in which they appear.
3. Note when one event causes another event.

Vocabulary Strategy

Word Origins Sometimes if you don't know the meaning of a word, you can often find clues in the word itself. For example, in this section you will learn about *apartheid*. If you don't know the word's meaning, what part of the word gives you a clue?

A word's origin is where a word came from. In this case, *apartheid* originated in Africa. It means racial segregation, or when people are separated by their race.

Can you think of another word that has "apart" in it? How about apartment? An apartment building, for example, contains several living spaces that are **apart** from each other. The next time you're not sure of a word's meaning, see if the word's origin or studying the word's parts can help you.

Target Reading Skill

In a few words, sum up the section titled "Arab-Israeli Conflict."

____

____

____

✓ Reading Check

What are the struggles that Africa faces?

____

____

____

Section 4 Summary

New Nations in Africa and Internal Struggles

The years after World War II brought hope to Africa. Ghana became the first nation in **Sub-Saharan Africa** to become independent. During the next 20 years, more than 40 African nations achieved independence. By 1990, all the colonies were free.

Dictators often took control and tried to force different ethnic groups to live together. Throughout the 1990s, though, most African countries had elected governments.

All-white governments controlled South Africa until 1994, even though most of the people are black. These governments had a policy of **apartheid**. It forced people of different races to live separately. In 1993, a new constitution was adopted doing away with apartheid.

Beginning in the 1980s, the **HIV/AIDS** crisis arose. It has hit Africa harder than almost anywhere else. In several African countries, more than a quarter of the adult population is infected.

Africa is rich in natural resources like oil and diamonds, but it is still the poorest continent because of unfair trade policies and poor farming conditions. Africans are working to improve their nations. ✓

Arab-Israeli Conflict

After the Holocaust, many Jews wished for a land of their own. Their wish came true in 1948 when Israel was created in Palestine (PAL us tyn).

Israel is a small democratic nation. It has a Jewish majority and a Muslim Arab minority. It is surrounded by Arab nations that are led by nondemocratic governments. Israel has fought several wars with its neighbors.

Key Terms

apartheid (uh PAHR tait) *n.* a system of strict racial separation
HIV/AIDS (aych i vee aydz) *n.* a virus that leads to the gradual collapse of the immune system and is fatal
Sub-Saharan Africa (sub suh HA run AF rih kuh) *n.* the part of Africa south of the Sahara

Israel has won all four wars with its neighbors. It has political ties with only one Arab country, Egypt. They signed a peace treaty in 1979. ✓

The Palestinians are fighting for their own independent state in the Israeli-controlled areas of the West Bank and Gaza Strip.

The Importance of Oil in the Middle East and the Persian Gulf

Without oil, industrial economies could not function. But the most advanced countries must find oil elsewhere.

In 1960, Middle Eastern oil powers formed the Organization of Petroleum Exporting Countries (OPEC). It was formed to give exporters more control over the world price of oil.

The United States is the largest oil consumer. Japan is the second largest. Much of the oil used by these nations comes from the Middle East and the Persian Gulf, which together contain 65 percent of the world's known oil reserves.

The three countries with the most oil are Saudi Arabia, Iraq, and Iran. The United States has supported a conservative monarchy in Saudi Arabia. It is run according to strict Muslim laws. The United States has also been involved in Iran, on the Persian Gulf. In 1990, Iraq invaded the oil-rich kingdom of Kuwait (koo WAYT). The United States led an international military force to drive Iraq's troops out of Kuwait. Ten years of international pressure did not change the policies of Iraq's dictator, Saddam Hussein (suh DAHM hoo SAYN). In 2003, the United States overthrew Saddam's government and captured Saddam. ✓

Review Questions

1. Which historical event led many Jews to wish for a homeland of their own?

____

____

2. Which two countries are the world's largest consumers of oil?

____

____

✓ Reading Check

With which Arab country does Israel have political relations?

____

____

____

Vocabulary Strategy

Why does *OPEC* stand for?

____

____

✓ Reading Check

Why do many countries have an interest in what happens in the Middle East and the Persian Gulf?

____

____

____

Prepare to Read

Section 5
The World in a New Century

Objectives

1. Explain the impact of TV and computers.
2. Learn about the global economy.
3. Find out about threats to the world's security.
4. Explore environmental concerns.

Target Reading Skill

Summarizing You will learn more from your text if you summarize it. When you summarize, you use your own words to restate the key points. A summary includes important events and details in the order the events occurred. It also makes connections between the events.

A good summary:

- includes all of the important events and details.
- keeps the order in which important events occurred.
- indicates connections among events or details.

Vocabulary Strategy

Word Origins Abbreviations and acronyms are two examples of how words can be shortened. Brief forms are another example.

Sometimes the brief form becomes more common than the full form. For example, *fax* is used more frequently than *facsimile*. In fact, many people may not realize *fax* is a brief form.

In this chapter, you will read the word *e-mail*. Did you know that it is a brief form for *electronic mail*?

What other short forms can you think of? Add them to the lists below.

Full Form	Brief Form
automobile	*auto*
bicycle	*bike*
medications	*meds*
telephone	*phone*

Section 5 Summary

TV and Computers

After World War II, television became very popular. In 1950, about 9 percent of American homes had a television. Today, the figure is near 100 percent.

At first, TV was mainly for entertainment, but Americans soon turned to it as a major news source. Cable TV expanded choices to dozens of networks.

The first home computers were available in 1975, but by 1990, only 15 percent of American homes had computers. By 1997, 35 percent had at least one computer, and in 2004, the figure had risen to 79 percent.

A major force in the growth of computer use is the Internet (IN tur net). It has changed the way the world communicates. With e-mail, instant messaging, and chat rooms, people communicate in seconds. ✓

A Global Economy

Globalization (gloh bul ih ZAY shun) began with the creation of the **United Nations** in 1946. The U.N. is a place where nations discuss and act on the world's political problems. ✓

International trade is another important part of globalization. Several trade organizations have been created. The North American Free Trade Agreement (NAFTA) lowered tariffs among the United States, Canada, and Mexico. The World Trade Organization (WTO) makes rules to help increase international trade. It also resolves international trade disputes.

Threats to the World's Security

Some radical groups have sponsored **terrorism**. On September 11, 2001, a radical Muslim group hijacked and crashed airplanes into the World Trade Center in New York City.

Key Terms

United Nations (yoo NYT id NAY shunz) *n. pl.* an international organization that discusses and acts on world issues

terrorism (TEHR ur iz um) *n.* the deliberate use of violence to achieve political goals

Target Reading Skill

Write a summary for the section with the heading "TV and Computers."

Vocabulary Strategy

What term is *e-mail* short for?

✓ Reading Check

How has the Internet affected communication?

✓ Reading Check

What is the purpose of the UN?

Another plane crashed into the Pentagon in Washington, D.C. A fourth crashed into a field in Pennsylvania after passengers overtook the hijackers. It was the worst act of terrorism to strike the United States.

In response, the United States launched a campaign against terror and led a coalition of forces into Afghanistan (af GAN ih stan). A brutal regime called the Taliban (TAL ih ban) ruled there and was believed to support the al-Qaeda (ahl KY duh) terrorist group—the group blamed for the September 11 attacks. ✓

✓ Reading Check

What terrorist group was blamed for the September 11 attacks in the United States?

____

____

____

The U.S. government created a Department of Homeland Security and passed the USA-PATRIOT Act, laws aimed at catching potential terrorists.

Environmental Issues

There has been a growing interest in the **environment** for the past 30 years. Concern about pollution led to the first Earth Day in 1970. That year, the Environmental Protection Agency (EPA) was formed. Pollution still threatens the environment. Acid rain and global warming also pose risks. ✓

✓ Reading Check

When was the first Earth Day?

____

____

____

Acid rain is caused by sulfuric acid (sul FYOOR ik AS id) that is released into the air from factories and power plants. Acid rain can harm lakes, trees, and crops. Global warming may be caused by "greenhouse gases" from cars and factories. These gases trap the sun's warmth in the atmosphere.

Review Questions

1. When did television become popular in the United States?

____

____

2. How does NAFTA help increase trade?

____

____

Key Term

environment (en VY run munt) *n.* the elements that surround all living things and make life possible

Chapter 22 Assessment

1. What was the result of the war in Korea?
   A. North Korea defeated South Korea and united the country under a communist government.
   B. South Korea defeated North Korea and united the country under a noncommunist government.
   C. The Soviet Union took over North and South Korea.
   D. The country remained divided.

2. In which Latin American country did the military wage a "dirty war"?
   A. Argentina
   B. Brazil
   C. Cuba
   D. Mexico

3. India and Pakistan have fought for years over which territory?
   A. Gaza Strip
   B. West Bank
   C. Iraq
   D. Kashmir

4. What kind of government does Saudi Arabia have?
   A. It is a democracy ruled by an elected president.
   B. It is a monarchy run according to Muslim law.
   C. It is ruled by a harsh communist dictator.
   D. It is a constitutional monarchy.

5. What causes acid rain?
   A. sulfuric acid released into the air from industrial and power plants
   B. carbon dioxide released into the air by trees and other plants
   C. carbon monoxide released into the air by cars
   D. greenhouse gases

Short Answer Question

What steps did the United States take to protect itself against terrorism?

____

____

____

____

____